Beneath Haunted Waters
The Tragic Tale of Two B-24s Lost in the
Sierra Nevada Mountains during World War II

Peter Stekel

Guilford, Connecticut

An imprint of Globe Pequot

Distributed by NATIONAL BOOK NETWORK

Copyright © 2017 by Peter Stekel
All photos by the author unless otherwise noted
Maps by Jim Reed, PhD

British Library Cataloguing in Publication Information available

Library of Congress Cataloging-in-Publication Data available

ISBN 978-1-4930-2530-5 (paperback)
ISBN 978-1-4930-2532-9 (e-book)

∞™ The paper used in this publication meets the minimum requirements of American National Standard for Information Sciences—Permanence of Paper for Printed Library Materials, ANSI/ NISO Z39.48-1992.

Printed in the United States of America

The Hammer Field Boys

During the 1930s and 1940s, those who we know today as "young men" in their late teens through their late twenties were commonly referred to as "boys." You hear it in movies of the era and read it in diaries and journals of the day and letters sent to and fro between parents and their children. The term is used in the memoirs written during and immediately after World War II. Today's ears may find the term a disparaging or childish reference for soldiers old enough to risk and encounter death on the battlefield. But "boys" is what they were called, and boys they will always be, forever locked in the capsule of their time. Especially the ones who never grew old enough to officially be men in the eyes of culture and society.

The Crew of B-24 Liberator #41-28463 (aka, 463)

Departed Hammer Field, California, at 8:50 a.m. on December 4, 1943, on a high-altitude celestial navigation training exercise of approximately six hours and ten minutes to Tucson, Arizona. Last sighting, and presumed killed on their return flight, sometime after 2:10 a.m., December 5, 1943.

461st Bombardment Group (H), 765th Bombardment Squadron

2nd Lt. Charles Willis Turvey Jr., pilot
0-582921, Reesville, Ohio
Born: July 23, 1921; age 22 years, 4 months
Unmarried

2nd Lt. Robert Mellor Hester, copilot
0-735344, Los Angeles, California

Born: December 13, 1919; age 23 years, 11 months
Married; one daughter

2nd Lt. William Thomas Cronin, navigator
0-691961, Olean, New York
Born: October 15, 1919; age 24 years, 2 months
Unmarried

2nd Lt. Ellis Homer Fish, bombardier
0-752711, La Crosse, Wisconsin
Born: June 12, 1916; age 27 years, 6 months
Unmarried; one son

S/Sgt. Robert Oakley Bursey, flight engineer
11084894, Rutland, Vermont
Born: December 17, 1921; age 21 years, 11 months
Unmarried

S/Sgt. Howard Wandtke, radio operator
15354576, Toledo, Ohio
Born November 30, 1923; age 20 years, 1 month
Unmarried

THE CREW OF B-24 LIBERATOR #42-7674 (AKA, *EXTERMINATOR*)

Killed approximately 9:50 a.m., December 6, 1943.

461st Bombardment Group (H), 766th Bombardment Squadron
Capt. William Howard Union Darden, pilot and squadron commander
0-389288, Portsmouth, Virginia
Born: June 28, 1918; age 25 years, 6 months
Married; one daughter

2nd Lt. Samuel J. Schlosser, navigator
0-797409, Brooklyn, New York

Born: March 18, 1918; age 24 years, 9 months
Married; one daughter

S/Sgt. Franklin Nyswonger, flight engineer
16009396, Green Bay, Wisconsin
Born: February 23, 1922; age 20 years, 10 months
Unmarried

Sgt. Dick Erwin Mayo, top turret gunner
35448517, Prestonsburg, Kentucky
Born: July 25, 1920; age 22 years, 5 months
Unmarried

Sgt. Richard Lee Spangle, bottom turret gunner
19013003, Gazelle/Weed, California
Born: February 13, 1924; age 19 years, 10 months
Married: no children

Sgt. Donald C. Vande Plasch, tail gunner
36279044, Wauwatosa, Wisconsin
Born: May 29, 1913; age 30 years, 7 months
Married: no children

2nd Lt. Culos Marion Settle, copilot
0-806149, Wilkesboro, North Carolina
Born: July 13, 1917; age 26 years, 4 months
Married; three children born after the war
Died: April 26, 1957; age 39 years, 9 months

Sgt. George John Barulic, radio operator
32565369, Newark, New Jersey
Born: April 13, 1922; age 21 years, 8 months
Married after the war; two sons and two daughters
Died: June 22, 2014; age 92 years, 2 months

Dedicated to
Eugene R. Fletcher (1921–2013)

Major, USAF (Ret.)
B-17 Pilot, Lucky Sherry
8th Air Force, 95th Bomb Group (H), 412th Squadron
Horham, England
Distinguished Flying Cross
Air Medal with Five Oak Leaf Clusters
Author of Mister *and* Fletcher's Gang

During World War II, Major Fletcher flew thirty-five combat missions
and eighteen air force weather missions.
Fletcher said the highlight of his service occurred on
December 27, 1944, when he flew his final combat mission.
"It was the last time I was under enemy fire, and the day I sent my entire
bomber crew home without a scratch."

War not only takes its toll of the participants, it decimates the lives of those who are left to grieve.
—R. W. "BILL" BULLEN DFC (1919–2006), POET AND
RAAF PATHFINDER NAVIGATOR,
NO. 102 SQUADRON AND PFF

It is community and it is respect, of course, but the dead have more claims on you than what you might want to admit, or even what you might know about, and the claims can be very strong indeed.
—CORMAC MCCARTHY, *NO COUNTRY FOR OLD MEN*

The passage of time all too often muddles reality by implanting preconceived notions and biases generated by those with no direct experience.
—JOHN L. STEWART, *THE FORBIDDEN DIARY:
A B-24 NAVIGATOR REMEMBERS*

There are thousands of men and women that have no known grave and most will never be recovered and given a decent burial. However, we owe it to the families and our nation to do our best to bring home the ones that are recoverable. If we are able to locate, identify, and return home with honor any one of those missing, we should ensure that happens without delay, before there is no one left to remember them.
—DANNY I. P. KEAY, *ROSCOE RED THREE IS MISSING*

The public dearly loves a hero; but the men who have been both heroic and lucky must share their honours, as they are the first to insist, with others whose courage was not less, though their luck failed them.
—SIR WALTER ALEXANDER RALEIGH, *THE WAR IN THE AIR*

Contents

PROLOGUE

On December 11, 1960, the United States Department of the Interior, Board on Geographic Names, christened a remote and inaccessible body of water high in California's Sierra Nevada, "Hester Lake." Not long before it had been known via newspaper reports as either an "unnamed lake," or as "LeConte Lake." The naming process happened quickly, with some gentle encouragement by the management at KCBS in San Francisco, the announcement coming from Secretary of the Interior Fred A. Seaton. The Associated Press reported on "the appropriateness of this name, in view of the father-son devotion it symbolizes."

CHAPTER 1

Discovery in a High Sierra Lake

ALONG THE STEEP AND NARROW SHORE, AND SUBMERGED IN THE WATER of the unnamed alpine lake, James Moore, Frank Dodge, and Leroy Brock could see lots of aluminum pieces. Twisted chunks of metal mostly, but also broken bits of tubing and wiring. The lake was shallow for only a few feet out before the dark blue of impenetrable deepness began.

After finding a yellow oxygen bottle, part of a flight suit, and other aircraft debris while climbing the treeless granite slope below the lake, the three men had expected to see something like this. It was hard to say with any certainty what happened here—only that it hadn't been pretty. An airplane crash for sure. But what kind of airplane? How big, and when?

This 1960 field season in Kings Canyon National Park had been both productive and exhausting for Frank Dodge. As a Stanford University graduate student and field assistant with the United States Geological Survey (USGS), all he had to do was follow lead researcher, Dr. James G. Moore, around the High Sierra. Except that following James Moore was never an easy task. Since they were collecting rock samples for a geological mapping project of the national park, they spent little time on trails. It was always up one mountain and then down the other. Mountain-climbing experience was not a prerequisite for the job, but it should have been.

Dodge and Moore, with all their food and equipment, had been carried into the backcountry by Rainbow Pack Station from Bishop, California. They rode horses over 11,972-foot Bishop Pass into Kings Canyon National Park and dropped into Dusy Basin. There they set up a

Dr. James G. Moore, summer 1960.
COURTESY DR. JAMES G. MOORE

base camp. The next morning they awoke and realized they hadn't hung their food high enough in what passes for a tree in Dusy Basin. A bear had raided their food cache, taking all the choice bits like bacon, chocolate, and butter, and leaving everything else. The two geologists were not happy with losing all their high-caloric food, but the loss didn't dissuade Moore; they would push on.

After several days of mapping and gathering samples, Moore and Dodge left their cozy canvas-wall tent, secured their remaining good food properly, and packed up their clothing, equipment, and backpacking food. Shouldering backpacks they began an extended hiking trip of climbing peaks and clambering their way over, around, and through some of the roughest country in the Sierra Nevada. For more than a week they never set foot on a trail. Highlights during the following days included tracing the route taken by Joseph N. LeConte in 1903 in order to climb and map 14,242-foot North Palisade, and evading an electrical storm on 12,151-foot Mount Shakespeare. Eventually, Moore and Dodge dropped down

Palisade Creek to the Middle Fork Kings River, where they made their way upstream along the John Muir Trail to the remote LeConte Canyon backcountry ranger station, below Little Pete Meadow. Their plan for the following day was to "map part of the east side of the craggy Black Divide, so named from abundant outcrops of black and ancient volcanic rocks."

It was July 27, 1960.

At the ranger station the two geologists met Leroy Brock, the Kings Canyon National Park seasonal ranger living there with his wife and six-month-old daughter. In its second year of operation, LeConte Canyon Ranger Station consisted of a rough wooden frame with plywood floor and sides, topped by a canvas tarp. The park service called it a "tent cabin." Life in the one-room cabin was simple and basic. The young family hauled water from the Kings River for drinking, cooking, and bathing,

LeConte Canyon Ranger Station, circa 1957. The station itself is a one-room "cabin," with plywood sides and a canvas top. Notice all the horse-packing accoutrements. Meals were cooked in the wood-burning rock fireplace and oven.
COURTESY LEROY BROCK

and made use of an outdoor privy. They burned all the trash they could burn and buried the rest.

In front of the ranger station / cabin was a large canvas tarp, handmade table and benches, and rock fireplace. Not far away was a corral for the ranger's horses. It could have been 1860, not 1960—that's how spartan and primitive were accommodations for living in the Kings Canyon National Park wilderness.

That July, Leroy Brock was eager to break the monotony of his ranger work, which consisted primarily of patrolling up and down the John Muir Trail through LeConte Canyon on horseback. There were also frequent excursions up the trail to Dusy Basin. Brock had met Moore and Dodge before, and when they showed up at his station that July day in 1960, he asked to accompany the scientists on the next leg of their study. "I wanted to go with them on one of the hikes that would be dangerous for a single person."

Frank Dodge recalls, "We'd go by there [the ranger station] occasionally, and it was *something* to see somebody else. I mean, we wouldn't see anybody for days on end when we were working back there. So, we'd stop and talk to Leroy for a while. He kept bugging us, and he wanted to go out with us. So, Jim [Moore] said, 'The next day is going to be an easy day. We'll ask Leroy if he wants to come.'" The geologists were accustomed to traveling alone as they mapped and collected specimens on their expeditions. As Frank Dodge had already learned that summer, Moore kept up too grueling a pace for any but the hardy to follow.

As Brock recognized in his request to the two geologists, it was uncommon in those days for hikers to leave the trail with nothing but a map and compass and vague ideas of where they wanted to go. For one thing, though the maps were accurate enough, many of the places on the maps had never been visited. Terrain could be guessed, but routes were unknown.

Opportunities for injury abounded, whereas help for the injured did not. On July 16, 1952, twenty-one-year-old Charles Bays Locker fell to his death while leading three teenage Boy Scouts from San Diego on a climbing trip, traversing a ridge to an unnamed peak on the Black Divide very near where Moore and company planned to go.

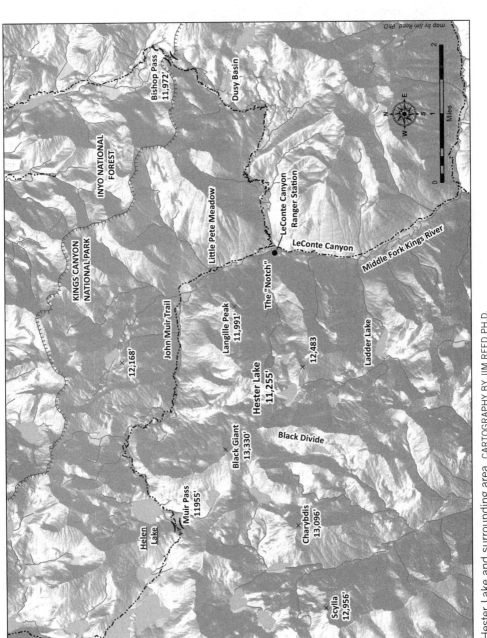

Hester Lake and surrounding area. CARTOGRAPHY BY JIM REED PH.D.

Seventeen-year-old Donald Albright and fifteen-year-old Karl Hufbauer dispatched thirteen-year-old Gary Hufbauer on a search for any help he could find. At nearly sunset the boy found newlyweds Douglas and Ballard Engelbart camped near where the LeConte Canyon Ranger Station would be built seven years later. Leaving young Gary behind, fed and sheltered by their fire, the Engelbarts made a rough nighttime trek, barely lit by a waning crescent moon, across steep and rocky slopes, intercepted by treacherous fields of snow and unbridged, fast-moving streams over Bishop Pass. They arrived at Parcher's Camp at dawn, seeking help.

In the meantime, the two traumatized elder boys had scrambled around the ridge in search of Locker. They found their friend at the bottom of a couloir and dragged his body over snowfields for some 4 miles before darkness and exhaustion forced them to stop a short distance from their base camp at Ladder Lake. After sadly burying their friend in a snowbank, they ate a meager dinner and settled into their sleeping bags for a restless night.

With no official or organized search-and-rescue organization within the national park at that time, the recovery effort involved many volunteers, including Rainbow Pack Station owner, Dudley Boothe, sheriff John Joplin, Dr. Robert Denton, and game warden Stephen "Lou" Lukacik. The party's horses could not make the last 2 miles to Ladder Lake, so they continued on by foot, carrying a Stokes basket. Recovering and transporting the body of Charles Bays Locker took the party two full days.

In those days before off-trail routes were popularized, marked, and written up in guidebooks, the Kings Canyon National Park wilderness was a much more dangerous place for the uninitiated than it is today. Few rangers patrolled the park, and they rarely left the trail. Radio contact was spotty and helicopter rescue unheard of. Hard to believe today, but some backcountry ranger stations actually had telephones! Hikers were few, and the preferred method of travel was on horseback.

In 1960, when Moore and Dodge called upon Ranger Brock and his family, they could have been visiting a homesteader on the frontier. Rangers had a lot of leeway in their duties because they were isolated from any kind of central authority and reliable communication. Leroy Brock was free to make up his own schedule and define his own job description. Though tethered to his radio set back at the ranger station, Brock was his own man elsewhere.

What James Moore considered an "easy" day entailed a strenuous climb of more than 3,000 vertical feet in less than 3 miles to an unnamed lake basin with several unnamed lakes. They began by crossing the Kings River behind and below the ranger station. The thigh-deep ford was cold, the river bottom with loose cobbles the size of grapefruits. The three men then climbed steeply through a thick conifer forest, with Moore and Dodge making notes on the geology. On the way they passed a beautiful waterfall that sprang through a crack in the granite canyon wall. The torrent leapt nearly horizontally from the rock, set free from the force of gravity before falling, tumbling loudly over granite slabs.

Reaching a small, open bowl with a wet meadow ringed by mountain hemlock, the men were confronted by a vertical granite wall extending from right to left. On their extreme left a rocky slope of scree and talus, choked in places by shrubby willows and large patches of snow, led upward with no visible summit. Before them lay a deeply incised, 300-foot-tall, narrow notch in the rock. As they soon discovered, the Notch was even more narrow higher up. A thin stream of water cascaded down through it over room-size boulders. Two hundred feet of talus slope, covered in some spots by snow, and in others, by willows, led up to the Notch. It looked like the only—and therefore, most obvious—route up, so Moore, Dodge, and Brock slowly made their ascent.

That way was steep but not life-threatening. Their biggest concern was the water that flowed through the Notch, making the rock slick. There were a few places where they had to climb hand over hand. Toward the top it was difficult to find their way, as the three men bashed through prickly gooseberry and over matted willows and loose talus. In a couple of places one or the other of them slipped and slid through the vegetation. By the time they finally reached the summit, the men were sweating profusely and breathing hard.

The Notch below Hester Lake that has discouraged so many visitors to the lake. Peak 12,483 visible behind the Notch. PHOTO BY PETER STEKEL

Above the Notch the way flattened out into a wide rock bench, and they hiked steeply over giant slabs of granite toward their lake basin target. Pretty soon they began seeing pieces of something that could have only been an airplane. Brock found what looked like a stainless-steel bicycle chain. He recognized it as a chain used to move the ailerons on an airplane wing. Next, the men discovered a yellow oxygen bottle, the kind used in unpressurized aircraft so the crew could breathe at high altitudes. "Jim Moore or Frank Dodge had been in the air force, I think, during the Second World War, and recognized it immediately," Brock recalled years later. "It was unusual to find it in this location," so they knew something terrible had happened sometime in the past. The questions were: How long ago, and did anybody else know about it?

They began to find more debris. Farther up the drainage they found the remains of a flight suit jacket. Attached to it was a piece of partially decomposed plywood with a bailout bottle. Bailout bottles were green cylinders, about the size of a thermos flask, that clipped onto an airman's flight suit. Aviators used them when they had to bail out at high altitude so they could breathe oxygen on the way down.

Reaching the unnamed lake they found it frozen over in places, but the three men could see plenty of objects along the shore and in the water. At the lake outlet Moore found a wooden chock, a wedge used to block an aircraft's wheels from rolling. Dodge spotted a boot in about 6 feet of water. There was an open parachute, too, suspended in the water like some huge jellyfish. Brock saw another yellow oxygen bottle and waded into the lake to retrieve it, thinking it might have an identification number on it. No such luck.

After a bit of consultation, Moore stripped off his clothing and waded, then swam, in the frigid lake water. He grabbed the white fabric of the parachute; the rotten silk ripped and tore as he pulled it free from the lake. Dodge and Brock helped to haul the sodden sheet onto the shore. Moore decided to retrieve the boot Dodge had spotted earlier. He dove into the water and grabbed the boot but couldn't bring it to the surface because there were cords attached to it. These were electrical cords attached to the boot, part of an aviator's heated flight suit.

Returning to the lake with his knife, Moore cut the cords and brought the boot to shore and made a gruesome discovery. "It was a flight boot that contained a human foot, broken off at the ankle. The skin of the foot, though slightly wrinkled and bleached, was otherwise almost perfectly preserved, as was the hair and flesh." The men were shocked. Because of the remarkable preservation of the foot within the boot, "Our first reaction was that we were dealing with a crash a year or two old." Later they realized the preservation had less to do with time and more to do with the lake being frozen over during the winter and spring, and its temperature remaining just above freezing the remaining months.

They expanded their search. Brock says, "Around the lake we found the remains of the plane. Pieces, just different pieces. A wing. A brief-case." Beneath the unnamed peak at the lake's southwestern end was a major part of the airplane's empennage, or tail assembly. Brock found a 15-foot section of wing and the tip of a wing. It was difficult to see the wing because its brown color was camouflaged against the rocks. On it was labeled "FORD B-24." So, now they knew what kind of airplane they were looking at.

The briefcase they discovered was 30 feet upslope from the water's edge, and the side facing up was extremely weathered. But turning it over they could easily read "Lt. William T. Cronin," embossed on the cover. According to James Moore, "Papers within, though caked with mud and barely legible, revealed that they had belonged to the navigator of a B-24 bomber, the four-engine World War II Liberator."

Moore, Dodge, and Brock considered the evidence before them and its location:

- Pieces of a B-24 Liberator's wing and tail section were located in the rocks above the lake but below the tall mountain, Peak 12,483 (so-named for its elevation marked on the 1948 USGS Mount Goddard 15-minute topographic map).

- An oxygen bottle, pieces of a flight suit, and a bailout bottle were found below the lake.

- The wheel chock was discovered at the lake's outflow, and there were bits and pieces of other debris scattered everywhere along the northeast shore . Lieutenant Cronin's briefcase was found in the rocks, above the northeast shore.

Putting it all together, the men created a scenario to fit their observations.

- They judged the B-24 Liberator came in low over the mountains flying northwestward.
- It clipped Peak 12,483 immediately south of the lake.
- After impacting the peak or, maybe, the ridge, the aircraft tumbled through the sky, disintegrating and throwing off parts as it cartwheeled 1,240 feet earthward.
- Hitting what they assumed was the frozen surface of the lake where the three men now stood, the plane then skidded across

Hester Lake, with Peak 12,483 in the background. PHOTO BY PETER STEKEL

the ice, ramming into the cliffs on the northeastern shore. Debris, such as the navigator's briefcase, was thrown high onto the rocks above the lake. The majority of the airplane must have come to rest on the surface of the frozen lake.

• Once summer came and the lake melted, all the wreckage sank to the lake's bottom.

Moore recalls, "We returned the boot to the lake, took the papers from the briefcase, and noted the inscriptions on other small pieces of the aircraft. I had difficulty resuming geologic work that afternoon." The party returned to the ranger station late in the day, and Leroy Brock radioed park headquarters of their discovery.

With work to do, Moore and Dodge left Brock the next day and performed a grand sweep off-trail through rugged High Sierra territory, mapping as they went. The geologists returned to the LeConte Canyon Ranger Station about a week later. Over dinner and a campfire, Leroy Brock filled them in on what, exactly, they had discovered. The information from park headquarters was slim but definitive. On December 4, 1943, a B-24 with the registration number 41-28463 departed the US Army Air Forces base at Hammer Field in Fresno for a training mission to Tucson. It had disappeared in poor weather the next morning, without a trace, during the return flight.

The name on the briefcase they found, Lt. William T. Cronin, showed where the plane had come to rest. Cronin, from Olean, New York, was navigator on the missing plane. The other crew were pilot, 2nd Lt. Charles W. Turvey, from Reesville, Ohio; copilot, 2nd Lt. Robert M. Hester, from Los Angeles, California; bombardier, 2nd Lt. Ellis Homer Fish, from La Crosse, Wisconsin; flight engineer S/Sgt. Robert O. Bursey, from Rutland, Vermont; and radio operator S/Sgt. Howard Wandtke, from Toledo, Ohio.

Brock told Moore and Dodge, "Clinton Hester, the father of the copilot, had become obsessed with searching for the plane and his son. He spent every summer season combing the vast reaches of the alpine Sierra. He traveled from one trailhead to another by motorcycle and then searched the trails on foot. This passionate search was not successful. Eventually he died in 1959, just a year before we discovered the plane."

In all likelihood no one had ever visited the lake before or since the crash, though the closest to come to it were Charles Bays Locker and his three Boy Scouts, when they were the first people to climb Peak 12,483, in 1952. The airplane had rested, unmolested, for seventeen years in that unnamed lake high up on the west wall of LeConte Canyon. All of this was about to change. The legend and myth of the plane in the lake were about to take off.

CHAPTER 2

The Reporters

THE MYSTERIOUS B-24 LIBERATOR BOMBER WAS BIG NEWS, AND THE national media jumped on the story. Everyone wanted to know how the airplane had ended up at the bottom of the unnamed wilderness lake in the Kings Canyon National Park. Even before the army could notify families or get a dive team organized to explore the possibility of recovering the crew's remains, fast-moving reporters and photographers from the San Francisco Bay area made their way to the crash site.

First to the lake were James Benét and photographer Barney Peterson from the *San Francisco Chronicle*. Three days after the discovery of the B-24, on July 30, 1960, the newspapermen flew over the crash site, snapping photos, before landing at their jumping-off point in Bishop. At 5:00 a.m. they showed up on the front stoop of the Rainbow Pack Outfit, asking owner Dudley Boothe to take them to the lake. Benét's article about the trip would appear two days later in the *Chronicle*. In a front-page story above the fold Benét called the crash site a "grim corner of the High Sierra."

Having presented themselves to Dudley Boothe, Benét and Peterson told him they wanted to leave immediately. Boothe's son, nineteen-year-old John, was there—home on leave from the US Army, and helping his father with the usual duties of a pack outfit: taking tourists, but mostly fishermen, into Kings Canyon National Park over Bishop Pass on horseback. John Boothe recalls that, "After a quick breakfast the two newspapermen, my father, and I threw some supplies together, packed our mules, and got on our way."

That first day was consumed in riding the 15 or so miles from the South Lake trailhead, over Bishop Pass, through Dusy Basin, and down to LeConte Canyon and the ranger station. Leroy Brock and the Boothes were well acquainted, and after dinner there was a bit of jawing around the campfire about the plane, its discovery, and what might have happened.

The next day, guided by Ranger Brock, the *Chronicle* men and the Boothes made the difficult hike to the lake where the B-24 had crashed. John Boothe recalls three hours of climbing the "sheer side of the canyon," on "hands and knees" in some places, and "hand over hand" through "a steep narrow chute."

At the lake they found lots of airplane parts and pieces. Benét dove into the lake and swam around in the shallow part, looking for significant debris. In his *Chronicle* article, Benét described seeing hundreds of fragments on the lake's northeast shore, strewn about as if from a careless hand. There were "bits of sheet metal, twisted instruments, a propeller blade. The force of the impact snapped the heavy aluminum castings to which a seat belt was fastened, and tossed half the seat belt and half the casting, still bolted together, a hundred feet up the slope." All the airplane parts in the lake were clean and looked new, the instrument panel dials readable and switches functional. Across the lake, on the ridge to the west, Benét came upon the wing seen by Moore, Dodge, and Brock. Echoing the site's discoverers, Benét proposed that the bomber had struck Peak 12,483 directly south of the lake and tumbled into the water.

In 2011 Benét, then ninety-seven years old, but still spry and enthusiastic, had only dim memories of his trip to the unnamed lake with the airplane crash. "It was one of those things, at the time, you're really thinking how exhausted you are, doing all this climbing. But it was an interesting trip. You know, if you're working as a daily newspaper reporter, you have to expect to be put in some places that require a lot of energy. That's just part of the job."

In his Monday, August 1, 1960, article for the *Chronicle*, Benét wrote, "We know the B-24 radioed its Fresno base, Hammer Field, as it returned from a training flight to Tucson, Ariz., that it was caught in one of the Sierra's terrible winter storms. It strayed too low." Benét draws a

John Boothe holds a propeller blade from 463 that was fished out of Hester Lake in July, 1960. COURTESY JOHN BOOTHE

line from Peak 12,483, the wing wreckage, and other crash debris to the lake and says, "The peak that caught its wing and dashed it down more than a thousand feet into the lake—then frozen and piled high with midwinter snows—stands among much higher ones." Ominously he adds, "Below 13,000 feet the bomber didn't have a chance."

Benét reports that the airplane was last heard from on Sunday night (actually, early Sunday morning), December 5, 1943, and that a *second* B-24 was lost the following morning while looking for it. This sister ship had vanished in the Sierra Nevada foothills, "about 10 miles west and a little south" of its Hammer Field, Fresno, base. Two of eight crew members from this second aircraft had parachuted to safety, but the other six were lost. This second B-24 wasn't found until 1955, when the reservoir at Huntington Lake was drained so that retrofitting could be performed on the dam structure and, "there it was."

John Boothe was impressed by what he saw at the lake. "Some moving parts we found that were still together worked like new." He was more impressed after examining the flight boot first brought to shore by James Moore. "The flesh and even the hair were still in place, as though it had happened only the day before." He was convinced, and so were the men from the *Chronicle*, that the lake had been frozen over when the plane had careened into it. When the ice melted, the plane sank to the bottom of the lake. John Boothe didn't doubt the lake may have been frozen over all year, nearly every year since 1943, when the bomber crashed. "It is quite common for locations in the higher elevations of the Sierra to be covered by snow year-round, except after the occasional light winter."

After exploring the lake for several hours, Benét and his photographer colleague returned with Brock and Dudley and John Boothe to the ranger station below, in LeConte Canyon. Leaving Brock to his family in their wilderness home, the four other men saddled up and made the long trek back to Bishop that evening.

Two more reporters arrived on the Boothes' doorstep the morning after the *San Francisco Chronicle* crew departed. They too wanted to visit the crash site at the unnamed lake above LeConte Canyon. The new arrivals were Fred Goerner from KCBS News in San Francisco and the *San Mateo Times*, along with photographer Bob Fischer, who had brought skin-diving gear. They had driven all night from San Francisco. Dudley Boothe turned to his son and told him, "Well, you know the way; you don't need me," and the younger Boothe was elected to return to the crash site.

The three men rode horses, with two mules carrying the party's heavy load of scuba equipment, still and movie cameras, and tape-recording gear. Like the previous trip they stopped at the ranger station in LeConte Canyon and spent the night with Leroy Brock and the ranger's family.

At five the next morning Boothe, Goerner, and Fischer departed the ranger station for the crash site with Ranger Brock. What had been on the mule's backs the previous day was now carried by the men. Fred Goerner got halfway up the Notch and, overcome with exhaustion, refused to go any further. Boothe bluntly told him, "You made it this far, and you're going." Emphasizing his point, Boothe shouldered Goerner's pack and continued climbing. Leroy Brock remembers struggling to get the two newspapermen up to the lake. "The photographer, he just totally zoned out." Tired beyond belief, Fischer became angry and uncooperative. "But he made it. He made it all the way up."

Finally at the lake, Brock and Boothe, Goerner and Fischer, met up with Peter Schuft, chief ranger for Sequoia & Kings Canyon National Parks. Schuft had been ferried in from park headquarters in Three Rivers via helicopter to supervise the affair.

After the difficult and arduous trip to the lake, Goerner and Fischer had little interest in doing much of anything. When it came time for Fischer to use all of the scuba gear they had hauled in, John Boothe says, "I don't know if he was scared or what, but he just wouldn't do much. Brock had some diving experience, so he finally put on the gear," and "wound up doing most of the diving."

Fred Goerner wrote two articles based on his ordeal. The first, a front-page, below-the-fold, uncredited article in the August 2, 1960, issue of the *San Mateo Times*, features a large, staged photograph. The caption identifies Bob Fischer, standing waist-deep in the lake, wearing a wet suit, weight belt, and face mask, handing a piece of airplane fragment to Leroy Brock. Chief ranger Peter Schuft looks on, holding a poorly coiled lariat. John Boothe says, "The diver in the water is none other than Leroy Brock, and the person he was handing something to was none other than me. The only one they identified correctly was Peter Schuft."

Goerner's first article explains that he and Fischer "carried 50 pounds apiece of the diving and survival equipment up 3,000 feet through 'almost straight up' rocky inclines." Also, that the pack trip before that had required "nine hours on horseback" and then "six hours of climbing, often hand-over-hand." Goerner declares, "We found the actual spot where the bomber crashed, about 200 feet below the highest point of the Black Divide." Actually, the lake and crash site are 1,500 feet below the Black Divide, so the reporter's description can't be accurate. He must have been confusing the rim of the lake basin for the Black Divide, because between the Black Divide and where the B-24 Liberator was found is a large lake basin where debris would have come to earth.

Speculating on the route of the B-24, probably from information derived from Leroy Brock and John Boothe, Goerner figures the airplane was heading northeasterly, though its destination was Fresno, to the west. "The pilot appeared to be guiding the plane in the wrong direction." Goerner specifically says that the plane crashed during a snowstorm, which he says he verified after returning home. "The bomber did not crash against the mountain and then slide down. Instead, it bounced after hitting, and flipped, possibly end over end, a quarter to half a mile. Then it slammed down onto the ice-covered surface of the 600-yards-long lake, and skidded across the ice to smash into a rocky cliff at the other (i.e. northeast) side. There it disintegrated." Echoing others, Goerner says the wreckage sank to the bottom when the lake later thawed.

Goerner makes some interesting observations. Channeling later explorers who actually investigated the lake bottom, Goerner says, "We found the lake about 50 feet deep. Bob [Fischer] dived and we located the fuselage, intact but badly smashed; and the motors. The crystal-clear, frigid water perfectly preserved both the plane and the bodies of its occupants. It looked like it had crashed yesterday. Paint and bright-metal parts were like new. The conditions of the bodies—severely mutilated as they were—still surpassed any embalming process known." He goes on to say that the water was so cold, even wearing a heavy diving suit, "Fischer

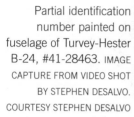

Partial identification number painted on fuselage of Turvey-Hester B-24, #41-28463. IMAGE CAPTURE FROM VIDEO SHOT BY STEPHEN DESALVO. COURTESY STEPHEN DESALVO

was able to stay underwater only four to five minutes at a time, but he was able to survey the remains of the tragic accident."

Fred Goerner's description of the airplane *in* the lake and the bodies of the crew sitting in their seats is tantalizing, because what he reports is so close to what subsequent searchers would describe. Yet both Brock and Boothe steadfastly maintain that Goerner's diving companion, Bob Fischer, never got anywhere near the wreck. Boothe says, "The day we went up there Fischer didn't go out beyond the shallow water, and only spent a little time in the water." He also steadfastly maintains, "We didn't find anything else of any significance that day." As for either Goerner or Fischer knowing the lake's depth and finding the majority of the plane with bodies in it, "All I can say is, it just plain didn't happen." And yet, Fred Goerner seemed to, mostly, know what would eventually be found.

In his *San Francisco Chronicle* article, James Benét had noted, "Under the water, then, the torn bodies lie as carefully preserved by nature as Egyptian pharaohs. And even better, for the pyramids have been despoiled by men for centuries." Benét removed no wreckage. The geologists who discovered the crash site had necessarily removed items to be used for identification purposes.

Goerner returned home with a "section of instrument panel containing the serial number of the B-24 bomber (4128463)," plus other material, including "a section of the navigator's manual" and "a misshapen mechanical pencil." Other items removed included gloves, shoes, personal effects, and numerous plane parts, which were cataloged by Goerner, who tape-recorded each finding. The souvenirs were later displayed at the newspaper's booth at the San Mateo County Fair, along with airplane relicts Goerner had brought back from Tanapag Harbor in Saipan several weeks earlier, "by this paper's Amelia Earhart expedition." It's unknown where these historical artifacts from the lake are now, or whether they still exist.

Goerner's second account is a mix of heroic adventure writing, journalism, drama, and speculative fiction, mixed with inconsistently presented details. This Sunday, August 6, 1960, *San Mateo Times* article is entitled, "The Angry Mountains—A Radio Newsman Fights the High Sierra," and is illustrated by Robert Fischer's photographs.

After an "assault on that 3,000 feet separating us and the Liberator's crash site," the lake reminds Goerner of a "big rock quarry filled with water." The climb took "five minutes more than six hours," packing "that Aqua-Lung, diving suit, lead diving belt, face mask, snorkel, fins, underwater light, tools, tape recorder, still cameras, motion-picture camera, and a good amount of film."

For drama, "We scrambled, clawed, and crawled our way up." Then, they "stopped, rested, and fought" their way before reaching the crux, that gash or notch in the granite constituting LeConte Canyon's western wall that would come, over the years, to stop many a traveler to the lake. Here, "We climbed straight up the rocks hand over hand for better than 400 feet." Goerner truthfully admits that he and Fischer were woefully unprepared for the expedition. Reaching the lake, "Bob [Fischer] and I threw down our packs and stretched out from sheer exhaustion."

In Goerner's account, "Bob Fischer with his protective diving suit slid into the icy water of the lake," and does all the exploration underwater. No mention is made of Leroy Brock doing any diving. Goerner has Fischer needing an hour to locate the wreck in 50 feet of water, at the deepest part of the lake. To the surface he brings "many articles, including parachutes, gloves, boots, warning lights, instruments."

At 4:00 p.m., the reporters and their guides loaded up their equipage and backed down the mountain. There is a photograph in Goerner's second article of four men snaking down a steep granite slope above the

Notch. Two have daypacks, a third carries some sort of handled case in his left hand, and bringing up the rear is a fellow with a cowboy hat, carrying an Aqua-Lung.

At the Notch, Goerner injured his ankle, but says, "I managed to make it to the plateau below," before collapsing. "My legs were so tired they wouldn't support me no matter how I willed them to do so." He writes that the three other men left Goerner there, promising to send a rescue helicopter. After cooling his heels and watching the sun dip below the peaks behind him, Goerner decided, "I'd better try to make it down on my own power." He panicked, not knowing if he could find his way, somehow managed to, and, "Two hours later I came out within forty yards of the ranger's tent." No further words about the helicopter. Goerner and Fischer packed out the next day with John Boothe and returned to San Francisco.

In retrospect, Brock understands how physical limitations made it difficult for Goerner and his cohort to reach the lake. "They traveled all night and got to the pack station and wanted to go in. They were tired to begin with." On top of being fatigued, the inexperienced flatlanders had to deal with the high altitude and an excruciating off-trail climb while hauling heavy packs. No wonder they were unable to do much at the lake except watch John Boothe and Leroy Brock do all the work.

The day following his second trip to the lake, John Boothe switched on the television to watch Fred Goerner's account of the trip on the San Francisco CBS affiliate. "The one or two minutes [of the report], it made me wonder how it was all worth it, considering what we all went through."

Goerner's description of his journey to the lake might come across as overblown at first, but not within the context of an inexperienced city dweller on his first adventure in the High Sierra. All things considered, and even if they bit off more than they could chew, both he and Bob Fischer were good reporters. They did well enough to get their story and return home to tell it.

Despite his ordeal, Goerner found time in his *San Mateo Times* article to be poetic. Reflecting upon where the six boys had been buried for nearly seventeen years, he wrote, "God must love them very much. He chose one of the most desolate spots in the world as their resting place. I like to think He wanted them to himself."

CHAPTER 3

The Divers

WITH THE BAY AREA NEWSPAPERMEN GONE, FOLLOWING THE DEVELOP-ing story of the bomber in the lake fell to the local newspaper in Bishop, the *Inyo Register*. For the next two weeks the newspaper kept tabs on what was happening at the crash site. It was interesting enough that the wire services picked up the story, giving it national coverage. This had to be the first news any of the families had received about the lost airplane since the boys' disappearance nearly seventeen years earlier.

Wednesday morning, August 3, 1960, the *Register* reported that Stephen Lukacik flew over the B-24 crash site in a fixed-wing airplane with a Major Hamil from Stead Air Force Base in Reno. Their purpose was to investigate whether it would be possible to land a helicopter near the lake. Had they known to communicate with chief ranger Peter Schuft, they could have saved themselves a trip.

During the reconnaissance Lukacik spotted a "large cargo parachute with four packages attached approximately two miles northwest of the unnamed lake where the wreckage of the B24 was found." Lukacik identified the parachute and packages as likely "survival equipment which a plane crew would throw out first before bailing out." Reporting that the parachute "appeared to have been there for some time, as the orange-colored chute had faded," Lukacik concluded it had nothing to do with the recently discovered B-24. The parachute was on the ground in upper LeConte Canyon, "at about the 11,200 ft. level," which would place it somewhere below Helen Lake, south of Muir Pass.

Peak 12,483 (front) and Hester Lake, on collision course. PHOTO BY PETER STEKEL

Later that summer, Ranger Leroy Brock located the parachute in upper LeConte Canyon. He found four cases of intact and eatable C rations from Hill Air Force Base in Utah. Brock knew the base had a Boy Scout troop, and that they were doing an extended backpacking trip through the Sierra. Brock figured some of the fathers had arranged an illegal food drop in the Kings Canyon National Park wilderness. He's sure the food drop was not part of rescue supplies because "It had napkins in it," from the officers' club.

Unaware of Lukacik and Major Hamil, on August 3 came a three-man US Army team from the Presidio in San Francisco. Major John E. Thayer, assistant Sixth Army operations officer, arrived to survey the lake and assess what would be needed to recover the crew. Along with Thayer were Lt. Robert C. Hartmann and S/Sgt. Henry M. Waskavitch, two divers with the 561st Engineering Company at Fort Baker. The army men drove to Bishop from the Bay Area, hopped aboard a waiting helicopter, and were flown to the lake. An initial survey made with

Scuba diver prepares to enter Hester Lake. Note the wing panel wreckage to the right of the diver. COURTESY SHIZUE MCCOY, PAUL MCCOY AND MCCOY FAMILY

"shallow diving equipment" determined that the lake was too deep for scuba diving.

The army men decided that helicopters were needed to bring divers, deep-sea dive suits, air compressors, food and camping equipment, and support staff into the High Sierra. The recovery operation became a major expedition occupying many days and a crew of twelve men, including two civilians and an identification technician. Their equipment would allow the divers to go down to 300 feet.

The type of diving they proposed is extremely dangerous. Even under highly controlled situations, deep-diving is chancy. Adding high elevation to the mix increases that danger. Robert Mester and Mark Allen are both highly trained and experienced divers who have gone as deep as 250 feet, either with scuba or hard-hat diving, while recovering or salvaging sunken aircraft and marine vessels. Both agree that the conditions and complexity of deepwater diving at high elevation means anyone attempting it is risking their life.

The biggest worry is decompression. Atmospheric air is a mixture of about 78 percent nitrogen, 21 percent oxygen, and 1 percent other gases. Animals need oxygen to survive, but all that nitrogen in air is inert and not utilized. However, nitrogen is still absorbed into the bloodstream and distributed throughout the body. That's where the trouble begins. "Oxygen and nitrogen can and will become toxic and eventually fatal unless their partial pressures are carefully monitored during decompression, or by adjusting the breathing mixture to keep them at safe levels under pressure."

When a diver descends from the surface to, say, 200 feet, the gases breathed in at depth enter their bloodstream at extreme pressure. Returning to the surface, those bloodstream gases expand as the pressure of the water decreases. The same effect is seen when opening a bottle of carbonated beverage. The sudden release of pressure allows the highly saturated carbon-dioxide gas to come out of solution and make bubbles.

The same bubbling happens to a diver ascending too rapidly from deep water, and the result is called "decompression sickness," or "the bends." The bends are caused by saturated gases in the blood leaving solution. They leak into the body's tissues and joints and lodge there. The result is painful, and can be fatal.

Peter Hunt, retired navy fighter pilot and a veteran of deepwater expeditions to explore the *Andrea Doria* shipwreck, points to an insidious environmental factor *before* a diver even enters the water that leads to, or exacerbates, the bends. If you climb too quickly from low to high elevation, you're subject to a range of symptoms known as "altitude sickness" that result from a lack of adequate oxygen to the brain. The most salient symptoms include dehydration, headache, fatigue, difficulty thinking or concentrating, and a feeling of being lightheaded.

The army intended on diving at an elevation of 11,255 feet, which is 1,255 feet *above* the altitude where pilots are required to use supplemental oxygen when flying. Acclimating to such high altitude puts stresses on a person's body and increases a diver's risk for decompression sickness. Dehydration from altitude sickness adds to that risk, as does being tired and chilled, such as from exposure to cold water.

For deepwater, hard-hat diving, an umbilical cord runs from the diver's helmet to the surface and then to an air pump, which delivers air

A Mark V diving helmet similar to what was used in 1960 by army divers at Hester Lake. PHOTO BY PETER STEKEL, HELMET COURTESY OF FOSS WATERWAY SEAPORT MUSEUM

to the diver. Within the cord is a microphone and speaker wire, enabling the diver to communicate to the dive supervisor topside. The diving suit used in the 1960s was made of vulcanized rubber covered with an inner and outer cotton-twill layer. The Mark V helmet of that era was made of brass, with four tempered-glass windows. Some divers likened it to being in a cave with the walls inches from your face.

To counteract their natural buoyancy, the lake divers had to wear 35-pound lead-weighted shoes. Without the shoes, air inside the diver's suit would make his legs float above his head. Also helping to counteract buoyancy was an 84-pound weight belt and the 54-pound breast plate where the helmet attached to the suit. Adding to all the dangers and discomfort, deepwater diving isn't swimming. It's *walking* along the bottom, usually in the dark, stirring up muck. Essentially, divers work in zero visibility.

If the diving wasn't dangerous enough, there was also the interaction between altitude, atmospheric pressure, and 1960s helicopter technology to consider. Even today, flying and landing rotary aircraft at elevation is tricky, requiring skilled and experienced pilots. The issues involve the aircraft's engine, ability to hover, payload size, topography, updrafts and downdrafts, and winds.

Atmospheric pressure decreases with altitude and warmer air has less pressure than colder air. Aircraft performance suffers with less atmospheric pressure, and propellers have less "bite" because the air is less dense. It's like whitewater kayakers trying to paddle through foamy rapids that are more air than water.

Helicopters can hover close to the surface because of "ground effect," the added aerodynamic buoyancy produced by a cushion of air pushed beneath the aircraft by the helicopter blades. As atmospheric density decreases, the angle of attack of the helicopter's rotor needs to keep increasing in order to get a bigger bite of air. When the helicopter reaches a stall point for the rotor system, it can't hover out of ground effect, and at that point the helicopter ceases to become an aircraft and becomes a rock.

Helicopters in the 1960s were all piston-driven and didn't have the oomph to do the work the dive team needed done. They were going to an elevation of 11,255 feet—out of hovering range for most 1960s-era helicopters. This made it necessary to fly the dive team into the backcountry in one helicopter and then shuttle them in small groups in another.

First, a Piasecki H-21 "Flying Banana" was used to transport everything and everybody to 8,960 feet in Little Pete Meadow, about half a mile up-canyon from the LeConte Canyon Ranger Station. The Piasecki was far too large to find landing space in the vertical world around the crash site, and was also far too underpowered to carry all the men and equipment up there. Designed in the late 1940s when helicopters were first built, The H-21 was only effective at low altitudes and in cold weather, where the air is thicker—that is, more dense. "The service ceiling [the highest altitude an aircraft can fly] for the 1,425-horsepower, single-piston engine was only 9,450 feet, and was limited by the power of the engines, and the aerodynamics of the rotor system," as well as the load. This meant that the landing-zone elevation at Little Pete Meadow was dangerously close to the Piasecki's limits.

A factor necessitating logistical creative thinking with the H-21 was its empty weight of 8,950 pounds. Its maximum gross weight (at sea level) was 15,200 pounds, so that didn't leave much room for its payload of divers, diving gear, support staff, food, and camping gear. The shuttle from Bishop to Little Pete Meadow required several runs.

Once they reached Little Pete Meadow the men and equipment were moved to a smaller helicopter—a Kaman HH-43 Huskie. The Huskie had its own set of limitations. The HH-43 vibrated terribly due to its dual intermeshing rotors. Unlike our normal perception of helicopters, the Huskie lacked a stabilizing tail rotor. This function was performed by intermeshing rotors which compensated for the yaw (side motion) caused in all single-rotor systems. "This also allows all of the engine power to be turned into lift rather than expending a percentage for yaw control," resulting in the HH-43 having "an edge in high-altitude performance." Given the task it needed to perform, the Huskie needed all the edge it could get. However, "The HH-43 would not have had much lifting capability at 12,000 feet." The payload for each run would have been equivalent to only two team members.

The Huskie lacked landing skids; instead, it had four castor-type tires. "This made the little helo top-heavy, with a high center of gravity,"

Transferring men and equipment from Piasecki H-21 "Flying Banana" to HH-43 Huskie. Note the size difference between the two aircraft. Little Pete Meadow, August 1960. COURTESY SHIZUE MCCOY, PAUL MCCOY AND MCCOY FAMILY

making it unstable on the ground. Takeoff from a high mountain site had to be done carefully and slowly, with the pilot then needing to gain forward airspeed quickly by aiming downslope.

Complicating matters for the helicopter pilot was that he would be flying above 10,000 feet, where regulations required the use of supplemental oxygen. Since the Huskie was not pressurized, the pilot had to carry a "walk-around" oxygen bottle, which was quite cumbersome for a pilot to use. Everybody else on board, divers included, therefore arrived at the lake already in decompression mode, off-gassing their sea-level nitrogen.

The HH-43 from the late 1940s through the 1950s had a single-piston engine and a service ceiling of 25,000 feet. Even when a turbine-powered model was introduced late in the 1950s, it had a low maximum speed of 120 miles per hour and a range of only 185 miles. Therefore, frequent refueling was necessary. Given the limited payload of the Huskie, it's reasonable to assume a lot of shuttles were needed to carry a team of twelve, plus gear, up to the lake.

Soldiers ferrying dive gear upslope to Hester Lake, August 1960. Peak 12,483 in background. COURTESY SHIZUE MCCOY, PAUL MCCOY AND MCCOY FAMILY

For the dive team, the shuttle from Little Pete Meadow to the crash site would have been mercifully short, though unmercifully unpleasant. "The HH-43 is not comfortable for passengers—they were either sitting on the aluminum floor or on fold-down web seats." Inside, the cabin was cramped and smelled constantly of aviation fuel. With the engine immediately above the cabin, noise was extreme. The Huskie's two large rotors make an extremely loud, *wompety* sound, and the vibration of the rotor system is so bad it causes the human body to be fatigued quickly.

"The flight to the site would have been okay, but the landing would be 'sporting,' given the extremes of high mountain landings." Setting down on the uneven and rocky ground around the lake would be ticklish. If the pilot bumped the ground on landing, the low swinging blades would come in contact with the rocks and disintegrate the helicopter.

Reaching the lake on August 4, 1960, the Huskie pilot decided it was unwise to attempt a landing. Instead, while he hovered over an area approximately 700 yards below the lake, equipment was dumped out from a height of 8 feet. The soldiers then followed. Three hours later they had hauled themselves and all their gear to the lake and were performing their first dive.

The earlier survey trip had estimated the lake to be 50 feet deep, but the two divers, Sergeant Henry Waskavitch and his assistant, Sergeant Douglas McCoy, soon determined this to be in error, finding that their equipment was "inadequate for a complete job." Heavier dive equipment would be needed, and while they waited for it to arrive, they continued exploring the shallower water.

Sergeants Waskavitch and McCoy were brothers-in-law, and Paul McCoy remembers stories related by his father and uncle about their lake assignment. "They were told they were going to go up and retrieve some bodies and remove parts from the plane to positively identify the plane." Weighted down with men and equipment, their first pass with the helicopter was almost their last. The machine barely had enough lifting capacity to get them out of there.

With all the men and gear at the lake, the next challenge for the soldiers was to find a place to camp among the rocks. The largest, nearly, flat spot was a little meadow beside the lake. The air compressor and hoses for the divers went there. The men spread out as best they could. Unlike today, there were no high-altitude fire restrictions in Kings Canyon National Park in 1960, but there also weren't any trees at the lake crash site—or anywhere near it. Without wood for a fire, the nights were cold, and all cooking had to be done on portable liquid fuel stoves.

In addition to the army divers and support crew working at the lake, the army had another support crew of six men stationed at the staging area in Little Pete Meadow. The soldiers at Little Pete were as sorry a lot of campers as Leroy Brock had ever seen. "They didn't have enough gear. They didn't have anything to cook with. All they had were C rations. That was pretty grim!"

The lieutenant in charge of the meadow team visited the ranger station and asked to borrow some pots and pans. "My wife said, 'Why don't you come down here and use our fire?'" Brock had built a rock fireplace and they had a grill on top. "They came down and they were extremely polite."

After heavier diving equipment arrived, the lake bottom was searched on a pattern basis, and all portions of the wreckage were examined and

Sgt. Douglas McCoy suits up for his dive into Hester Lake.
COURTESY SEQUOIA & KINGS CANYON NATIONAL PARK

checked. The divers found the lake water to be "crystal clear." There were parts of the airplane strewn about on the lake bottom, and it looked like the B-24 had just crashed the day before.

Despite the clearness of the water, conditions on the bottom of the lake were not ideal. A deep layer of silt exists everywhere. Any movement stirred up the muck, eliminating visibility. Wearing their lead boots and claustrophobic suits, the divers sank to the bottom of the silt and began lifting their legs up and out, like "post-holing" through deep snow. Movement was deliberate, difficult, and laborious.

The two men mostly worked by touch but could occasionally see what was around them. Douglas McCoy told his son, "You could see where the guys were sitting in their seats." McCoy can't remember if his dad said whether any of the boys were out of the plane, but did note that "there were a couple of them in the plane itself." He said, "For as many years as they'd been in there, they looked awful fresh." Naturally, "They never talked much about removing the bodies, about how they did it. He never talked about that."

The official report from the expedition says that after eight days of searching the lake bottom and surrounding area, the only identifiable recoverable remains were those of S/Sgt. Robert O. Bursey, the flight engineer. He was found in 35 feet of water near the edge of the lake. "Other remains" were recovered from many areas of the lake, but were not identifiable to any individual.

The entire army expedition was a testament to the tenacity of the people working around the lake. The conditions were difficult and primitive, the location remote, and the dangers manifest. "The various commanders ordering the work to be done were likely unaware of the difficulty of the tasks they were assigning." The divers, pilots, and support team involved in the operation probably accepted it as something that they were assigned to do, likely brushing off any hazards and labeling the assignment a "tough one" before moving on.

On August 18, 1960, the *Inyo Register* reported that the search for bodies in the sunken B-24 had been called off. "The team decided that nothing more could be accomplished." Maj. John E. Thayer said, "The plane had been identified positively as the one that crashed December 5, 1943, while on a training mission." Plans for a memorial service for the six crew members had not yet been formulated.

At the end of their field season James Moore and Frank Dodge petitioned the Board on Geographic Names to christen the lake where the plane was found. They chose "Cronin Lake," since it was the navigator's briefcase with his name on it that provided the first clue as to the airplane beneath the lake's haunted waters. Instead, "Hester Lake" was chosen, to honor 2nd Lt. Robert Hester, the copilot, and his father, who had died the previous year after a sixteen-year search for his son.

Robert Hester's sister received a telegram on August 21, 1960, from the Office of the Quartermaster General, Department of Army:

Reference your brother Second Lieutenant Robert M. Hester who lost his life 5 December 1943. His plane was recently discovered in a lake high in the Sierra Nevada Mountains, California. Army has investi-

gated and results will be available by end of August. Army recognizes you as Roberts [sic] legal next of kin, and letter furnishing details will be dispatched as soon as possible.

Next of kin of the other crew members received similar messages.

The impact of Hester Lake on the first people to reach the crash site in 1960 was profound. There was something about that place. James Benét, from the *San Francisco Chronicle*, felt the power of the lake and wrote about it in his newspaper article. "Now come the newspapermen, the Air Force with, perhaps, a helicopter to try to give the bodies a burial more reverent, though no more dignified and safe than the one the mountains gave."

For the remainder of their lives, army divers Henry Waskavitch and Douglas McCoy told the story of Hester Lake over and over to their children. And their children have continued the tradition with their own children.

Ranger Leroy Brock has spent a lot of time over the years talking to people about the Hester Lake B-24 Liberator. It's a story that interests and excites people everywhere, not just hikers in the national park. He says, "I feel that I'm doing a service to the families and other people."

A few years after the Hester Lake discovery, Leroy Brock was coming out of the backcountry from LeConte Canyon, through Dusy Basin and over Bishop Pass, when he came across two men hiking up the trail in orange flight suits. Since this attire was so unusual, Brock stopped to talk with the two strangers. They were on their way to Hester Lake. "One was the brother of one of the men who was aboard the plane. I can't remember what position it was. And this brother died in the crash." After the plane crash had become public in 1960, Brock would frequently see a large military cargo transport plane over the backcountry. "It would come circle, and circle, and circle." One of the men in the orange flight suits was that pilot.

The pilot told a sad story. He and his younger brother had met for the last time shortly before the brother disappeared. The pilot had told his brother that he could arrange a transfer from combat aircraft to military transport if he wanted, so they could be close. "But he said, no, because he

Ranger Leroy
Brock on Mather
Pass, circa 1957.
COURTESY LEROY
BROCK

wanted to stay with his crew, because they were deploying overseas and he felt very strong ties to them."

The man in the orange flight suit was Lt. Col. Harold J. Cronin, older brother of Lt. William T. Cronin, navigator of the B-24 Liberator #41-28463 that came to rest at the bottom of Hester Lake.

CHAPTER 4

One of Our Airplanes Is Missing

VERY EARLY IN THE MORNING OF SUNDAY, DECEMBER 5, 1943, 2ND LT. Charles Willis Turvey Jr., pilot, and 2nd Lt. Robert Hester, copilot, muscled their B-24 #41-28463 (known as "463") back into the sky. They were on their way home from Davis-Monthan Army Air Forces Base in Tucson, Arizona, heading back to Hammer Field in Fresno, California. The boys were leaving Tucson for Hammer Field, completing a navigation mission begun the previous morning.

Built at a cost of $306,592 by the Douglas Aircraft Company in Tulsa, Oklahoma, 463 had come off the line in June of 1943. In her short life 463 had visited Kelly Field in Texas for use at the advanced flight school, Pocatello in Idaho, and Wendover Field in Utah. Turvey and Hester, along with their navigator, Bill Cronin, and bombardier, Ellis Fish, had been delegated—along with several hundred others at Wendover, on November 11—to their proper duty station at Hammer Field. It's possible they flew there in 463; it's hard to know. In any event, the plane and its crew were in California by mid-November.

With all four Pratt & Whitney R-1830-65 Twin Wasp fourteen-cylinder air-cooled turbo supercharged radial engines running, Turvey and Hester felt the whole world trembling. Charley and Bob felt the vibrations in their chests and in their souls. They slept with that feeling. They dreamed of it late at night, tossing and turning in their bunks, thinking of their girlfriends, wives, children, their mothers and fathers, sisters and brothers, and what little they knew of this war and why they were fighting in it. An in-line engine hums, barks, and coughs. But a radial engine growls. It grumbles like a hungry stomach. It pulses and beats like your heart. A radial engine lives and breathes while an in-line engine is simply a machine.

On takeoff, the B-24 Liberator was truly a two-pilot aircraft that flew only with teamwork. Though the pilot was the airplane's commander, he could not fly it by himself. There were too many instruments to pay attention to, in addition to performing the basics of flying the aircraft. When the flying was most difficult one man would fly the instruments while the other flew visual contact with the ground. This kind of flying was "[a] critical and a very risky game of I'll-Pull-You-Push and visa versa [*sic*]," wrote Truman Smith in *The Wrong Stuff*. "It was two human nervous systems interlocked as one in total harmony, any conflict of action or reaction—within a fraction of a second—could result in disaster. It took guts, sensitivity, strength, and complete confidence in each other." There was no stronger bond.

Behind the two pilots their flight engineer, S/Sgt. Robert Bursey, stood and monitored the big bomber's gauges, calling out airspeed and manifold pressure. It was also Bursey's responsibility to monitor the loading of fuel before takeoff and calculate fuel consumption during flight. He knew they would eventually reach their target—if they carried sufficient fuel, that is. Bursey had enough experience with the Liberator to subscribe to the old barnstormer's philosophy about fuel: "I firmly believed the only time there was too much fuel aboard any aircraft was if it was on fire."

Leaving Tucson, scattered town lights below them speckled the earth like grounded stars. Somewhere in the distance were the Catalina Mountains, and the pilots made sure they had more than enough altitude to clear those rocks. When they reached Phoenix, a galaxy of lights in the otherwise mostly dark desert, Turvey and Hester turned, aiming for their next checkpoint, the army airfield at Muroc near Lancaster-Palmdale, California.

Flying west, the only sensation of progress for the boys in the noisy and drafty airplane came from watching scattered pinpricks of light move beneath their wings. From his vantage point in the Plexiglas bubble of his bombardier's station, 2nd Lt. Ellis Fish watched the ground pass away and imagined the horizon unfolding. The experience made him feel as if the Liberator dangled like a toy by a string, but from the heavens.

Flying the B-24 by hand required vigorous attention. And when the crew moved around the cabin, upsetting the center of gravity, the plane required constant re-trimming by the pilot because the aircraft was so sensitive to pitch. "The workload is demanding and requires constant attention to the engine temperature and pressure gauges, navigation, and talking to ATC (air traffic control)." The pilot's most challenging chore was synchronizing the propellers with the electric governors into a pleasant hum that didn't cause jaws to clench, power to surge, and fuel to be wasted.

Once they had settled into their course and altitude, Turvey switched on the C-1 autopilot for 463. Finally, he and Bob could relax. The crew settled in as well, each quietly alone in his thoughts. With the Liberator's propellers synchronized, there wasn't much for Turvey, Hester, and Bursey to do for the time being except monitor the dully green luminous dials on the instrument panel. Cylinder head gauges: Check. Oil temperatures: Normal. Vacuum up: Check. Fuel pressure: Maybe a little low, but sufficient. Oil pressure: Good, and steady. Power settings for manifold pressure and tachometers: Set to give a slow cruising speed and low fuel consumption. Magnetic compass: Holding steady. Radio compass: Kaput.

The boys would have loved to remove their uncomfortable oxygen masks, but there wasn't enough air to breathe at their nearly 20,000 foot cruising altitude. It was cold, too, and they were thankful for their electrically heated leather and lamb's wool–lined flight suits.

At 0210, Turvey's navigator, 2nd Lt. William Cronin, gave the ship's captain a new course home to Hammer Field in Fresno. The lieutenant turned 463 westward and had his radio operator, S/Sgt. Howard Wandtke, tap out a message in Morse code to Hammer Field with their position: 35 degrees 06 minutes North Latitude, 116 degrees 50 minutes West Longitude—50 miles east of Muroc; their new heading, 280 degrees; and altitude, 18,500 feet. This heading would take them over Tehachapi Pass, then over Bakersfield, 72 miles away, in the southern San Joaquin Valley. From there it would be a straight shot north to Hammer Field.

Preparing for their last leg, Turvey dropped his speed to 200 miles per hour and lowered 463's nose. Below 10,000 feet the boys could rid themselves of their uncomfortable oxygen masks. He began his descent, assured there were no high mountains between his position and Hammer Field. They would be home on time, at 0300.

Somehow, nothing worked out right. Shortly after making their last radio call to Hammer Field, Turvey and Hester were diverted. They didn't know it at the time; it would probably be half an hour before the boys in the cockpit could confirm something was up. They had lately been flying through patchy clouds and heavy undercast that obscured the night sky and the ground. Flying on instruments was okay; they had their weather forecast, and what they saw out the cockpit window was what they had been told to expect. High scattered clouds 8,000 to 12,000 feet as they proceeded north, but CAVU (Clear Above, Visibility Unlimited) around Muroc. High winds at 12,000 feet. A cold front west and north of Fresno was expected to pass Hammer Field between 0100 and 0800, bringing the freezing level—and therefore, the chance of wing icing—down to 10,000 feet.

So, they should have seen a glow of lights signaling Bakersfield by now. Instead, they were hurtling through the night, blind and in the dark, with increasing cloud cover. What they didn't know was that by then they were on the wrong side of the Sierra Nevada Mountains. They *should* have been on the *west* side; instead, they were on the east.

Weather creeps up on a pilot who isn't paying attention. There's something about being in an airplane that makes the decision to deviate, or especially, to turn around when the weather is getting worse, a difficult one. Author and pilot William Langewiesche says, "You can see the weather coming at you up ahead. It never takes you by surprise. You know what is happening. You see it." And, as the weather gets worse, with clouds blowing in and rain falling, a pilot will either want to rise above it or descend, looking to the lights on the ground or in the sky for comfort.

"Flight is a forward progression." Unlike a car, you can't stop and pull off to the side. You have to keep going. "It takes enormous and surprising mental energy to make the decision, especially for beginners, to deviate or turn around." That's how pilots get into trouble. Through basic inertia or the mental momentum of flight, they allow the airplane to fly *them* rather than the other way around. There is a window of escape from disaster that gets narrower and narrower until the window shuts. Once a pilot is in trouble, that trouble either takes the form of hitting the ground or flying into a mountain.

The problem is that pilots don't experience bad weather like banging against a wall. Bad weather grows. There are gaps. "It comes at you like a suspicion of the weather." Then, a little more weather, and a little more. "In flying heavy weather, watching your stern is a major occupation." There may be layers of cloud and weather, and the pilot wants to stay between them or on top or bottom. But what happens when the layers close off?

Faced with problems in flight, "There are many times when it is better (even though it can be more difficult) to stop pushing and to just slow down, or even stop, if that is possible." Airplanes can't stop flying or they fall to earth. What a pilot *can* do is stop whatever it is he's doing when what he's doing isn't accomplishing anything.

An hour past their last reported position and beyond their estimated arrival time, Charlie Turvey and Bob Hester knew they were lost. They had been lost before during training; everybody had. But not *this* lost. There is lost and not knowing where you are, and there is lost and not knowing how to get found. Turvey and Hester were both kinds of lost. And they also knew it would do no good to tell anybody about it. Flying the airplane was more important than radioing their plight to someone on the ground incapable of understanding their situation or doing anything about it. The boys were on their own. That was okay. Both Turvey and Hester knew it would be worse in combat. This was still training. It was good experience to figure out what was wrong and how to fix it.

Forward and below the flight deck in his little nook behind the bombardier, navigator Bill Cronin worked at figuring out what had gone wrong. That was his job—to get them from point A to point B and back again. If they were lost, Bill felt it the deepest. He was *responsible*. They were a crew, and everybody relied on everyone else to do their job and do it well. As navigator, the other boys on board relied on him to get them home.

They were deep in the clouds now and Cronin couldn't take a celestial fix. He couldn't see the ground either, so pilotage was out of the question, and, not knowing where he was, he couldn't use dead reckoning either, because he had no single point of reference. Because flight is a forward progression, the problem with aviation navigation is that you never know where you are, only where you've been. All Bill Cronin could do was check his compass, his math and figures, and calculate backwards in hopes of placing himself somewhere on a map.

The three of them, pilots and navigator, knew they were not where they should be. But where *were* they, exactly? That was Cronin's job, and he bent to it with a will. Into the universe they flew forward, never thinking for a minute that they could turn around to their last known fix, and start over.

They were committed to their course. That was their mistake. They didn't know it, but 463 was flying the airplane, not them. Because flying is a forward progression, navigators and pilots can be fooled into only thinking forward. But when you're in trouble, the closest safe place might actually be *behind* you. "A B-24 does not fly backward. There was something inevitable, irrevocable about a plotted course."

When you're stuck in the soup, altitude is an ally, and Turvey and Hester may have thought of climbing above the clouds so Cronin could, possibly, get a celestial fix. The B-24 service ceiling was over 30,000 feet, and they knew they might fly that high in combat, but there was no way of knowing how deep in that soup they were. For altitude to be your ally it must be below, not above, you. A world of sky above you won't help when the object is to keep from hitting the ground. Turvey and Hester, perhaps discussing what to do in their situation, probably forgot this axiom. Instead, they continued losing altitude as if still on their approach to Hammer Field. Or, maybe they nosed down, hoping to pick up some kind of ground reference. It was a fatal mistake.

The crew of 463 should have arrived at Hammer Field in Fresno, California, at 0300 on December 5. Though they didn't, and they were assumed crashed and missing, probably in the Sierra Nevada Mountains, it required another day for a search party to be organized. One reason for the delay may have been confusion with another Liberator from Hammer Field lost the same morning as 463, and in the same vicinity. South and east only a few miles as the crow flies from 463's final resting place, "A huge B-24 Liberator bomber made a forced landing at Manzanar airport last Sunday morning (5 December) about 4:30 o'clock, overshooting the runway and nosing over on the north end of the field."

Caught in overcast near Las Vegas, Nevada, 1st Lt. William H. Zumsteg was flying on instruments with a failed radio. Running low on fuel, Zumsteg was forced to put down at the auxiliary airfield adjacent to the Manzanar War Relocation Center in Owens Valley. Because the field was too short for a B-24 Liberator, Zumsteg ran off the end of the runway, causing unspecified damage to his plane.

Lieutenant Zumsteg's mishap was added to another B-24 bomber forced landing at Manzanar a week earlier. On November 28, 1943, 2nd Lt. Stanley A. Sagert had to make an emergency landing, "after two motors on the ship had gone out while they were on a mission out of Muroc Army Air Base."

Accidents and deaths were ever present during training. Given their extreme youth, many boys figured accidents and death happened to other people. The full weight of what could happen often didn't sink in until years later. Charles Watry recalled the profoundly tragic and intensely sad experience forty years later of losing friends to fatal training accidents. "I believe, though, that most were philosophical about the occurrence—we knew that it could happen and that we couldn't let it affect our performance in the program. Most of us carried on, even though the memory of our classmate stayed with us for a long time."

John Boeman wrote of the "pervasive sense of danger that seemed to accompany every flight," at all the airfields where nineteen- and twenty-year-old boys were now learning how to fly airplanes. Boeman knew students who had run out of gas while trying to fly around a storm. He knew pilots who crashed after losing control of their aircraft. He knew of others who lost control and were killed while slow-rolling. He knew boys who crashed due to mechanical faults such as engine failure. Any accident without a rational explanation was attributed to "gremlins," and the boys early on developed the fatalistic attitude that "When your number's up you go; when it's not you don't."

For anyone in the Owens Valley in late 1943, it must have seemed like a lot of aircraft were falling out of California's sky. The frequency does seem high, based on newspaper reports, especially compared to other places in the country, like Wisconsin or Montana or Mississippi. That was mostly due to the number of training fields located in the state. There were around fifty major airfields in California, along with hundreds of sub-bases and auxiliary fields.

Issues complicating the search for 463 were the loss, search, and discovery of other B-24s missing within California around the same time. Even though all the boys were eager to do something to help their buddies, it was difficult to find available aircraft and crews not already involved in training exercises. If any of them yearned to do something important, something that mattered, that opportunity had come.

Perhaps this is why a ten-airplane element with nearly full crews was chosen for the search. The search could become a training mission as well as a search for the missing crew. Fortune does not smile on the unprepared or the too eager, and the search party experienced its own tragic accident which resulted in the loss of another B-24 and six more deaths.

CHAPTER 5

Another of Our Airplanes Is Missing

ON THE MORNING OF DECEMBER 6, 1943, A DAY AFTER 463 FAILED TO return, ten B-24s from the 461st Bombardment Group left Hammer Field to search for their buddies in the missing plane. One of these searching Liberators was #42-7674, an aircraft known as *Exterminator*. It was piloted by Captain William H. U. Darden, commanding officer for the 766th squadron. On board as copilot was Lt. Culos Marion Settle, navigator 2nd Lt. Samuel J. Schlosser, flight engineer Sgt. Franklin C. Nyswonger, radio operator Sgt. George J. Barulic, and gunners Sgt. Dick E. Mayo, Sgt. Donald C. Vande Plasch, and Sgt. Richard Lee Spangle.

Exterminator left Hammer Field at 0912, ninth in line. Their mission, with the rest of the squadron, was to search an area comprising a large diamond of mountains and desert plus a small rectangle of California's Central Valley. The search pattern was predicated on where 463 would have flown had it overshot Hammer Field. It was also based on the last known position of 463, radioed in Morse code to Hammer Field. At 0210 Sergeant Wandtke had radioed their location as 35 degrees 06 minutes North Latitude, 116 degrees 50 minutes West Longitude, or 50 miles east of Muroc and heading home.

The pattern was also determined from a statement given by 2nd Lt. John K. Specht. Like 463, Specht was on a night celestial navigation training mission on December 5. The lieutenant and his crew had left Tucson one hour after 463, but on a different route, passing over San Diego. Flying over Muroc at 0145 Specht had encountered

Capt. William H. U. Darden. PHOTO IN AUTHOR'S COLLECTION, COURTESY OF BIG CREEK
SCHOOL 4TH GRADE PROJECT

high scattered clouds and "quite a bit" of turbulence. There were 40- to
50-mile-per-hour winds from between 270 to 290 degrees (that is, from
the northwest) at 12,000 feet. As a result he had been blown 40 miles
off course to the southeast. When landing at Hammer Field at 0300
Specht had not experienced severe weather. The field was overcast, and

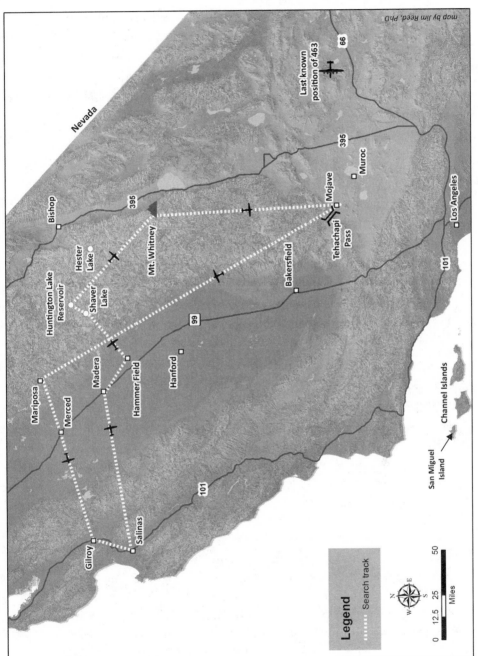

Search grid for Turvey and Hester's B-24. CARTOGRAPHY BY JIM REED PH.D.

he encountered light rain at 3,000 feet, with the cloud deck being 2,000 to 3,000 feet thick. Other than some high scattered clouds, Specht said it was clear on his route as far north as Hanford (about 30 miles south of Fresno).

When pressed for a reason to account for the loss of 463, Specht volunteered that he'd heard from another pilot, "The compass radio in 463 was not in very good operating condition." Lacking a functional radio compass on a night celestial navigation training mission "could have been a very good reason for them to get quite a ways off course without realizing it," said Specht.

The first section of search was a triangular chunk of mountains, deserts, and valley on both sides of the Sierra Nevada and represented the area 463 could be in if they had been blown off course by bad weather. Starting from Hammer Field the searchers were to fly northeast to Shaver Lake. Fifteen miles farther northeast of Shaver Lake, the squadron would begin peeling off at fifty-second intervals on a south-southeast course, taking them down Owens Valley. Near Mount Whitney they would turn again, heading farther south to the town of Mojave. From there the squadron would turn once again, north-northwest, heading up the southern Central Valley on the western edge of the Sierra Nevada to Mariposa, passing Hammer Field, and beginning their second search area.

This second search pattern assumed 463 had entered the Central Valley and had either overshot Hammer Field or drifted nearly due west of the Field. From Mariposa, the squadron's plan was to fly southwest to Salinas via Gilroy, where everyone would rendezvous. The searchers would then head east to Madera and the California Bombing Range, and then return to Hammer Field.

The search was the archetypal needle in a haystack. The searchers were expected to survey broken terrain in lower elevations of the Sierra Nevada, river valleys everywhere, and the wintry, snowbound, high-elevation glaciated canyons and rocky crags. Altogether they created a texture that could hide a dozen planes—even when you knew where to look. From the air, every large chunk of talus, reflecting a bright sun, resembles a sheet of aluminum. Add to that virgin forests of 200-foot-tall pine and fir in the middle elevations and unbroken stands of shrubby chaparral in the Sierra foothills, and a lesser man would have given up without a try. Col. Frederic E. Glantzberg, commander of the 461st, was not a lesser man, however. The boys in the missing plane were his boys, and he wasn't going to give up on them unless he knew they were dead and gone. Colonel Glantzberg therefore piloted the first ship in the squadron. He would not follow when he could lead.

Leaving Hammer Field, the squadron followed their predetermined course to Shaver Lake and began peeling off as Huntington Lake reservoir appeared. The reservoir lies in a broad and undulating valley at an elevation of 6,995 feet. The squadron's planes were still gathering altitude, reaching for 11,000 feet, in order to pass over the eastern crest of the Sierra Nevada when they reached Huntington Lake. Approaching 0950 *Exterminator* was at around 8,000 feet—a scant 1,005 feet above the reservoir, and dangerously low for what was about to happen.

In the cockpit were Captain Darden and Lieutenant Settle, assisted by flight engineer Sergeant Nyswonger. Settle was the usual pilot for *Exterminator*'s crew; they had been commandeered by Captain Darden for the search party. Settle's usual copilot, 2nd Lt. Richard Behrens, was displaced and did not fly that day. The crew's bombardier, 2nd Lt. Earl F. Ostrander also was not flying, presumably because a bombardier wasn't needed, although he did represent another pair of eyes for searching the ground. Not only that, but the bombardier position, with its big windows, also represented the best vantage point in the aircraft.

Culos Settle wasn't the only lieutenant to be bumped from the left seat that morning. Of the ten B-24s conducting the search, five were piloted by squadron leaders or senior officers. This suggests less a heroic mission of mercy and more of an opportunity for the officers to get some much needed flight time before overseas deployment to combat.

Captain Darden finished peeling off over Huntington Lake, and then events got out of control. And fast! Apparently, *Exterminator* lost its propeller governor on the #2 engine. Aircraft like the B-24 had variable pitch propellers that changed relative to engine rpm. By changing a propeller's pitch, or angle, a greater or lesser amount of atmosphere is grabbed by the propeller, and by extension, power is greater or lesser and so is fuel consumption.

Lieutenant Settle, in the copilot's seat, was monitoring engine power and performance. He checked the tachometer on #2 and he looked at the props. He told Captain Darden that "it sounded all right."

Although it was unclear to Lieutenant Settle, Captain Darden seemed to sense that something was seriously wrong. Darden's subsequent behavior indicates that he didn't believe his copilot's assessment about the #2 engine. Worryingly, *Exterminator*, only 1,000 feet above the terrain, began to dip and lose altitude. Captain Darden said, "All right, hell, get out of here," ordering the crew to bail out. At the same time, he ordered the flight engineer, Sergeant Nyswonger, to change some fuses, and then changed his mind and didn't say what fuses he meant. Magneto failure was an issue in the Liberator's Pratt & Whitney R-1830-65 Twin Wasp engines, requiring constant fuse changes. Perhaps this was Darden's intention.

Darden repeated his order for the crew to bail out. Settle and Nyswonger, following orders, left the cockpit and worked their way past the radio operator to the bomb bay. As he moved through the cramped interior within the airplane, Sergeant Nyswonger must have struggled to get his parachute strapped on.

There are several emergency exits from the Liberator. Navigator and bombardier leave through the nosewheel hatch. Tail and left waist gunner exit via the belly hatch. The rest of the crew jump from the bomb bay doors. Positioning was important to ensure surviving the bailout: Face forward and roll out, headfirst. Don't pull the rip cord until well clear of the airplane. It was not uncommon for a parachute to wrap itself around the tail and empennage of the B-24 if the rip cord was pulled too soon. You could also hit the tail of the Liberator as you jumped and the airplane swept past you. Another exit point from the Liberator was the top hatch on the flight deck behind the pilots. It was an ideal escape route if the ship ditched, but slipstream from the airplane during flight made the flight-deck hatch exit problematic.

The bomb bay doors were the best way out and were activated electrically. To manually open the bomb bay doors, which resembled the corrugated cover of a rolltop desk, a man had to work a hydraulic lever on the starboard side of the bay. There were huge drawbacks to opening the bomb bay doors with this method. Opening the bomb bay created aero-dynamic drag that knocked the aircraft out of trim, making the Liberator difficult for the pilot to control. For the crew, an open bomb bay brought terrific winds inside the airplane, the force of which worked against the poor soul working the hydraulic lever.

All of these problems came to the fore in *Exterminator's* crisis moment. Lieutenant Settle couldn't get the electric switch to function. There he was, standing against the empty bomb racks, and he wasn't able to get the bomb bay doors to open. He stepped back on the thin catwalk that traversed the bomb bay, not knowing what to do next. A warning horn sounded, signaling that the Liberator's landing gear was coming down. Later, Settle told a committee investigating *Exterminator's* emergency, "The engineer opened the doors." Culos Settle bailed out by stepping through the open bomb bay doors. The last thing he heard was "the captain . . . repeating to bail out all the time [until the point] when I got out."

As events were unfolding, back in the tiny radio operator's compart-ment behind the copilot's seat, Sgt. George Barulic was trying to figure out what was going on. Only thirty minutes into the flight and the ship's skipper all of a sudden starts screaming over the interphone (intercom) for everyone to bail out. "I could hear him yelling," George Barulic told the team investigating the crash. "The first time I heard him say 'Bail out,' I took off my headsets and started getting ready." He saw Lieutenant Settle trying to open the bomb bay doors and moved to help. He could hear the warning horn blowing, announcing that the landing gear was lowering.

Barulic succeeded in manually opening the bomb bay doors. "He [Settle] put it on manual and tried to crank it. But I was watching when he was doing it. He wasn't strong enough to open it. So I opened the thing up and he just jumped right out." That's when Barulic realized he lacked a parachute of his own. He crawled toward the back of the aircraft and fortunately found a loose seat-type parachute and quickly strapped himself in. Barulic says, "You know, luck is just like that when you're fly-ing [in combat]. You can move one way or another and you're alive and . . ." The sergeant's luck was in full swing that morning on *Exterminator*

S/Sgt. George J. Barulic. PHOTO IN AUTHOR'S COLLECTION, COURTESY OF BIG CREEK SCHOOL 4TH GRADE PROJECT

over Huntington Lake because, "I wasn't supposed to fly that day. I had the day off." He was sitting around the base, thinking about making a trip into Fresno, when a Jeep drove up and picked Barulic up as is; no flight suit, and, of course, "I didn't even have a parachute with me."

The lack of any movement within *Exterminator* convinced Barulic that he and Captain Darden, who was still flying the plane, were the last ones inside, and that everyone else had left. But of *Exterminator's* boys, only he and Lieutenant Settle made it out. Why the others chose to stay on board is an unsolvable mystery, but there are several possibilities to explain their behavior.

The decision to ditch or bail out was not taken lightly by experienced Liberator pilots. "Where the low-wing B-17, with its bridge-truss wing structure and strong circular fuselage section, fared somewhat better in water landings, the high-wing B-24 was prone to breaking up, its flexible bomb bay doors proving to be only about a fifth as strong as the rest of the fuselage." A calm-water ditching didn't guarantee the Liberator wouldn't snap like a matchstick, "as the bomb bay doors collapsed under the impact."

With their superior range over open water, Liberators became the workhorses of the Pacific air fleet. But even crews who had been in the Pacific for a long time had little to no experience with ditching or bailing out. On the other hand, ditching—making forced landings on water—is mentioned in war memoirs, so crews learned about it somewhere. Ditching was also covered in the war department's *Pilot's Training Manual for the B-24 Liberator*, so Darden and Settle had at least some academic exposure to what might happen when *Exterminator* hit the drink.

Second-guessing Captain Darden's decision to evacuate and the crew's decision to stay is futile. Darden obviously believed there was a reason to bail out the crew. He had little leeway on where to land, since Huntington Lake was the only place in his immediate vicinity which wasn't carpeted in trees. Without a doubt, attempting a forced landing in a forest would have been fatal. Captain Darden was faced with precious little in the way of options, and he did the best he could with what he had.

George Barulic chose to follow Lieutenant Settle out the bomb bay and parachute to safety. When asked for a reason why the other boys might have chosen to stay behind he said, "I never had any kind of training about bailing out or anything like that. So, some people don't feel like jumping out. They'd rather take their chances they'll land okay." Practice in jumping out of airplanes was not part of a crew's training. Even paratroopers had minimal practical experience, and they were considered experts for their time.

Experienced jumpers also didn't jump so low to the ground as Settle and Barulic. They were barely 1,000 feet above the ground when Darden ordered the crew to bail out, and between 300 and 500 feet when Settle and Barulic bailed out. According to Sergeant Barulic, "When I jumped, I must have been awful low. I hit underneath the plane on the tail end and I opened the parachute and I don't remember anything and the next thing I'm on the ground. It just opened up and, Bang!"

Lieutenant Settle reported to the accident examining board that events transpired so quickly, there was little Captain Darden could do to keep from losing altitude. "We were going down at that instant. Prior to that time, we were fixing to climb over the mountains ahead around 11,000 feet. Fixing to fly 2,000 rpm and 32 inches Hg. Would have been enough power to climb if something hadn't gone wrong. Naturally didn't know what was happening because we should have been climbing."

When Culos Settle bailed out, he noticed a few things. First was, "We had changed direction from south back to west," meaning that Darden was attempting to come about, perhaps to line up with the west-east trending reservoir. "We were down between the mountain peaks when I bailed out." Settle reported that Captain Darden was pushing the bailout button and continuing to call over the interphone for the crew to bail out, but, "I didn't hear the bells in the nose tail and tail turret." From his position at the bomb bay, Settle could see into the cockpit. He clearly noted that engine manifold pressure appeared normal.

William Darden was considered an experienced officer and flier. Leaving Virginia Military Institute a fraction of a point from winning his degree, Darden enlisted in the Army Air Corps on July 26, 1940. He was sent to flight training and received his wings in 1941 at Maxwell Field, graduating at the head of his class. Before arriving at Hammer Field, Captain Darden had served as a flying instructor. He had 1,453.05 hours of flight experience, with 235.4 hours in the B-24. In the previous ninety days he had accumulated 128.3 of those B-24 hours, along with 39.55 instrument hours in the previous six months, and only 1.25 hours of instrument flying in the previous thirty days. Darden's nighttime hours were 28.55 over the past six months, and 2.4 hours during the past thirty days.

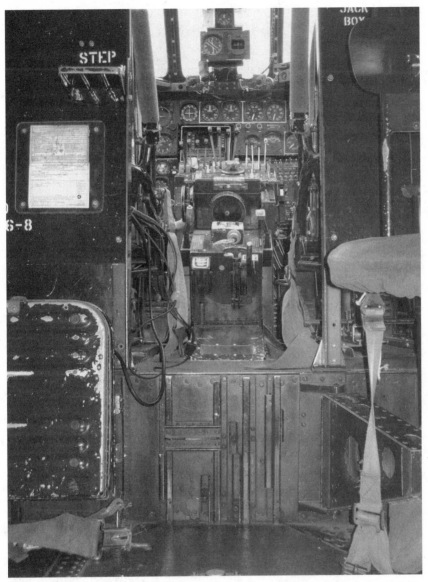

View from the bomb bay to the instrument panel in a B-24. Lt. Culos Settle could have easily read the instruments before bailing out of *Exterminator*. In his testimony to the accident investigation board, he stated he could clearly see that engine manifold pressure appeared normal (two gauges located beneath the compass).
PHOTO BY PETER STEKEL

Questioned about whether the throttles were changed during the peeling-off maneuver (a decrease of power would have caused the ship to lose altitude), Lieutenant Settle replied, "No." *Exterminator* was Darden's plane, and Settle had no problems with it either, telling the board that it was "slower than other type E's," but also contradicting himself by adding, "Ran as good as others, just as fast."

The lieutenant was asked whether he noticed any "unusual atmospheric changes," to which he responded, "[There was] only a cloud," and because they had to avoid two high peaks directly in front of them, "if we hadn't turned, we would have hit the cloud." As if anticipating the next question, Culos Settle defensively added, "I am a first pilot but was acting copilot, and in no position to take over, as he was the commanding officer."

The interrogation turned to focus on the weather. "Was there very much cloudiness that morning?" The forecast for the search route on December 6, 1943, had been for "broken clouds in the San Joaquin Valley at 5,000 to 6,000 feet, visibility 3 to 5 miles, increasing to 5 to 7 miles by 10:00; low clouds obscuring the Sierra Nevada peaks, with rain showers and snow possible along the rest of the route." Pilots were given the following instructions: "Instrument conditions will exist in San Joaquin Valley in dense fog, lowering ground visibility in [search] area to less than 1 mile at 0900," and then continuing to get worse. Not really ideal conditions for a search, but they went anyway. Lieutenant Settle didn't see any of this bad weather, however; only the one cloud, and it was 2 miles distant. That, and a strong wind blowing west across the reservoir.

The examiners wanted to know if Lieutenant Settle noticed anything unusual about *Exterminator's* speed, such as the aircraft slowing down. All he observed was the aircraft losing altitude. Were the searchers briefed about the mountains? Settle replied that they knew the danger, especially since they were to search at 500 feet above ground level.

The questions again circled back to the weather, and Settle's answers became acutely brief.

Examiner: "Was any mention made of type of weather?"
Settle: "No, sir."

Examiner: "No velocity of wind?"

Settle: "Don't know; may have been mentioned, I do not recall."

Winding down, finally, someone thinks to ask about the crew. "Where were the other men riding?" Lieutenant Settle's incomplete answer only accounts for "[t]wo in the tail and two in the nose. The men in the tail could have gotten out . . . We could have been over the ridge, saw the trees, and decided they would rather risk the lake than the trees." The lieutenant didn't see anything of those four men. "There was no scrambling around in the nose, no one trying to get out. That's the reason that I thought they had jumped. It seemed that they hadn't. No evidence of anyone else having jumped." The only ones found by searchers were Settle and Barulic.

Having landed alongside the reservoir's shore, Sgt. George Barulic found a road and started hiking out. "I figured since everybody jumped out ahead of me, they must be up towards the mountain. So I started walking north. Up instead of down, because there was a little road there. And then I met Settle, coming down." The two men talked things over a bit, deciding what to do. They couldn't figure out where everyone else could be. Then a truck came down the road. "Somebody checking some electrical stuff up there in the mountains." This was an employee of the company that owned and maintained the dam that formed Huntington Lake reservoir. It was a quick drive to a telephone, and Lieutenant Settle called Hammer Field to report that another of the squadron's B-24s was missing.

Then, Culos Settle had himself driven back to Huntington Lake. Along the shore and in the reservoir he could see badly damaged oxygen bottles, parts of *Exterminator*'s nose section, Sergeant Nyswonger's jacket, part of Sergeant Barulic's radio operator's logbook, bits of radio equipment, first-aid kits, and an engine tag belonging to *Exterminator*'s #4 engine. It was obvious to Settle from the amount of airplane debris floating on the reservoir's surface, and what had washed up onshore, where *Exterminator* had to be.

Settle had several hours to wait before a vehicle from Hammer Field could reach Huntington Lake. Borrowing a boat, Settle ventured out into the reservoir to collect what hadn't washed up onshore. There was a strong wind blowing east to west and large waves almost capsized him. He gave up and rowed back to shore.

The next day an air search over the area began in case any of the other six on board *Exterminator* had bailed out and were awaiting rescue. Airplanes flew overlapping strips of sky, 3 miles wide and 80 miles long, while people on the ground searched along the reservoir's shore. No other members of *Exterminator's* crew were found. On behalf of Hammer Field commanding officer, Col. Guy Kirksey, Lt. Col. Glantzberg reported to the Office of Flying Safety that Capt. William H. Darden, 2nd Lt. Samuel J. Schlosser, S/Sgt. Franklin C. Nyswonger, Sgt. Dick E. Mayo, Sgt. Donald C. Vande Plasch, and Sgt. Richard L. Spangle, were "still missing."

The search for Turvey and Hester's B-24 was a disaster and was terminated. It was bad enough losing 463, but commanders of the 461st Bombardment Squadron at Hammer Field now had a second airplane lost while searching for the first.

The investigation as to what went wrong with *Exterminator* slowly continued. On December 27, 1943, the examining board determined culpability for losing an airplane and six men was, "Pilot 50%, Undetermined 50%." In the narrative accompanying the determination of cause for *Exterminator's* loss, the three accident board examiners commended Captain Darden with lukewarm praise for sensing "some difficulty, which is not clearly defined by the testimony of the copilot, and [then ordering] the crew to jump." They concluded, "A strong wind from the southeast is believed to have caused a downdraft, which confused the pilot momentarily. It is believed that the low altitude with reference to surrounding terrain and the pilot's lack of familiarity with the terrain caused him to commit himself to a landing in the lake as an emergency procedure. He was apparently unable to maneuver so as to avoid a downwind landing. There is no definite evidence to show mechanical difficulties resulting in a lack of power."

The tragic loss of one airplane and crew while looking for another was, sadly, all too common. The chain of events involving the loss of B-24 #42-7011, *Hat in the Ring*, is important because they are tied to a future search for 463 and the Turvey and Hester crew. The *Hat in the Ring* boys were lucky; eight out of ten survived to tell the tale.

At 7:00 p.m. on July 4, 1943, *Hat in the Ring* left the Salinas Army Air Base near Salinas, California, for night-navigation training. In transition training to bombers, twenty-five-year-old Lt. Thorel "Skip" Johnson was well trained, but had only forty-four hours of experience flying Liberators at night. That would equate to three, maybe four, flights.

Johnson was supposed to head 400 miles down the California coast before turning inland for Bakersfield. Fuel consumption was exceeding the Liberator's range, so Johnson changed course. Cutting inland west of Santa Barbara, at about Point Arguello, Lieutenant Johnson lost power to three engines and gave the order for his crew to prepare to bail out. The Liberator's airspeed dropped off and gravity began to reassert itself. Without waiting for orders, the navigator and bombardier chose to bail out over the ocean, exiting through *Hat in the Ring*'s nosewheel well.

Facing a bleak future, Johnson waited until confirming he was over land before ordering the crew to abandon ship. It was 2:00 a.m. with a moonless night. Exiting the Liberator north of Santa Barbara, near San Marcos Pass, the boys came down in rough mountains. *Hat in the Ring* flew on without its crew and soon crashed in Camuesa Canyon, near Santa Barbara.

With *Hat in the Ring* overdue, a flight of three Liberators was dispatched to look for it. One of those, B-24 #42-7160, vanished. That Liberator's remains, along with its twelve crewmen, were found eight months later on San Miguel Island, some 40 miles southwest of Santa Barbara. The cause of the crash was never determined. The pilot, 1st Lt. Douglas J. Thornburg, had survived another B-24 crash just three weeks before, in which six of the ten crewmen perished. This time his luck ran out.

The *Hat in the Ring* navigator and bombardier were never found, though rescuers located two parachutes floating in the ocean near Goleta, some 10 miles up the coast from Santa Barbara. It was assumed the missing boys had tried to swim to shore, drowned, and were washed out to sea.

A board of inquiry investigating *Hat in the Ring*'s loss placed full responsibility on the pilot's shoulders. Lieutenant Johnson improperly set

Propeller wreckage from *Hat in the Ring* on San Miguel Island. The bent blades indicate the propeller was turning when the aircraft crashed.
PHOTO COURTESY G. PAT MACHA

the airplane's cruise-power settings, which led to excessive fuel consumption. He also didn't question the flight engineer's fuel-level reports, which fluctuated during the crucial time that engine power was lost. Nobody was punished, and nothing was said about the two boys who had jumped the gun and evacuated the aircraft too soon.

The story of *Hat in the Ring* demonstrates how some people were lucky, some less so, and others had no luck at all. As for *Exterminator*, it would be another eleven years before she was heard from again.

CHAPTER 6

The Phantom Rider

BOB HESTER WAS A LOT LIKE HIS FATHER, CLINT. BOTH LET LOVE RULE their lives. But it was loss of love that influenced each of them the most. Neither Clint nor Bob could accept that death takes away forever those closest to you. For Bob, it was losing his mother, Frances Hester, in 1938, during his senior year in high school. She lived just long enough to see him graduate, and he was heartbroken to lose her. For Clint, it was losing his son in 1943 during a training flight. He, too, felt that the light in his life had been irretrievably dimmed. From that moment onward, Clint Hester's life would be one of sadness, tragedy, and finally, irony.

Both Clint and Bob faced their sorrow the same way: by retreating into wilderness. Following graduation from University High School in west Los Angeles, Bob relocated to Juneau, Alaska, with a close buddy for a seasonal job with the United States Forest Service. Clint had always wanted to see Alaska, and it must have rubbed off on Bob, that it would be a good place to bury his sorrow. Anyway, he headed there, and that is where he met Miriam Puranen and was married.

Like his son, Clint Hester needed wilderness to cleanse his soul. He and Bob had spent time exploring the Sierra Nevada and, with his only son missing in those mountains, the Sierra is where he now began to search. Clint persuaded someone at the Army Air Forces base at Hammer Field to supply him with the flight plan and the last radioed position for his son's aircraft. This encouraged him to center his search in the Mount Whitney country, along the Sierra's steep eastern escarpment. In the days following 463's disappearance, Clint searched wherever winter snow didn't keep him out of the mountains. He told those who knew him, "I'm going to find them. I can't rest until I've found that ship. They could still be alive. Bob knows those mountains. They might have survived that crash."

A month after 463 disappeared, Clint Hester received a letter from Mrs. Charles W. Turvey, the mother of Charles Turvey, pilot of the missing Liberator. "There [aren't] any words that can do either of us any good; we just want you to know we are thinking of you." Her son had made it home only once in the eighteen months since he'd enlisted and left for training. During that visit, "the last of October," he was "anxious to get back, and mentioned how well the boys worked." Charles Turvey also mentioned about the boys getting promotions and "how they deserved it," and that during training, "When they bomb at such a high altitude their hands and feet get numb, but he said, 'Never once have I heard any boy complain.'"

The enormity of what the searchers faced was unknown to Mrs. Turvey. "It seems as though they could find a plane as large as a B-24." A Midwesterner her whole life, Mrs. Turvey had never been to California, nor seen mountains as tall and rugged as the Sierra Nevada. She can be forgiven for not realizing how easily an airplane as small as a B-24 Liberator could be swallowed up in that enormous area of forest, rock, water, and ice. Clint knew what he was up against. But he had to see it through.

"I can think of nothing worse that could happen to us," Mrs. Turvey continued, adding that the anguish of losing her eldest son *was* worse, because it happened "in our own U.S.," and "the worst part [was], there is nothing we can do for own boy." Charles was as lost to her in California as if he had died in Europe or the south Pacific.

There was something important about her son's death that Mrs. Turvey didn't know. "In early 1943 the Army Air Forces was aware of an uneasy public becoming concerned over the ever increasing number of accidents in training." General of the air force, H. H. "Hap" Arnold, was worried that the "American public did not grasp the tremendous increase in hours and miles being flown and were only being told about the accidents." Historians point to the miraculous industrial capacity of the United States being a huge contributing factor to winning the war.

But they gloss over the incredible success with shortened training programs for aircrews. Reginald H. Thayer Jr. served as a B-17 bombardier on seventy-nine missions. At one time, bombardier school was eighteen weeks long. By the time Thayer got there in late 1942, the class was compressed to eleven weeks because the need for bomber crews was so great. In 1989 he recalled, "Those training programs were one of the miracles of the war."

Arnold callously viewed training accidents as a public relations issue. "The accident problem is serious, but it is far from being as alarming as regular reading of newspapers would lead the average citizen to believe." Of course, Arnold hadn't lost a son in an aircraft training accident. For the duration of the war, a public relations campaign by the Army Air Forces assured the public that all steps were being taken to make flying as safe as possible.

The only people who knew anything definite about deaths and injuries from aviation training accidents were those who had lost a child or spouse in such a manner. And it was unlikely that even those family members received the full story of how their loved one died. That was the case with Henry Neil Henson, who lied about his age and enlisted as a gunner in the US Navy at the age of sixteen. His airplane was lost over San Francisco Bay while practicing aircraft carrier takeoffs and landings. Henson's family received no information about the accident except that nothing from the airplane was found but the tail section and a wing. They didn't even know what kind of aircraft it was.

Flying is inherently risky. Between the first flight of an airplane in 1903 and forty years later, flying, and learning how to fly, had always involved a culture of risk. Deaths were inevitable in a profession that saw advances in design and aviation technology often surpass the training, knowledge, and experience of the people flying the airplanes. Before World War II, overall injury and death in the US Army Air Corps (precursor to the US Army Air Forces, and the US Air Force) was low in numbers, but represented a high percentage of personnel because there weren't that many qualified pilots.

That all changed in 1942 as the army geared up and began training tens of thousands of pilots, navigators, bombardiers, and other crew

members for the ten-man B-17 and B-24, and smaller crew comple-
ments for medium bombers, air transport, and fighter planes. Arthur
Artig flew in a B-26 squadron and recalls, "I graduated from pilot's
school and I couldn't even drive a car."

"Death in combat is tragic but can be justified," writes historian
Marlyn Pierce. More tragic is death during training, because, "The perception of training, among most participants, is that it is 'safe,' or at least a
controlled environment where accidents occur but where steps are taken
to reduce them."

Even after he was sure Bob could no longer be alive, Clint Hester didn't give up. Once the spring of 1944 arrived, Clint followed the
snowmelt into the high country. He began taking time off from work
and spending weekends, then weeks, searching for Bob's airplane. He
communicated his plan to keep up the search to the other families, and
Mrs. Turvey wrote again to Clint, thanking him for a letter from Mrs.
Fish, mother of Ellis Fish, bombardier on 463, and a map. "I wouldn't
take anything for the map. It was considerate of you to send it." She also
asked Clint what he had learned during his search, "or if you have started
in any way."

Having spent Mother's Day in her native state of Indiana with her
own mother, Mrs. Turvey also disclosed that her son Charles had planned
to marry in 1945. The girl's name was Jane, and the Turvey parents had
just met her for the first time during their Indiana excursion. "She was so
sweet and just won't give up that the boys are dead." According to Mrs.
Turvey, Charles had told his girl, "Bob is a fine fellow and is a better pilot
than myself."

It had been six months since 463 disappeared, and Mrs. Turvey
admitted, "We are still so broken up we can't live normal yet, and I'm
beginning to fear we will never know." Perhaps that fear of never knowing prompted Mrs. Turvey's next comment, or perhaps it was the fear that
Clint Hester might have to give up his search for lack of funds. "We feel
we should help in some way with the search. I see no reason you should
do it all when our boy is there too." So, she offers to help with some of
Clint's expenses, confessing, "We haven't so much, but we all work and
would be glad to spend our money in that way. Money means so little

anyway, now. So, tell us anything, and I'm sure the rest [of the families] feel as we do."

Clint Hester wasn't a wealthy man, but he made a decent living as a physical trainer and masseur at the Hollywood Athletic Club. He would also supplement his income collecting and selling rare coins and by buying older, sporty cars and fixing them up. Since many of his clients at the club were top-line actors and directors and other movers and shakers in the film business, he had a ready market for the automobiles once they were up and running. Still, the offer of some financial assistance had to be welcome, because Clint wasn't working much anymore. Most of his time was spent searching for Bob.

Clint Hester responded quickly to Mrs. Turvey and she wrote back from her Reesville, Ohio, home on June 28, 1944—two weeks after her initial offer. "You'll never know just what you've meant to all of us. To know there is someone out there who cares and is trying to find them means more than words can tell." She shared some choice words about the official searchers from one of her son's high school friends, now preparing to be an army pilot. "I don't think they are trying to find them. The government doesn't give a damn now. I'll bet if I was out there I'd find Charlie, or know the reason why."

Clint had always been interested in airplanes, and so had Bob. They would frequently spend weekends at local air shows in southern California, admiring the prowess of the pilots and the beauty of their machines. Both father and son enjoyed going fast, especially on motorcycles. Long before riding motorcycles was fashionable and anything more than a curiosity, Clint had been riding America's quintessential two-wheeler, the Harley-Davidson. In fact, in addition to his duties of helping the Hollywood elite keep buff, whenever an actor needed instruction in how to ride motorcycles in a movie, it was to Clint Hester they came.

Following their marriage, Bob and Miriam returned to west Los Angeles and Bob took up flying. In 1939, as part of Roosevelt's New Deal economic program, and part of war-preparedness, the Civilian Pilot Training Program (CPTP) began offering aviation classes to civilians. The idea was to prepare a pool of civilian pilots for military service in the eventuality of war. "The program was one of the largest government-sponsored vocational programs of its time."

It was likely at nearby Clover Field, in the tiny resort town of Santa Monica, where Bob took lessons. During the 1930s there were no less than eight flight schools located there. In any event, Bob and Miriam Hester were living with Clint, and the airfield was just ten minutes away from the Hester home, at 11237 Graham Place.

Bob Hester had managed to scrape up enough money to purchase an airplane, a Retz R-10 with the tail number of NR-157551. The Retz was a "homebuilt" airplane, meaning the plane was constructed either from "scratch," using a set of plans, or from an assembly kit. It was like buying

Aviation cadet Robert Hester. COURTESY OF JANET HOVDEN AND ROBERT HESTER FAMILY

and assembling a model airplane, except the R-10 was full-size and fully operational.

Clint Hester hung on to Bob's Retz until late 1945, when he decided it was time to sell. A man named Al Hanes wanted to buy it. As it turned out, Hanes lived in the Hesters' neighborhood, and had been a combat pilot during the latter part of the war. He was about the same age as Bob Hester would have been. He and Clint hit it off immediately, and it wasn't long before Clint had told Al the complete story of Bob's disappearance.

Hanes already owned one airplane, a Stearman PT-19. The Stearman was used extensively for training new pilots during World War II because of its forgiving nature. The PT-19 was a biplane, like the Retz R-10, but with two seats, not one, and definitely not built for speed. Al Hanes asked Clint Hester, "Why not hunt for the ship from the air?"

Starting at Clover Field they flew east and north to Lone Pine to begin their search. From the air the enormity of the Sierra Nevada was on display. Every road and trail, each canyon, lake, glacial cirque, and stream was visible. There was no way Clint could ever cover all that territory. It had to be a tremendous blow to Clint's confidence to truly see what he was up against. "But I can't give up," he told Hanes. "I can't stop looking." So, it was back to hiking the trails during the summer and exploring the back roads and lower, snow-free country whenever he could get away from work. Time marched on, and Clint's quest continued. Love never left his heart. Finding room for romance, Clint Hester remarried in 1948.

These days, the length of State Highway 395 in the Owens Valley on the east side of the Sierra Nevada is nearly all four-lane highway with wide shoulders. In Clint Hester's day Highway 395 was a remote and dangerous at night, poorly marked and illuminated, narrow, two-lane blacktop county road. During the summer of 1947, returning from a weeklong search in the Sierra, Clint hit a patch of bad road and spun out of control, landing in a ditch and wrecking his car. He required several weeks of hospitalization. As soon as he was discharged, Clint was back in the Owens Valley, this time on his motorcycle. Hitting a rut in the road he was catapulted into the air and the big, heavy Harley came crashing down on top of him. He escaped with his life but not without injury. During his search for Bob, injury would follow injury. It seems his luck was always bad.

Tragedy continued to stalk Clint Hester. His second wife died in 1949 from a cerebral hemorrhage. Gladys Estelle Brooner Hester was only thirty-five years old.

Now in his early fifties, Clint Hester was also developing health issues. Though he never smoked a day in his life, Clint had the early signs of heart disease and emphysema. This was quite a blow for a man who had been a wrestler in his youth and who took pride in being physically fit.

Clint Hester, circa 1955.
COURTESY OF JANET HOVDEN
AND ROBERT HESTER FAMILY

In 1950, Clint Hester bought several acres of property in Lone Pine, within sight of Mount Whitney and the locus of his search for Bob. By 1952 he had built a 960-square-foot, two-story, two-bedroom, one-bath house, and had retired from the movie business. To some he said, "Lone Pine's a beautiful spot for a retired man," and to others, "I won't have to go so far to look for Bob." In the front yard, within sight of the highest point in the Lower 48, and the main area of his search for Bob and the B-24 Liberator's mountain grave, he erected a flagpole. Every morning for the next few years Clint Hester raised the colors to salute his son. The bond between Clint and his son and daughter was unconventional for the time. Part of it surely revolved around the children losing their mother at a very important time for young adults, but there was something else, too. Neither Bob nor Janet referred to their father as anything but "Clint." Janet recalls, "He was never a strict father. We were pretty much on our own, which is good—when I come to think about it. He was just one of us."

Clint Hester had relocated to Hollywood in the early 1920s from Lincoln, Nebraska, with his wife and children. They moved into a cabin in Laurel Canyon, a stone's throw away from the glamour and the studios that provided a steady income for a husband and father. Eight homes later, when employment was more secure, Clint bought a house with a large backyard on Graham Place in west Los Angeles, and the family settled in.

Love told Clint that although his son's plane was lost, Bob could be found. Love told him his duty was to find his son. During World War II, duty meant everything. Duty was an expression of honor. Like Odysseus, for that generation, Clint's quest was not only acceptable but celebrated. Not to seek a better world, nor any world at all, but to find his son. As George Eliot wrote, "Our dead are never dead to us until we have forgotten them."

Clint's quest consumed him to his death, never to be forgotten not only by family but strangers as well. Over the years, from 1943 until his death, Clint Hester came to be known by hikers, anglers, hunters, and the denizens of eastern Sierra Nevada towns in the Owens Valley as the "Phantom Rider." He may have appreciated the sobriquet, but certainly never let the nickname distract him from his mission. His quest may have been an interesting topic over coffee in Owens Valley towns or in the gossip of hikers, but his determination never wavered.

His health in decline, in 1953 Clint returned to live in Los Angeles with his third wife, Bernice. Midway through that year he suffered a near-fatal heart attack. His days were now confined to dreaming of places he would search for Bob if only he could.

In September of 1954, the US Air Force contacted Clint Hester with what they thought was great news. Hikers had discovered the wreckage of a B-24 Liberator on San Miguel Island, off the coast of Santa Barbara. There were still two unresolved missing B-24s that the air force knew about, and they were sure this airplane had to be one of them. A search of records had found the December 1943 missing airplane report for Turvey and Hester's B-24. In that report somebody had read the last position report of 463 as:

TWENTY-FIVE DEGREES ZERO SIX MINUTES NORTH LATITUDE CMA ONE HUNDRED SIXTEEN DEGREES FIFTY MINUTES WEST LONGITUDE. MAKING GOOD TRUE COURSE TWO HUNDRED EIGHTY DEGREES.

A further note in the accident report points out how terribly incorrect this heading had to be.

OBVIOUSLY THIS POSITION REPORT WAS NOT COR-RECT BECAUSE IT WOULD PLACE SHIP APPROXI-MATELY TWO HUNDRED FORTY MILES SOUTH OF GUADALUPE ISLAND HEADING WEST.

Guadalupe Island is 337 miles south of San Miguel Island. In 1954 the air force didn't seem to notice the discrepancy. Clint must have wondered how they could get something so wrong.

Why the air force thought the San Miguel wreckage belonged to 463 is indecipherable, since the sighting was 557 miles away from the coordinates they found in the 1943 accident report. As they soon discovered, the airplane was #42-7160, the Liberator lost back in July of 1943, while looking for *Hat in the Ring*. At least that mystery had been solved.

On February 16, 1959, Clint Hester died quietly in his sleep. He was a month shy of sixty-five years old. The cause of death was listed as "heart failure." Anybody with a trace of love and romance in their soul who had paid attention from 1943 to 1959 would have said Clint Hester died of a broken heart.

Clint's military history shows that he served a year in the US Army medical department stateside during World War I, and was discharged as a sergeant. In 1931 he had been admitted to the Soldiers' Home in west Los Angeles (now the Veterans Administration Greater Los Angeles Healthcare Center), where he received treatment for arterial hypertension, cardiac hypertrophy, and adenomatous thyroid condition. It would appear that Clint had issues with his heart going back for a number of years. All that time in the mountains and all those years of worrying about finding his son likely shortened his life. Unhealthy cardiac hypertrophy is the response to stress or disease such as hypertension.

Mrs. Turvey never forgot Clint Hester and his quest. In 1961, after the boys had been found and their remains interred in Arlington National Cemetery, she wrote to Clint's daughter Janet, commenting on the *Time* magazine article, "The Long Search," which documented Clint Hester's quest. She especially liked "that he [Clint] was recognized for his great effort in searching for the plane."

The Turveys had made their own long journey from Ohio to eastern California the previous November to visit as close to the plane-crash site as they could. They stopped in Lone Pine, within view of Mount Whitney, to visit the house Clint Hester had built so he could be closer to Bob. "It looked so lonesome," Mrs. Turvey wrote to Janet. Thinking about the geography but not comprehending the difficulty of getting anywhere in the mountains, she added, "He really was not too far from them after all." But always close in his heart.

One of the most complete and well-researched articles about the crash of 463 was published in 1961 by author and screenwriter William Lansford. Thoughtful and sensitive, Lansford had stumbled upon the Hester Lake story by chance and was deeply affected by its irony and pathos. A combat veteran of two wars, Lansford felt an immediate connection to the boys on 463 and their families because he had witnessed not only the physical destruction of war but how it wounded and scarred families through the generations to come. In a letter to Bob Hester's sister, Janet, on January 2, 1961, William Lansford reflected on the idea of "dying for one's country" and how it carried but one reward: "the fact that one has died for one's country." Lansford was trying to explain to Janet Hovden why he found the story of her brother's death so interesting, so tragically sad, and yet, so compelling. And why he believed the story needed telling.

Any belief that war came with glory or heroism vaporized for Lansford after his experience as a combat soldier during two wars. He recognized that if we're going to have war, some men will die. "But each time I come upon a case I ask myself: Why did this particular man have to die?

Graveside service, Arlington National Cemetery, October 3, 1960.
US ARMY PHOTOGRAPH, COURTESY CRONIN AND HESTER FAMILIES

Why couldn't it have been some stranger?" He answers his own question as seventeenth-century poet John Donne might have:

> *The inescapable fact is, of course, that no man who has died that you might continue to live can ever be a stranger. By the act of dying, in this manner, he makes himself an integral part of you; he shares in all your future life. It is a right which he has bought in the highest way imaginable. What remains of you is all that there will ever be of him. And so, this is the way my wife and I have come to think of Bob and his friends and crewmates.*

Nothing ever cuts through grief. As Mrs. Turvey wrote to Clint Hes- 1944, "Everywhere you look or anyone you talk to has sorrow these

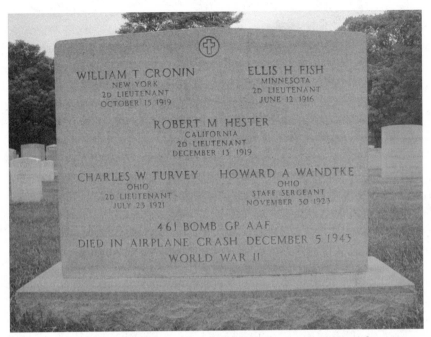

Headstone for five of six crew members from 463 at Arlington National Cemetery.
PHOTO IN AUTHOR'S COLLECTION, COURTESY JEROME ZECH SR.

days. Sometimes I wonder if life is worth living. Just when you get your family raised and can enjoy them, a war has to take them, and for what?"

In October of 1960, after the boys had finally been found, Janet Hester Hovden journeyed to Arlington National Cemetery with her husband and two children. They were there for the interment of her brother and four of the five other boys from 463. For the first time, since December 6, 1943, people with the names of Turvey, Hester, Cronin, Fish, and Wandtke would be together, albeit briefly, and in grief.

With that meeting in mind, and hopeful the families would stay in contact with each other, William Lansford ended his letter from January 2, 1961, to Janet Hovden with a request. Consciously echoing the words of George Eliot, Lansford asked Janet to convey his regards to the families of the other boys from 463, and explain his reasons for writing their story: "for we've come to join them in their memories; in cherishing those who have departed, yet are still with us."

CHAPTER 7

Training for War

UNTIL THE JAPANESE KNOCKED THE STUFFING OUT OF THE US PACIFIC Fleet at Pearl Harbor, most Americans were content in the isolationist attitude that the wars in Europe and Asia had nothing to do with them. With declarations of neutrality, Congress was more than happy to go along with those feelings. For these citizens, the Japanese attack was less a wake-up call than a stunning surprise. Not everyone was surprised, however; portions of the United States military had been preparing for a European war for years. And President Roosevelt had been getting ready for another conflict with Germany by helping the British since 1940 in any way he could.

For the average citizen, everything changed overnight. Immediately, opinion coalesced behind the president: The United States of America could no longer hide its collective head in the sand. It was best expressed by prominent isolationists like Charles Lindbergh, who dropped their America First affiliation to take up wholehearted support of US intervention. As the next four years demonstrated, self-interest and parochialism disappeared as America truly came together with a unified national purpose to fight common enemies. For, when you are attacked, you fight back. But how? And with what?

The Pacific Fleet, though not decimated by the Japanese, was in abysmal shape. That "Date of Infamy" pointed out our country's vulnerabilities. The army was understaffed and poorly outfitted—still wearing puttees and Great War helmets. What passed for an air force was 20,000 enlisted personnel and a small fraternity of 2,000 officers. Granted, our forces fought extremely well over the next few months in the Philippines, at Guam, Wake Island, and many other places foreign to our citizens. But our boys were overwhelmed by superior forces using superior military equipment. "American weakness was very apparent after Pearl Harbor in Washington. US leaders knew that the United States was desperately short of every military asset, from infantrymen to battleships." In short, we were miserably unprepared for global war.

Political policy dictated a significant, if symbolic, response to the Japanese attack; Colonel Jimmy Doolittle's April 18, 1942, raid on Tokyo took care of that. It was militarily insignificant but provided a much-needed morale boost for American citizens, and it embarrassed Japanese commanders. They now knew they were neither safe nor secure from attack.

Lacking a large standing army and navy, choices for what the United States could do next to prosecute the war were limited. However, it had to be done, and it *was* done. "Americans cut corners, rationalized procedures, shortened training schedules, and created a serviceable military within nine months of Pearl Harbor." It was an amazing achievement in human resources, dwarfed only by industrial might. The ranks of the army and navy swelled with volunteers—men and women of all ages and experience. American industrial output, long delayed by the Great Depression, kicked into overdrive. This kind of increased productivity in manpower and industry meant that safety—at least, in the twenty-first-century sense—took a backseat to getting things done. Training accidents and industrial accidents claimed thousands of lives, and injured many thousands more.

As that serviceable military developed, it was decided to follow the United Kingdom and Doolittle models of bringing the war directly to the enemy. The United States would build an air force dedicated to attacking the homelands of the Axis powers: Germany, Italy, and Japan, and their affiliate and co-belligerent states. This immediately required a large force of pilots and bomber crews. It also required airplanes and munitions to rain down upon the enemy. Neither manpower nor aircraft were in great supply in 1941 as the United States entered the war.

In 1939, not really thinking of global conflict, the army expected to train 1,200 pilots per year by 1941. In 1940, with war in Europe on the horizon, they upped those numbers to train 7,000 pilots that year and, in 1941, changed plans again, increasing the number to 30,000. It would not be enough.

The boys charged with accomplishing political policy and military goals found the process arduous and fraught with danger and death. During training, US Army Air Forces (USAAF, or AAF) aviation cadets were pushed to limits they never believed possible, or thought existed. The boys were continually barraged with tests—physical, mental, academic, and emotional. Because of the huge numbers of American boys involved in training, most tests were executed in a systematic, assembly-line fashion. The army made use of the results to teach, probe, prod, classify, categorize, and judge.

All boys in flight training were called "aviation cadets." These cadets lived in fear of "washing out" and being forced, due to some failure or other, to leave the pilot training program. For the first years of the war, a pilot who washed out was transferred to another school, either to learn navigation or to be a bombardier. This was done with the thought that pilot washouts still had accrued valuable training which should not be discarded, forgotten, or wasted.

When cadets first began training in 1942 with the USAAF, they were told that one in three of them would not make it through the program. "Between July 1939 and August 1945, some 317,000 students entered AAF pilot training. Of these, 193,440 (61 percent) were successful in graduating from advanced (training). More than 124,000, or roughly two out of five, washed out along the way."

There were plentiful opportunities for washing out. According to Charles Watry, who trained (successfully) to fly B-17s, 50.3 percent of the boys who took the qualifying exams to *enter* the cadet program failed the initial physical and written exams. "Planning factors for procurement of men for the flying training programs were based upon the projection that only one out of five (20 percent) who took the initial mental and physical qualifying exams would qualify. Of those who did qualify, no more than 40 to 50 percent were expected to successfully finish the course." Those were cruel numbers for the boys who failed to make the grade.

Due to the planned washout rate, "Cadet recruiting in 1942 aimed at attracting ten times the number of applicants that were eventually expected to graduate." Achieving the *prewar* goal of attracting 30,000 pilots a year meant that 60,000 students had to enter training. "It meant further that the number of applicants to the program would be on the order of 300,000 a year. By October 1942, the goals for graduating pilots had been successfully increased and had reached nearly 100,000 a year. Almost one million applicants would have to be sought." The task of reaching these numbers was truly formidable.

The pass rate for cadet qualification and course completion increased from 26.8 percent in 1939 to 49.7 percent by 1942. The reason had nothing to do with smarter students and everything to do with changing the course structure and examinations so more students passed. As a result, "washout rates for pilots actually averaged 39 percent rather than the projected 40 to 50 percent."

The results of this shift in training and increase in manpower was nothing short of fantastic. "In 1938, the Air Corps (precursor to the USAAF) represented but 11 percent of the United States Army, with a total strength of just over 20,000 personnel." Six years later, reflecting the importance of airpower when it came to winning the war, 2.4 million men and women were serving in the Army Air Forces. This represented nearly one-third of the army's ranks.

The fact that all of these boys had to be trained with such astounding speed was a major factor in the number of aviation accidents and deaths that occurred during the war. Following the attack on Pearl Harbor, the Army Air Forces became the largest single educational organization in existence. Across the United States schools were set up to train not only pilots, but also navigators, bombardiers, gunners, and mechanics. Support staff had to be trained as well to fill such positions as office workers, cooks, janitors—you name it.

By late 1943, crews for the heavy bomber B-17 Flying Fortress and B-24 Liberator consisted of ten specialists. There were four officers (pilot, copilot, navigator, and bombardier) and six noncommissioned officers (radio operator, flight engineer, tail gunner, ball turret gunner, and two waist gunners). During combat every crewman but for the two pilots and bombardier manned the aircraft's defensive guns. After bomb's away, there was a machine gun for the bombardier as well.

A full B-24 crew complement. Pilot Lt. John K. Specht (far right, kneeling) reported that 463 had a faulty compass. COURTESY ROBERT SPECHT

Some fliers saw themselves as romantic "knights errant of the air." Others, like England's Leonard Cheshire, envisioned themselves as something like the seafaring captains of old. They were leaders of men, "in whose hands rested the lives of a crew," as well as the lives of "many hundreds of Germans on the ground." All of these people would feel and experience the captain's decisions and actions. "When I left training school I had pictured myself as a fully groomed operational pilot wanting but a short experience of gunfire to be complete."

Cheshire ruefully learned he wasn't as "fully groomed" as one would hope. Being a successful pilot and captain of his ship had everything to do with hard work. "Bombing is technical, a matter of knowledge and experience, not of setting your jaw and rushing in." Once that knowledge and experience are gained, "the crux of the issue is crew cooperation." And this didn't come from ordering the crew around. It sprang from the boys having confidence in their captain, that he wouldn't do anything stupid or get them killed. For that crew confidence to develop, a pilot needed confidence in himself. "You have got to be good, and they have got to know it, and they will only know it by results; for once you cannot bluff. I know what that trust is worth. It is worth working for." It began, "first and foremost," by learning how to fly.

Flying the B-24 was difficult and challenging under the best of conditions. Sometimes a pilot had a bad day. Maybe the airplane wasn't responding as well as he thought it should. Or other factors, like lousy weather, made flying difficult. He might get annoyed and take it out on himself, or, worse, his crew. John J. Hibbits had this experience during an instrument session, "flying under the hood." This was where an instructor sat in the copilot's seat, with the pilot's windows curtained off so that visual cues could not be followed. This was the best way to teach pilots to trust their instruments and drum out of their heads the old barnstormer habit of "flying by the seat of your pants."

After jerking the plane around too much, Hibbits had the controls taken away from him by his instructor. Hibbits was afraid that his poor piloting skills would be rewarded with a reprimand, or, worse, being washed out. Fortunately for Hibbits, his instructor didn't interpret one bad day as indicative of a trend. He saw it as a way to teach Hibbits how to be a good pilot. "If you become annoyed and lose control of yourself, you will destroy the confidence of your crew, not only in your ability as a pilot, but in you as a personality. If I were you, I'd refrain from any display of temper; for once you've lost the confidence of your crew, you have taken the first step toward breaking down their morale." And crew morale was "one of the most, if not *the* most, valuable asset you will have on a combat mission" (emphasis added).

The first of five pilot training levels was the five-week-long Preflight training at places like SAAAB, the Santa Ana Army Air Base (where there were no hangars, no runways, and no airplanes). In their 175 hours of instruction, aviation cadets learned military discipline and to march in drill. Because the brass believed in the power of physical training for building strong minds and agile bodies, there was lots of calisthenics and organized sports and athletics. Boys knuckled under an onslaught of academics covering a spectrum of subjects, including aircraft and ship-ping recognition, mathematics, meteorology, physics, map reading, and learning Morse code.

The washout rate at Preflight was tremendous, approaching 50 per-cent in some years. But anyone surviving those initial five weeks was one step closer to sitting in a cockpit and piloting an airplane. Those who did not wash out of Preflight moved on to Primary training, often under the instruction of civilian teachers.

As in the Army Air Corps before the war, "the pilot remained the most important of officers in a vastly expanded and greatly diversified wartime air arm." In Primary training cadets began to feel that impor-tance as they finally took to the skies with sixty-five hours of cockpit instruction. Here they learned not only how to take off, fly, and land, but also how to perform basic aerobatics, like loops and rolls. The airplane of choice during Primary was the docile but rugged Boeing biplane, the PT-17 Stearman. Cadets also continued with fifty-four hours of physical training, along with ninety-four hours of academic work.

Basic training, with seventy hours in the air, ninety-four hours in ground school, and forty-seven hours of military training, came next. The Vultee BT-13, affectionately known as the "Vultee Vibrator" for one of its in-flight characteristics, was the aircraft of choice.

Piled onto their previous training, during Basic training cadets were introduced to night flying, formation flying, and the Link Trainer. This first-ever flight simulator was designed to train pilots in "blind flying." This was their first taste of learning the crucial skill of instrument flying.

By the time cadets reached the next stage, Advanced training, their government had so much time and money invested in them, it's fair to say that "the only ones that failed to get their wings were those who managed to kill themselves flying." Cadets received seventy more hours of cockpit time focusing on instrument, day and night cross-country flying, and formation flying. There were sixty hours of ground school, and nineteen hours devoted to military training. Once they were finished, the boys were expected to be able to fly any single- or twin-engine aircraft.

Upon graduating from Advanced training and receiving their wings, a successful cadet had completed a minimum of 200 hours of flying, 248 hours of ground school, and 120 hours of military education. After being commissioned as second lieutenants or flight officers, they were thrilled to experience the first privilege associated with being an officer and a gentleman: more pay.

The next stage of a pilot's education was ten weeks of Transition training. Here, pilots were sent to specialized schools in either fighters, bombers, or transport. The lion's share of pilots ended up with heavy bombers, because that was where the greatest need lay. They flew without crews, only an instructor.

The first time a pilot got behind the wheel of a B-24 he was surprised by how completely different it was from anything else he had ever flown. "Now I discovered the big difference between the Liberator and the ships I'd flown up to then," John J. Hibbits wrote in his 1943 book, *Take 'Er Up Alone, Mister!* "It did not respond to the controls as quickly as the others had. When I turned the wheel, no matter how swiftly, nothing seemed to happen. I simply sat there and waited for a moment, and then watched the big ship slowly go into a smooth bank."

The interior of a B-24 was not a quiet place. Accustomed as we are today to flying in commercial airplanes, the B-24, like the B-17, did not have a pressurized cabin. It was a cold and windy environment. It didn't help that the waist gunners' windows were always open. And once the bomb bay was opened, "It sounded as if half a dozen subway trains were headed right up to the flight deck. The roar was terrific."

There were big problems in 1942 during Transition training, because "They were still having difficulty in getting enough B-24s to keep us all in the air." As a result, Lieutenant Hibbits, at Tarrant Field near Fort Worth, Texas, found himself training for the four-engine Liberator in the two-engine B-25 medium bomber. Backlogs in training also meant that senior pilots in the first phase of Transition training were given preference with the ships available, further retarding time in the heavy bombers for newer students.

Training backlogs occurred for two major reasons. First, the number of aircraft available for training was woefully lacking in the early years of the war. This remained the case until manufacturing was able to supply the needs of combat and training aircraft. Second was the number of boys involved in training, especially the increase in numbers as the war progressed. Even in combat, especially in the South Pacific, the difference between "paper strength" and "operational strength" meant there were always more pilots available than airworthy aircraft.

When they could get the airplanes, Transition training for B-24s involved an additional 125 hours of flying, with additional ground school. The course for B-17 pilots lasted nine weeks and included 105 flying hours because, during 1942 and 1943, the Flying Fortress was considered easier to fly than the Liberator.

Following Transition training, bomber pilots reported to unit training groups for Phase training. This is where they first met their crews. "Because bombing operations in combat units were normally done on a group basis, in training, too, the group became the fundamental unit." Between December 1942 and August 1945, 12,217 B-17 and 14,708 B-24 crews were trained.

The boys on *Exterminator* and 463 at Hammer Field were participating in unit training and had all been assigned to the 461st Bombardment Group that would take them overseas and into combat. *Exterminator's* crew was with the 766th Bomb Squadron, and 463 was with the 765th Bomb Squadron. Judging from letters written to their parents, Charles Turvey and Bob Hester thought they had a good, tight crew. They had learned the lessons Leonard Cheshire thought so important.

There is no extant record of how much flight time Bob Hester and Culos Settle had built up by 1943. What we know of Turvey and Darden's experience comes from their accident reports. Unlike Bob Hester, Culos Settle had trained as a pilot and gone through Transition training. As a copilot, Hester had not. Given his place in the educational food chain, it can be expected that Settle had at least as much experience as Turvey, who had 613 total hours of flight time, with 259 hours in the Liberator—150 hours within the previous ninety days. It also meant that squadron leader Darden, with 235 hours in the B-24, did not possess a superior amount of experience in that airplane compared to the men he supervised. That, and bad luck, would catch up with him.

Hester undoubtedly had less flight time than any of the others, since he was trained as a copilot. He would have graduated from Advanced training but not gone through Transition. That means that as unit training began, Bob Hester had never seen the inside of a B-24.

Also pointing to the disparity of experience between Lieutenant Turvey and his commanding officer is the fact that Turvey possessed ninety-seven hours of instrument training (fifty-eight in the previous six months), of which thirty-seven (seven in last thirty days) were nighttime flying in the past six months. Captain Darden had forty hours of instrument time, but only one hour in the previous thirty days, and twenty-nine hours of night flying, with a bit less than two and a half hours in the last thirty days. It's easy to see from these numbers that Darden's position of responsibility, flying a desk, had kept him on the ground quite a bit more than he would have liked. It's that kind of experience—or lack of experience, really—that could inspire a squadron commander to volunteer to get more flight time.

The accident reports for 463 and *Exterminator* do not specify when, or in what craft, the night-flying experience was gained, or if it had been credited to Link Trainers. Turvey, Hester, and Settle had been at Hammer Field since about October 20. That's forty-six days until 463's loss. With his seven hours of night flying within the past thirty days under his belt, Turvey's final flight returning to Hammer Field from Davis-Monthan could have been only his second, or (less likely), his third flying a B-24 in total darkness. Seeing that 463 had been crewing together since October, it's a sure bet that Turvey and Hester flew those most recent seven hours together, along with their navigator, Bill Cronin.

Combat and transport pilots during World War II had a tougher time of it than did their peers during the 1914–1918 conflict. During the Great War, "Flying was strictly a good-weather operation," and an aircraft's range was limited. Lacking navigation instruments and radios, pilots had to see the ground to know where they were and where they were going. Pilots during World War II flew long hours in all kinds of weather over all kinds of terrain for hundreds of miles. That required the services of a navigator, whose role was to get the bomber crew to their destination and back.

The army defined navigation as "the science of getting from one point to another, accurately and efficiently, despite weather and topography of the land." Before flying their first combat mission, the boys who became navigators were expected to get an airplane like the B-24 from their home base in the States to Europe or the South Pacific. This involved flying immense distances over land, and then even greater distances over open water, often in miserable weather, with nothing but their newfound skills to guide them.

It's amazing to consider that in 1943, it had been only fourteen years since Charles Lindbergh successfully made the first crossing of the Atlantic Ocean between New York and France. Long-range flights were still a new thing in 1943, made possible by the new and powerful engines designed and built in the late 1930s. "But on-board instruments and ground-based navigational aids lagged behind the new capabilities of the aircraft." Lindbergh's techniques for crossing the Atlantic weren't any different from what the boys used to get from North America to Europe or the South Pacific.

At the time of the war when Bill Cronin was navigating 463, navigators and bombardiers were mostly washed-out pilots. After failing as a pilot, in 1943, Cronin would have then begun a twenty-week course in navigation. He would have taken a practice flight on average once per week, for a total of 104 hours in the air. There were another 782 hours, increased after September 1941 from 470, in ground school. Emphasis was less on theory and more on practical knowledge; they weren't producing scholars.

On the oceans and in the air, navigators today rely on GPS. Placed in orbit by the United States Department of Defense, this space-based Global Positioning System consists of a network of twenty-four satellites. It's a wonderful system unless your enemy shoots down your satellites. In 1943, a navigator's tools were limited by the intelligence, training, and experience of the person and by inadequate instruments. Two primary tools for navigators were pilotage and dead reckoning. The first method is well known to any cross-country driver who navigates with a map on their lap, checking off landmarks as they are passed. Dead reckoning is also often employed by motorists. If you travel sixty miles at sixty miles per hour, you can expect to arrive at your destination in one hour.

It's the same thing in airplanes. Except it's different when you're flying across an ocean where there are no landmarks. Or where the wind blows at quarters to your course or in your face or behind you. Or if you're flying across enemy territory where they have done everything possible to obfuscate all ground references, all the while trying to shoot you down.

A third arrow in the navigator's quiver was celestial navigation, using an octant or sextant to make star and sun sightings. This technique was no different than the method used for hundreds of years by naval navigators to find their position on Earth relative to known fixed points in the sky. A major drawback of celestial is that it requires (mostly) clear skies, something a bomber crew traveling at 200 miles per hour, more or less, could not rely upon—unlike a ship traveling much slower at sea. At such a rate the world changes far too quickly to wait for clouds to clear. Reflecting its difficulty and importance, celestial took up 202 hours of a navigator's twenty weeks of training. By the end of those twenty weeks a navigator like William Cronin would have been as familiar with the stars as a motorist was with landmarks, curves, hills, and "the road that leads to his door." After graduation, Cronin was awarded his silver navigator's wings, commissioned as a second lieutenant, and was sent to Wendover Field in Utah, where he met Turvey, Hester, and Fish.

Training mechanics and the other boys who kept the airplanes in the air was as intensive as the training for flight crews. The numbers of boys trained for these positions are just as impressive. Between 1938 and 1939 the Army Air Corps graduated less than 900 soldiers from maintenance courses. By the time the war was over, that number had increased to over 700,000. From the attack on Pearl Harbor to the Japanese surrender, almost 1.4 million persons had received some kind of technical training. Many of the boys graduated from more than one course or discipline.

When the war began, nearly every one of these boys had as little experience in aviation mechanics as the pilots did in flying airplanes. George Barulic, radio operator on *Exterminator*, drives home this point better than any historian or statistician ever could. "Things, parts malfunctioned and planes went down. I think that's a big problem, and you got mechanics that aren't the best. They might have just gone through the school, and it's not like having a mechanic that does that for a couple of years and is qualified. I think a lot of the . . . well, that's just the way it is. A war is . . . you gotta go with what you've got."

Ground-duty enlisted men had a choice of thirty-four separate skills and eighty types of courses available to them. Communications (i.e., radio, telegraphy, telephone, and radar) had twenty-six courses from four to forty-four weeks in length. Aircraft repair and maintenance had fifteen courses, five to twenty-nine weeks in length. Flight engineers had eight courses running from four to twelve weeks. It doesn't really seem like that long a time to learn how to work on a machine as complicated as the B-24.

Despite the need for, and the speed of, training, each member of a bomber crew in 1943 received the best education possible for the job he had to do. However, there were plenty of holes in this education, and two in particular led to the loss of *Exterminator*. It's not difficult to see how lack of training in bailing out of an airplane and in how to ditch a B-24 led to the deaths of William Darden, Samuel Schlosser, Franklin Nyswonger, Dick Mayo, Richard Spangle, and Donald Vande Plasch.

The B-24 was one of the largest airplanes of its time. Indeed, seen from its exterior, the Liberator is formidable in size. However, a B-24 experienced from the interior is a completely different story. The Liberator's interior was cramped and small. There wasn't even a door! Crew either entered via the bomb bay or the front wheel well.

The interior walls were not finished as we see in modern airliners. They were lined with stacks of yellow oxygen bottles. Long lines of tubing, cabling, and wiring snaked everywhere along the walls. There were plenty of things sticking out that could hook or grab your clothing.

The catwalk over the bomb bay was 10 inches wide, so narrow a person needed to turn sideways to get through. Lack of interior space to move around is evident in photographs, and no more so than with the two waist gunners. They had so little room to maneuver that they routinely bumped into each other as they swiveled from side to side with their guns.

To reach the nose compartment and their stations, the bombardier and navigator entered the bomb bay and crawled through a 7-foot-long tunnel. The radio operator's head was level with the pilot's feet. Only the flight deck could be considered anything like spacious, and that was only in comparison to what the rest of the crew had available.

Imagine trying to navigate through this world wearing a seat-type parachute banging against the back of your thighs, or a heavy and bulky backpack-type parachute hanging up on everything while carrying an oxygen bottle at the same time so you don't die of anoxia. Even the smaller chest-type parachutes were difficult to maneuver through the airplane; it was like hauling around a huge belly. Flying as high as they did in an unpressurized cabin meant breathing supplemental oxygen, and the outside, and inside, temperatures were the same. The cockpit had a heater of sorts, but the rest of the airplane was, as they say, air-cooled. The crew, therefore, wore their sheep-lined leather jackets and pants, long underwear, and electrically heated flight suits. In combat they also wore body armor and their Mae West (life jacket). Look at photos of aircrews in front of their bombers, wearing all this bulky gear. The boys look like Teddy Bears in leather jackets with fleece collars.

With this world before you, consider how difficult it was to get out of an airplane, most likely on fire and pinning you by centrifugal force to your position. A Liberator was a tight fit everywhere, with no place to make a hurried exit.

Given how difficult it was for the boys to move themselves within a Liberator, is it any wonder only two members of *Exterminator*'s crew parachuted out of the plane? For the moment, assume that all the crew heard the order from Captain Darden to leave the ship. Also, assume they understood what that meant. Darden was not their usual captain—Lt. Culos Settle was. And Settle left the ship! This was probably only because he was already walking around the bomb bay, following Darden's order to figure out what was going wrong with *Exterminator*. Maybe the other boys had no idea what was happening.

Everything about the crew bailing out—or not bailing out—of *Exterminator* was odd. In his book about the B-24, William Carigan reviews what is *supposed* to happen with trained crews during a ditching, and is unequivocal about the procedure. "The pilot gives the crew the signal to take ditching positions," informing them of "the expected number of minutes before impact." Crew members are to loosen their shirt collars and remove oxygen masks and their heavy flying boots. When ordered to, the crew removes their parachute and parachute harness. The copilot remains on the flight deck and assists the pilot with flying the airplane. After ditching, "the airplane will usually remain afloat from one to five minutes." The job of the flight engineer was to deploy the life raft—if *Exterminator* had one, which is doubtful on a training aircraft. Then, "Crew should exit as fast as possible." The crew should have practiced all these procedures so they knew the drill when it was needed.

It's likely *Exterminator*'s crew suspected something wasn't right with their airplane, and just as likely they didn't know what was wrong. Perhaps they realized something unnatural was occurring. To be sure, they knew the airplane was falling out of the sky because of the ground getting closer and closer. Captain Darden was signaling for the crew to bail out. At least Lt. Settle and Sgt. Barulic heard the pilot's orders. Why did all but two of the boys choose to stay on board?

William Carigan, a Liberator and Flying Fortress instructor and pilot with fifty combat missions, strongly advised, "Never leave it up to the crew to decide whether they will bail out or not." Carigan's experience was that combat crews relied on their captain for their lives, "nearly always developed a strong confidence in him," and, "if left to their own choices, aircrewmen nearly always opt to remain with the pilot."

Carigan's operant words are "nearly always." On one hand, there is no reason to assume *Exterminator*'s crew lacked confidence in Captain Darden. In the December 1943 report for the 461st Bombardment Group, Darden was described as "a fine gentleman and an outstanding squadron commander . . . truly an outstanding leader of men . . . probably the best known, the best liked, and the most inspiring officer in the 461st Group."

But Darden's crew that day had never flown with him before. They knew Lt. Culos Settle and Lt. Richard Behrens as their pilot and copilot. Behrens wasn't with them that day; he'd been bumped by Captain Darden. Perhaps, as William Carigan wrote, the crew elected to remain with *Exterminator*, despite all commands and indications to leave, because they knew the pilot had done so too. But why didn't they follow Lieutenant Settle, their usual pilot? Perhaps they didn't know he'd jumped.

The meat of the matter was that *Exterminator*'s crew were probably just too plain scared to jump. During training aircrews were not given any instruction in parachuting—certainly not like what paratroopers received. George Barulic said, "I never had any kind of training about bailing out or anything like that."

As tough as pilot selection was, paratrooper selection was even tougher. In recognition of his elite status, the army paid a paratrooper an extra $50 per week. Like aircrews, the paratrooper was a volunteer. He had to be athletic. Enlisted men could be no older than thirty (officers no older than thirty-five), and no shorter than 5-foot-6 or over 6-foot-2, and weigh no more than 185 pounds. He had to be unmarried.

A paratrooper got plenty of jumping practice during his sixteen weeks of training. He made ground jumps from all sorts of heights and angles. Before going into combat, paratroopers got five or six actual jumps from an airplane. Despite all this training it wasn't unusual for a man to freeze and be unable to jump from an airplane thousands of feet above the ground. Imagine how it must have looked to the crew of *Exterminator*, which was only a few hundred feet above the thickly forested ground.

Leonard Cheshire's initial thoughts about bailing out of an airplane were, "Oh, well, you won't think anything [of] it, because if the situation arises where you've got to jump, you'll be so bloody glad to get out you won't give a damn about anything else." That was theory. Practice was different. When a situation arose where Cheshire might actually have to jump, he found he couldn't. "The thought of jumping is worse than anything. I'd rather stay here [in a stricken plane] and hope for the best."

For all but the bold and the brave, jumping out of an airplane is an unnatural act. It requires training and practice, neither of which were provided to bomber crews. That Lieutenant Settle and Sergeant Barulic left *Exterminator* should be considered an exceptional accomplishment by two incredibly courageous men.

Granted the crew's lack of training in bailing out of airplanes, ignoring Darden's command to leave *Exterminator* was not a good idea. A six-month survey of bomber ditchings around the time of the D-Day invasion showed that 22 percent of B-17s and 62 percent of B-24s broke up after hitting the water, and 6 percent of B-17 crews and 24 percent of B-24 crews drowned. Overall, 38 percent of 8th Air Force B-17 crews who ditched survived against 27 percent of B-24 crews. Clearly the numbers were against *Exterminator*'s crew surviving a water landing.

As William Carigan noted, B-24 Liberator crews were supposed to have some practical training in ditching. But the same D-Day ditching study mentions that only 16.8 percent of B-17 crews and 12 percent of B-24 crews had participated in a wet ditching drill of at least one hour.

Of the novels written about the air war, there are three that stand out. First is *Morotai*, by John Boeman. Another is *Face of a Hero*, by Louis Falstein. The third is *Goodbye to Some*, by Gordon Forbes. None of these thinly disguised fictional accounts mince words about the war their writers encountered—the killing and being killed, the abject fear, wastage, destruction, boredom, and tedium, and the men who led or failed to lead. Boeman and Forbes flew B-24s in the South Pacific, and Falstein was a B-24 tail gunner in Italy.

Falstein says once the boys got overseas, they quickly learned that Liberators were not designed nor built for crash landings. Hitting the ground with wheels up would crush the Venetian blinds that constituted the bomb bay doors, causing the plane's undercarriage to implode. Ditching made the same bomb bay doors collapse and the Liberator would snap in two.

Only after reaching Italy did Falstein's crew practice ditching positions. Experiencing a crash landing was harrowing, as Falstein captures in *Face of a Hero*. It could possibly be worse in a ditching, since the crew would have to contend with getting out of the airplane before it sank.

Gordon Forbes describes how poorly the Liberator fared during a water crash landing and the final moments before hitting the drink. "I have felt in rapid order the surprising shock and painful cutting pitch forward against my harness as we struck, the manhandling of the water as it ripped into the cockpit, the shouts, the noises like gongs, and then the final deep blubbering, with the crushing pressure singing higher and higher in my head."

Forbes then recounts the stifling claustrophobia of being trapped within the cockpit of a sinking airplane. "I am in a cage, rotating slowly and going down. I flip the seat belt buckle open and shrug off the shoulder straps. For a moment they cling to me and wave around my eyes like ribbons of white macaroni. Then I am out of the cage and pumping my arms and legs. But I don't know which way to go. The pressure is changing and it feels as though I am still going deeper. I scramble frantically, selecting one oblique direction after another."

The army was neither unaware nor unconcerned with the issues of ditching a B-24 Liberator. The problem was how little could be done about it. "Sometimes a plane would hit the water and float for a couple of minutes, letting everyone get out. Sometimes it would break in half and immediately sink. How do you tell?" It all had to do with the experience of the pilot, the angle the aircraft struck the water, the water's surface, and a lot of luck.

On September 20, 1944, the army tested the ditching characteristics of a B-24 on the James River in Virginia. The results were not encouraging, even though conditions for the test were highly favorable. The river that day was calm and only a slight crosswind was detected. The test B-24 was reinforced with steel plating around the flight deck, the pilots were very experienced, and the situation was not an emergency. The bomber came in as experience had taught pilots in a ditching—its nose up, with full flaps—and initially hit the water with the Liberator's tail. Nevertheless, when the big bomber set down on the river, its nose section broke off, the empennage and bomb bay were destroyed, and the fuselage collapsed in the middle. The pilots escaped the quickly sinking Liberator, which was eventually towed to shore and lifted out of the water using a crane.

Would it have made a difference to *Exterminator*'s crew if they had trained to ditch or crash-land? This is an important question, because the dangers inherent in training meant plenty of people got hurt. During World War II the US Army Air Forces lost more aircraft within the forty-eight states to training accidents than in combat with the Japanese. There is a reason why. It's because the USAAF took over a million young men and trained them to be pilots, navigators, bombardiers, flight engineers, gunners, and mechanics—among other professions. And they did it quickly. A total of 193,440 pilots graduated from pilot training between July 1, 1939, and August 31, 1945. "The peak was in December, 1943, when over 740,000 students were at various stages of individual pilot training." By the end of 1943, when the boys in 463 and *Exterminator* were in school, the army had already graduated 65,797 pilots,

The remains of a Liberator bomber is lifted from the James River following a test of the ditching capabilities of the B-24. COURTESY OF THE LIBRARY OF CONGRESS

15,928 navigators, 16,057 bombardiers, 91,595 gunners, and 544,374 technicians.

It's not as if accidents among aviation cadets went unnoticed. But there was an attitude of risk on the part of the cadets. It's an attitude that we, today, placing ourselves within the context of World War II aviation cadet training, would find unacceptable and difficult to comprehend. How else to explain the apparent cavalier attitude at the time about regular accidents, injuries, and deaths during training? Given the pace of training and the lack of background knowledge and experience in the field of aviation on the part of the boys during the 1940s, there had to be an acceptance on their part that somebody was going to die. With the ease and invulnerability of youth, they certainly thought it would be somebody else.

As different as the airplanes of today are to those of World War II, the contrast between pilot training and experience is even greater. In large part this was because after Pearl Harbor we desperately needed an immense number of trained pilots. The system the military came up with to provide these pilots developed not only out of need, but reality, because the United States was so far behind the curve in war preparation.

At the outbreak of hostilities between the United States and the Axis powers, the Americans believed that their 22,000-strong air force was technically excellent but far too insignificant for adequate protection. This was especially true given the experience of the French and Poles along with the British against the Luftwaffe. The Germans quickly demonstrated in 1939 that "air power had new meaning," and that "it was emerging as a separate striking force, with terrible power and range."

During the Great War, a striking force of fifty planes was considered significant. Navigation was so poor that aviators were forced to follow roads and railroad tracks to keep from getting lost. By 1942, the British and Germans were assembling hundreds of bombers to send against each other and, in one raid—the famous "Thousand Bomber Raid"—General Arthur Harris of the United Kingdom's Bomber Command succeeded in assembling slightly over one thousand bombers to attack Cologne, Germany, on May 30–31, 1942. While this was happening in the west, "The Nazis unleashed thousands of dive-bombers against the Russians to blast a hole for tanks and troops."

Even before the Japanese attack on Pearl Harbor, those in government and the military who were paying attention to world events knew a reckoning day would arrive when the United States must quickly build an enormous air force to counteract the Axis powers. The old way of recruitment and training had to end.

Always a volunteer force with strict admission standards, the Army Air Corps was a small, highly trained, and professional force that remained small by erecting artificial barriers to incoming recruits. On June 20, 1941, the Army Air Corps became the US Army Air Forces. Recognizing the dire need for change, the USAAF quickly adapted to the times. While maintaining the same strict physical requirements as the prewar Air Corps, artificial barriers were unceremoniously dropped. Gone were the requirements to be unmarried, between twenty and twenty-seven years of age, and to have at least two years of college.

In the "old days," admission requirements and the training regime were so exclusive that less than five hundred men per year were becoming pilots at the army's sole training center. This small number of graduates was one outgrowth of the Army Air Corps desire to "reduce the number of accidents and fatalities." As a result, the focus was on "slow, standardized training," which pushed washouts to the flight program's beginning. Gearing up for total air war, training accidents and deaths mounted with the increased number of students and the haste with which they were getting prepared for battle.

The number of mechanics and ground crews trained before the war were equally as small, but that also changed rapidly. "War has little respect of rules and regulations." War required millions of men, and quickly. Germany and Japan had taken years to build up their gigantic air forces, while the United States had only months.

Graduation numbers during the war were immense. According to General Henry "Hap" Arnold, "The training task we had undertaken was terrific. By the end of 1942 we had graduated 266,000 mechanics. By the end of 1944 we had graduated 997,000 mechanics." Pilot training, along with navigator, bombardier, gunnery, and any other kind of training you can think of to support the aircrews, also jumped sky-high. From about 9,000 pilots under instruction in 1941, the number jumped to 25,000 by the end of 1943, and by end of 1944, 226,000 pilots had graduated from flight school. The training program was so successful it created a glut of pilots. From graduating pilots "at a rate of 105,000 a year, we cut down our rate of training, until by March of 1945 we were back to a rate of about 30,000 a year."

These results were impressive, all the more so considering many of the boys were actually still children, not old enough to vote or drink—legally. As effective as the training was, not everybody was able to learn as fast or as completely as everyone else. In all the aviation trades there must have been plenty who measured up but were still not quite good enough. One can't help but wonder how many young men lost their lives because they either didn't have the training, experience, or emotional maturity necessary for them to do their jobs correctly and safely.

The boys still had a lot to learn after completing their training. Lieutenant General George Kenny, commander of the 5th Air Force, wrote to General Hap Arnold, commander of the air forces, about how unhappy he was with the boys and their combat readiness when they arrived in Australia. "Another disturbing element is the state of training of the B-24s coming from Hawaii. From the somewhat meager information I have to date, I find that their night flying is not up to scratch. The job here calls for night takeoffs with maximum loads, and often with crosswinds climbing through overcast to fifteen to twenty thousand feet in order to navigate." Kenny wanted to nurse along his new pilots before throwing them into battle. But getting considerably more night-flying experience was predicated on cooperative weather and other factors beyond his control.

Another indication of an incomplete education is that accidental deaths continued when the boys were overseas. It wasn't widely reported, and therefore has received little notice, but for every navy or marine pilot lost in combat in the Pacific, *another* pilot was lost either in training accidents or during nonoperational (i.e., noncombat) flights.

There was a time when flying was all about luck. Skill and training too. Practice, even. But luck was as big a part of flying as any of those other factors. Pilots may have intellectually disdained the belief in gremlins, but they eventually came around, because it seemed to them that experience supported superstition. How else to explain a perfectly good airplane with perfectly good engines just shutting down for no observable reason? Like boats, airplanes had personalities. They were capricious, yet tough. They needed to be babied; pampered. Loved and treated rough.

Would it have made any difference to their fate if the crew flying on 463 was more experienced in night navigation or if *Exterminator's* crew had been better versed in ditching a Liberator in open water? Sadly, probably not. The B-24 pilots flying out of Hammer Field in December 1943, when 463 and *Exterminator* were lost, had been flying for less than eighteen months, had less than a thousand hours of experience, less than a hundred hours of flying at night, and less than fifty hours flying on instruments, and yet they were considered experienced and ready for action.

CHAPTER 8

Not *Exactly* a Death Trap

THE B-24 LIBERATOR WAS MUCH MALIGNED DURING ITS SHORT LIFE serving the army and navy during World War II. History has treated the aircraft with similar contempt. Some called the B-24 "the crate the B-17 Flying Fortress was shipped in." Media of the day thumbed their noses at the Liberator. They considered it ugly, and facetiously likened it to a railroad boxcar. In memoirs written decades after the war, the underpinning of why pilots didn't favor the B-24 seems to be that they considered the aircraft difficult to fly. Some termed it a "Flying Coffin." Yet, for all its detractors, and for all the ill words it garnered, the Liberator had an outstanding war record, serving in Europe, North Africa, and the South Pacific.

The B-24 Liberator was designed and initially built by the Consolidated Aircraft Company of San Diego, California. Within five and a half years the Liberator was pushed from an unarmed prototype to a heavily defended combat-worthy bomber. Among its many innovations for the era, the Liberator's shining star was the Davis Wing, designed by David R. Davis. The wing was "characterized by a high-aspect ratio, which resembled the wing of a glider more than that of a powered aircraft." This meant there was less drag as the aircraft moved through the atmosphere, giving the B-24 more air time. The Liberator was also fuel-efficient. According to Royal Air Force figures, at a cruising speed of 160 to 170 miles per hour a lightly loaded B-24 could get 1.6 air miles per gallon. RAF data showed the top fuel efficiency for the B-17 was 1.2 air miles per gallon.

A Consolidated B-24 Liberator (294852) parked at Royal Air Force Station Mount Farm, 1944. ROBERT ASTRELLA VIA THE NORM TAYLOR COLLECTION/THE MUSEUM OF FLIGHT

In 1943 the B-24 Liberator represented the epitome of aircraft design, construction, and production. By the war's end it had "surpassed the production of every other single type of American military aircraft."

The number of Liberators needed for combat and the demand for the airplane led to an innovation in manufacturing the B-24. In addition to producing the airplane in its San Diego and Fort Worth plants, the Consolidated Aircraft Company licensed production to Douglas Aircraft in Tulsa, North American Aviation in Dallas, and the Ford Motor Company in Willow Run, Michigan. Turvey and Hester's B-24, #41-28463, was one of twenty-eight B-24E-10 models assembled by Douglas Aircraft. It was delivered to the army on June 23, 1943, at a cost of $306,592. Captain Darden's *Exterminator*, #42-7674, was one of 253 B-24H-1 models built by Ford at Willow Run.

Edsel Ford, president of Ford Motor Company, was convinced that airplanes could be mass-produced on an assembly line just like automobiles. And, from the army's point of view, just like pilots. Companies with years of experience in the aviation business scoffed at the idea that airplane and automobile production had anything in common.

Yet, by the war's end, "Willow Run finally created around 47 percent of all Liberators produced, either in complete aircraft or by manufacturing subassemblies for other plants to finish," and the plant could assemble a B-24 in sixty-three minutes. Another of Ford's innovations involved the use of dies, pressing sheets of aluminum into shape. This technique worked fine for steel but not so fine for the soft surfaces of aluminum parts, which the dies scratched, impairing the ability of the aluminum to withstand corrosion. Modifications were necessary, and eventually the process was successful.

Ford hired Charles Lindbergh as a test pilot to tell them what was right and what was wrong with the B-24 design and manufacturing at Willow Run. Blacklisted due to his prewar isolationist views, Lindbergh was happy to oblige Ford. The test pilot job was the only war-related work he could get. The "Lone Eagle" was not at all impressed with the Willow Run operation. Lindbergh said the Ford-built B-24s were "the worst piece of metal aircraft construction I have ever seen."

Lindbergh found the controls on the B-24 were stiffer and heavier than anything he'd ever handled. The Liberator was "unnecessarily awkward," and the instruments "more complicated than the keyboard of a pipe organ." Supporting Lindbergh's analysis, a B-24 training conference in 1943 concluded, "The actual flying of a B-24 airplane by a young [new] pilot was 30 percent more difficult than the flying of a B-17 airplane, as the B-17 was more conventional in design and operation," and more along the lines of what pilots had been trained to expect.

It got worse. At 20,000 feet, where the temperature could sink to -40 degrees Fahrenheit, Lindbergh said an icy wind blew through the cockpit. Any moisture on the pilot's face meant his skin would freeze to his rubber oxygen mask. The muscle power needed to get the B-24 off the ground and into the air meant pilots sweat a lot. Also, there were no windshield wipers. If it was raining during takeoff or landing, the pilot had to stick his head out the side window to see the runway.

At Ford's Willow Run facility, Edsel Ford had vowed to produce one bomber per hour. It was a production promise nearly impossible to meet for two reasons. First, there was a manpower shortage created by the surge in people signing up for the armed forces. Second, just like pilots and technicians in the Army Air Forces, the industrial workers who were available to fill the vacant slots on the assembly line were inexperienced and needed training in the worst way. In discussing this issue with the Ford executives during mid-1942, Charles Lindbergh laid it on the line: Their workforce was half of what they needed. "We have more than 30,000 employees at Willow Run now, and less than 400 of them had experience in aircraft manufacturing before they came here."

William Carigan was a contemporary of the 463 and *Exterminator* crews. He got his wings in December 1943. Like Capt. William Darden, Carigan was career military, starting in 1939 with the Kentucky National Guard. Carigan had some choice words for the Liberator. Fully laden with fuel, bombs, ammunition, and personnel, the Liberator was slow or sluggish to respond. "Heavy on the controls, the airplane tires the strongest teams of pilots on long missions." He recalled that during his Transition training, "We started with war-weary B-24Ds, operating on 91-octane fuel and supercharged with hydraulic turbo controls." The lower-octane fuel meant they had to fly at lower power settings, which meant longer flight times, which, in turn, meant greater fuel consumption—which might explain why so many pilots training with the Liberator seemed to run out of fuel. The lower-octane fuel was also responsible for shorter engine life.

Over its design life, the B-24 Liberator experienced many changes in appearance as turrets were modified, removed, or added, and as armament was changed and updated. Through all of its variants, the aircraft's length was 66 feet, 4 inches, to 67 feet, 3 inches; the wingspan was 110 feet; and the Liberator was 17 feet, 11 inches, to 18 feet tall. Empty, the B-24 weighed 32,605 to 36,950 pounds—65,000 pounds loaded—and could carry around 3,600 gallons of fuel. The powerplant was four Pratt

& Whitney R-1830-43 or -65 radial engines, each arranged in two banks of seven cylinders. Top speed was between 279 to 303 miles per hour, with a range of 2,100 to 2,960 statute miles. Service ceiling for the Liberator was between 28,000 and 32,000 feet. In 1941 the cost to produce a B-24 was $341,960. By 1944 the cost had decreased to $210,943.

Like its contemporaries, the B-24 Liberator was tailor-made to make war, not love. Plenty of people may have thought the Liberator resembled a crate but those people didn't fly the aircraft. Loved or not, pilots quickly learned the B-24 was not designed for comfort, though some Royal Air Force pilots thought otherwise. One RAF pilot by the name of John Musgrave wrote, "My first impressions of the Liberator were dominated by its enormous size in comparison with any other aircraft I'd seen or flown at that time. It was spacious and comfortable, making British-built aircraft seem very Spartan." Less than gracious appraisers of the Liberator felt the airplane was not designed for "crew or even aircraft survival in battle or emergency situations." Or, as a postwar study noted, "The design of military aircraft has been predicated on many factors other than safety."

For basic bodily crew comfort, the only thing approaching a bathroom on board was a urination, or relief, tube and a bag for defecation. It wasn't any better in the B-17, as Truman Smith wrote in his memoir, *The Wrong Stuff.* "Relief tubes were a devilish device that were best avoided because they consisted of a small rubber funnel on the end of a tube that was plumbed to evacuate the waste to the exterior." The smallness of the funnel coupled with the crewman having to practically disrobe the lower half of his body while carrying and breathing from a walk-around oxygen bottle guaranteed the man would make contact between the subfreezing rubber funnel and his private parts. Urine within the tube would freeze pretty quickly and block the opening.

There were no such conveniences aboard the big bombers if the call of nature involved something more urgent than urination. Truman Smith recalls a combat mission in his B-17 over Berlin where the flight engineer had such a need. The only accessible receptacle was his flak helmet. "He had to take off his flak vest; parachute harness; Mae West; flight

View from the bomb bay to the tail section in a B-24. Crew had to navigate their way using the narrow catwalk. The numbered canisters hold supplemental oxygen so the crew could breathe at high altitude. PHOTO BY PETER STEKEL

suit; electric flying suit; and long underwear, just to prepare for the task." Then, balancing and positioning himself perfectly, the engineer made his deposit. Finished at the bank, "The subzero temperature hastened him to reverse the entire process, while making sure to not dislodge his oxygen mask." By that time, the freshly produced contribution to his flak helmet had frozen.

The B-24 was an airplane of its time, designed quickly and under pressure; true, but nothing like the British twin-engine Stirling bomber, which was designed with only one factor in mind. "The Stirling was limited by a ceiling of about 16,000 feet as a result of design specifications drawn up to fit conditions in the late 1930s; its short 99-foot wingspan had been dictated by the 100-foot width of RAF hangar doors in those days." Along with the twin-engine Manchester, the Stirling proved disappointing and not up to its expected task.

Being the epitome of design for its era did not mean the B-24 Liberator was without design or mechanical faults and problems. Far from it. Though some of the airplane's problems were "simply" issues of comfort, some of the Liberator's faults were severe enough to cause accidents, injuries, and death.

One drawback to the Davis Wing contributed to problems at takeoff, landing, and flying at low speeds. "The wing area was smaller than that of the similar sized B-17, an aircraft which weighed about the same. This gave the Liberator a relatively high wing loading, which in turn led to higher takeoff and landing speeds and reduced low-speed control."

Engine failure was always a problem, especially at takeoff, and usually with an outboard engine. This resulted in "an immediate loss of directional control, requiring a skilled pilot to quickly trim up the ship to avoid smearing the landscape with a Liberator." Or, as William Carigan described it, "With all power off, the B-24 glides almost straight down."

In combat, loaded down with armament and fuel, while flying above 20,000 feet, the Davis Wing made for tricky formation flying. "So much so that formation combat boxes could not be flown as tightly as was possible by B-17s. At 25,000 feet the Liberator was struggling, whereas the Fortress was still controllable at 30,000 feet." Some pilots managed just the same. "Trimmed properly and with the smooth-running Pratt & Whitney engines, we could fly very tight with finger pressure on the throttles and yoke."

There are plenty of stories of pilots running out of fuel during their Transition training to B-24s. Not only were training aircraft using lower-octane fuel, but when not properly trimmed, Liberators would fly nose up, decreasing performance and increasing drag and fuel consumption. Importantly, "When airspeed was too low, the Liberator could easily lose a thousand feet when making a turn," a characteristic that could have affected both 463 and *Exterminator* in their respective moments of truth.

There were other problems with the Davis Wing. It was sensitive to ice loading, which would distort the airfoil and result in a serious loss of lift. With the tremendous weight of bombs, fuel, oxygen tanks, and everything else in addition to a heavy load of wing ice, the aircraft would spin earthward, out of control.

The Liberator nosewheel was notoriously weak. In North Africa, where runways were unpaved, following heavy rains there were instances of taxiing B-24s having their nosewheels buried in mud and collapsing. "Shimmy" (i.e., unstable lateral movement) was a problem, too, and recognized as a frequent cause for nosewheel failure in the early B-24s, like the "D" model. Anticipating this problem, the twenty-three Liberators sent over to North Africa to be used in Col. Harry A. Halverson's first Ploesti raid "carried a spare nosewheel when they left Florida." Including problems with the Liberator's nosewheel, there were 4,400 landing-gear failures covering all aircraft during the war that led to accidents.

The Pratt & Whitney engines used in Liberators were considered to be highly reliable, and "probably the best radials of the war." Overall, during the war there were 5,500 Liberator accidents caused by powerplant failures with magneto failure being the leading cause of Liberator engine failure. The magnetos required constant attention and the fuses required frequent changing. Captain Darden, according to Lieutenant Settle's testimony after the loss of *Exterminator*, had called for the crew to bail out and directed *Exterminator*'s flight engineer to change fuses, "and then changed his mind and didn't say what fuses." Darden might have known about this issue, and perhaps suspected a bad magneto fuse was the cause for *Exterminator*'s loss of power.

Another cause of engine failure was related to turbochargers. If one went out while at high altitude a serious drop in power resulted. This had significant impact on crews in combat. If an airplane couldn't keep up with the group it became a straggler. And stragglers were easy pickings when enemy fighters were about.

Not only were the boys flying Liberators new to the task, so were the mechanics. These recent graduates from the army's technical school were faced with the humongous task of maintaining aircraft with an inventory of spare parts grossly inadequate to the matter at hand. Included in this supply issue was a dearth of prop governors, that essential piece on *Exterminator* which may have caused the plane all of its troubles, resulting in the deaths of six boys.

The mechanics at Hammer Field were also swamped by the need to continually overhaul the squadron's engines due to the constant use of 91-octane fuel, lower than what the Liberator's Pratt & Whitney engines required. The need for frequent engine changes in turn retarded the flight training program, but not doing so threatened the B-24s with engine failure during flight. Records from the 461st Bomb Group show that training for the seventy crews at Hammer Field in December 1943 was delayed time and time again by an overall shortage of airplanes to fly.

Flying schedules at Hammer Field were arranged to provide six hours of airplane maintenance each day, but the poor condition of so many of the aircraft meant this wasn't enough time. Liberators judged unfit to fly led the list of reasons for the shortage of flyable aircraft. Records from Turvey and Hester's 461st Bomb Group show that from November 2 to November 14, 1943, nine of the Group's B-24s were not flyable, and the planes needed "long periods of maintenance and many engine changes." And between November 15 and November 28, 1943, Group airplanes were grounded 259 hours due to bad weather—meaning the crews fell further behind in their training, which raised their chances of making mistakes and having accidents.

Training delays due to SNAFUs with equipment or from maintenance slowdowns were hardly confined to Hammer Field. Across the training program were maintenance errors like installing the improper part, or installing the right part improperly. Mechanics sometimes left tools and other objects in the aircraft. Just as it wouldn't be fair to blame inexperienced pilots for making errors due to lack of experience or instruction, it's also not fair to accuse mechanics of making ignorant or careless mistakes. If you don't know what to do or what to look for, how can you be expected to do your job correctly? There were bound to be some inadequately trained maintenance personnel, just as there were inadequately trained aircrews.

Supervisory errors occurred continuously, contributing to maintenance errors. One investigation discovered that officers in the chain of command, usually the executive officer, would authorize an aircraft for use even though there were known mechanical problems. Kind of like letting pilots fly airplanes like 463 when "everybody" knew it had a faulty compass.

That these errors occurred is one indication that the number of maintenance personnel was expanding as rapidly as aircrews. It's inexcusable that mistakes were made that led to injury and loss of life. But blame, if blame should be laid, falls equally at the feet of the boys, the instructors, the vastly sped-up training programs, and the higher-ups who were willing (of necessity) to countenance this speedy training and its ultimate dangers. There was a war on, and a culture did exist that was willing to accept losses as part of the cost of doing business.

Mechanical problems primarily revolved around wear and tear and maintenance of the engines. Each of the four B-24 engines required twenty-six gallons of oil, and burned about one gallon of oil per hour. A flight between Davis-Monthan and Hammer Field for 463 was projected to be about six hours, and 630 miles. On their inbound leg home, as on their flight to Tucson, Turvey and Hester could expect to arrive with 23 percent less engine oil than when they started. Obviously, this oil-burn rate was not good for engine longevity.

There were other problems. Pilots were hampered in their duties by having limited views of their aircraft; unlike the B-17 or the two-engine B-25, neither wingtip is visible from the B-24 flight deck. Aircraft design such as weak brakes also introduced hazards that led to accidents upon takeoff and landing.

As difficult as the mechanics had it at home, once they got to their combat theaters they were faced with engine lives that could range between a few hours to many hundreds. As a result even a fairly new airplane like 463 was likely under-maintained as the demand for training aircraft grew ever higher. From beginning to end, from the States to overseas, ground crews worked long and hard hours keeping the B-24s up and in the air. Maintaining these machines required special skill and training, and the average age of a Liberator mechanic was twenty-five. Like their pilots, there was a lot of learning as you go because everyone was so young and lacking in experience.

The results of poorly maintained engines commonly meant death for the aircrews, as Philip Ardery recalls from his B-24 training. "The group that trained ahead of us at Biggs Field lost a number of planes and some crews during their training, partly because of their getting some poorly rebuilt engines. When the engines were put in their airplanes many of them failed in flight. The pilots were green and unused to emergency procedures in case of engine failure." When accident and fatality rates rose, "The effect of the combination of mechanical and personnel error sometimes produced near panic among pilots."

After Ardery became a flight instructor he turned his own negative training experiences into something positive for his students. He made it a habit to have his pilots spend time every day "planning how to meet emergencies in the air." He believed that "A pilot should have infinite coolness in emergencies, but also the caution to ensure that the only emergencies he ever meets are those not of his own making."

Ardery refused to accept the rotten reputation of Liberators for being unable to stay in the air on anything less than four engines. "You can fly okay on two engines," he wrote. "Sometimes you can keep aloft for a while on one." Putting philosophy into action, Ardery had all of his students practice three-engine operation and three-engine landings.

Ardery seems to be the exception to the rule. B-24 pilots like James Davis found less than four operating Liberator engines to create a dangerous situation. On a mission to France in 1944 Davis was forced to abort when he lost one engine. Then, over a populated portion of England, and with a full bomb load, he lost another. With full power to #1 and #3 engines, Davis and his Liberator were still dropping like a stone. Coming in to land he barely cleared a copse of trees and set down—several hundred feet in front of the runway. It was a close-call landing with no injuries or death or destruction. Flying with one engine out was not an easy task, as the plane needed to be steered and controlled by differential thrust to the remaining, functioning engines, plus hard use of the rudder. It required so much effort on the pilot's part that muscle fatigue would make their legs shake uncontrollably.

Fuel for the Liberator was kept in cells within the Davis Wing's center section. This "wet wing" design was considered innovative, since it meant that fuel was not kept in the crew compartment. More space to move around was a major improvement. The flight engineer transferred fuel during the flight from one cell to the others, keeping the weight in the wing balanced and the aircraft trimmed.

Some writers believe the "wet wing" design created a troublesome fuel-transfer system and a fire hazard. "Fuel seeping from tanks and connections drained down the wing and into the bomb bay." At altitudes below 10,000 feet, supplemental oxygen was not used by the crew. This meant that gunners in particular had to deal with noxious fuel fumes, although it's certain that fumes permeated the entire aircraft.

Liberators were known to catch fire or blow up when fumes within the fuselage ignited from an electrical spark, or even a crewman's cigarette. "No one smoked near the bomb bay, and armorers had to be especially careful when loading bombs [so as] not to cause sparks." If a fire did break out in the wing, it spread rapidly and engulfed the airplane in a huge fireball. Some B-24s had engine fire extinguishers—but not all of them.

Early Liberator models were known for their troublesome brakes. RAF pilot John Musgrave, who flew one of these earlier versions, recalls how easily the hydraulic expander bags (which operated the brake shoes) would burn, "if the brakes were applied for too long or too sharply." As a result, pilots were taught to steer the aircraft on the ground using differential engine power, keeping their feet off the brakes.

The abortion rates due to mechanical failure in combat for the 458th Bombardment Squadron was "around 22 percent." This meant that 22 percent of the aircraft leaving for a bombing run had to return to base without accomplishing their mission. Clearly, maintenance was an important matter for Liberators, and catastrophic mechanical failure probably led to many deaths.

Many Liberators that crashed on takeoff burst into flame, and there was nothing left for crash investigators to investigate. Others that disappeared in the air were not found for years, when either interest in the case had evaporated, or the wreckage was not able to give any clues as to cause.

Pilots are important to airplanes and usually seem to get all the glory, but no pilot worth anything let all that adulation go to his head. Each of the big bombers needed a crew of thirty-eight men in the air and on the ground to keep it flying.

Long before the cabin crew of ten boarded their B-17 or B-24, a crew of ten mechanics, with their ground-crew chief, combed over every inch of the airplane. Among the ground crew were two frame mechanics with eight engine men, two assigned to each engine. There were seven specialists on hand who checked instruments, radios, armament, parachutes, electrical equipment, propellers, and superchargers.

Distant from the actual airplane but just as important as the flight and ground crew were people located back in the office, where meteorologists and dispatchers worked. Before the bomber could leave on its mission, another crew towed bombs to the plane and another team of five loaded those bombs.

But maintenance was still the biggest issue. To facilitate overhaul, maintenance, and repair, Liberator engines were designed to be completely removed from the aircraft. While one engine was being worked on, another engine was bolted on and away you flew. "Normally the Liberator's Pratt & Whitney engines had a life of 300 hours." In arid and dusty climes, the air-cooled engines needed to be overhauled every sixty hours, because they were constantly sucking dirty air into the engine cylinders. Putting aside any lack of spare parts, it isn't difficult to imagine how a maintenance backlog would affect training.

A favorite nickname for the B-24 was "Flying Coffin." Henry Harley "Hap" Arnold, general of the US Army Air Forces, had strong feelings about airplanes that developed bad reputations for being "death traps," or other such designations. He saw that pilots developed a good rapport with some airplanes and not with others, and he knew this was an outcome of the aviator's direct experience, coupled with a healthy dose of superstition and distrust. Fatal flaws in aircraft design and construction contributed mightily to an aviator's conviction that a particular airplane was unsafe to fly. Even after those errors were corrected it was difficult to convince pilots otherwise. "In my long experience with airmen and airplanes, I have learned that if the flyers themselves come genuinely to believe that a certain plane is a 'Flying Coffin' or a 'Man Killer,' then it is definitely a 'Flying Coffin' or 'Man Killer' until they have been convinced otherwise."

The closest thing to truly making the Liberator a death trap was the aircraft's behavior in a ditching. As Truman Smith wrote, when shit happens, "There's usually more on the way." This fairly typifies what happens to the B-24 when "landing" on water, and who knows—knowledge of this fact might be what prompted Bob Hester to tell his wife how he both hated and feared the B-24 because, with practical experience, B-24 crews came to fear an open-water "landing," or ditching.

Ditching the Liberator was a disaster for two reasons. First, with the high wing, all the impact was absorbed by the fuselage. Second, the bomb bay doors were light-duty aluminum and designed like the cover of a rolltop desk. When the aircraft hit the water, the tail empennage broke off, the bomb bay doors collapsed, and the Liberator snapped in two. "Survival rates from ditching at sea were low."

In *Unbroken*, Laura Hillenbrand describes the experience of bombardier Louis Zamperini when his B-24 ditched in the Pacific Ocean. The "men behind the cockpit fled toward the comparative safety of the waist and rear of the plane." Life rafts didn't deploy automatically, and it was the duty of the flight engineer to stand behind the cockpit, "to pull the overhead raft-release handle." The engineer would have to wait for the actual crash before deployment, or there was no way to guarantee that the raft would remain close to the ship once it was ditched. This was a duty that served as a certain death warrant, because the engineer would have "little or no chance to get to a crash position, and thus, little chance of survival."

When they hit the water Zamperini's Liberator blew apart. The wings were ripped off, the tail separated, and the fuselage broke in two. Zamperini's body catapulted forward and he was wrapped in cables and wires from the broken aircraft. As the plane disintegrated around him and as the Liberator sank, it pulled Zamperini deep underwater. The downward motion stopped. Briefly buoyed by air trapped inside the fuselage, the bomber rose toward the surface before sinking once again, "as if yanked downward." Along with Zamperini, the only survivors were the pilot and tail gunner.

Ditching was not the only action that resulted in fatalities during a crash landing, but it certainly was the most catastrophic. When a Liberator was forced to land wheels up, the weight of the wing and four engines crushed the fuselage and the men within. In contrast, a lot of crash impact was absorbed by the lower-mounted wings of a B-17. The overall accident rates of B-17s and B-24s within the continental United States weren't much different (30 percent and 35 percent respectively, per 100,000 flying hours). However, casualty rates were double for B-24 crews, and fatality rates were about five B-24 men killed for every three B-17 men.

There were many ways to die in a B-24—or any other airplane, for that matter—that had nothing to do with its good or bad reputation. Enemy fighters and antiaircraft were the big killers in combat. But fliers could die in innumerable ways. Planes crashed while taking off or landing in fog. Pilots flew into storms and never flew out again. Errors in judgment, tired pilots, or careless pilots brought aircraft down. Not to mention inexplicable mechanical bugs, clogged fuel lines, malfunctioning controls, and other "gremlins." Crashes were also caused by flying too fast or flying too slow, over-revving engines, taxiing too fast, and so on and so forth.

Pilots and crews also died when mistaking landmarks or altitude, or when pilots flew into mountains, a characteristic engineers at Boeing Aircraft would eventually call CFIT: Controlled Flight Into Terrain. Formation flying, a necessary tactic in combat which afforded individual aircraft with the protection offered by the group, was never an easy operation. Collisions were common even with experienced pilots. Negligence, not paying attention, and simple mistakes were the primary causes of midair collisions. It will break your heart to read accident reports, learning of the myriad ways aircrews died within the United States as they trained for war.

Pilots were taught, and a good pilot learned, to keep thinking at all times, always anticipating what could (and would) go wrong, and how to get out of it. A good pilot learned there was no such thing as a "routine" flight.

Given the track record of the B-24 for accidents, many of them fatal or disfiguring, it's fair to wonder why crews didn't revolt and refuse to fly the things. The most basic reason probably has to do with not knowing any better. "For the majority of its aircrews, many of whom never had an opportunity to compare the Liberator with other big aircraft, its worth and worthiness were unquestioned. Unaware of the inherent design weakness that might lessen their chances of survival, they did their job as directed."

The B-24 Liberator wasn't the only airplane that suffered accidents, and fresh-faced pilots weren't the only ones injured or killed or almost so. While serving as a B-17 instructor in 1943 at Gowen Field in Boise, Idaho, Captain (and internationally recognized and bona fide Hollywood movie star) Jimmy Stewart had given up his copilot (instructor) seat to the Fortress's navigator so the boy could appreciate what went on in the cockpit. According to a magazine account written by Col. Beirne Lay, when the #1 engine flared out, Stewart yanked the navigator out, got himself situated, and put out the fire.

Sometimes the famous or well-known were killed. Harold W. Kulick, a war correspondent, photographer, and coauthor of the 1942 book, *He's in the Air Corps Now*, was killed in the crash of a Martin B-26 Marauder in England. He was returning from a mission with the 9th Air Force over France on August 10, 1944, where the plane suffered combat damage over the target. The aircraft crashed upon landing.

US Marine Corps major general William P. Upshur, a Medal of Honor winner for service in Haiti in 1915, was killed in an airplane crash on July 21, 1943, near Sitka, Alaska, while on an inspection tour of his command. Also on board was Capt. Charles W. Paddock, a member of the 1920 US Olympic Team. Paddock was known as the "World's Fastest Human," and held ninety-four separate track records, including the 100- and 300-meter runs.

Even those considered the best pilots were not immune to death or injury by accident—though not always aviation-related. In 1945 Col. John C. Meyer scored two aerial victories, bumping his total up to twenty-four for the war. "Soon afterward, he was grounded for the duration of the war—by injuries suffered in an automobile accident."

The beautiful and famous were not spared either. On January 16, 1942, a DC-3 carrying thirty-three-year-old actress Carole Lombard flew into "Double Up Peak" near the 8,300-foot Mount Potosi, Nevada. All twenty-two aboard the commercial flight, including Lombard, her mother, and fifteen army servicemen, were killed.

In the end, much of what we can say about the B-24 can be summed up by Peter Massare. Massare flew with the 15th Air Force on the Ploesti raid (Operation Tidal Wave) on August 1, 1943. He eventually logged 273 combat hours in a B-24, and says that he got around to liking the airplane. "I had nothing else to compare it with. It did the job, it got me back, and that's the main thing."

CHAPTER 9

Finding the Hammer Field Boys— *Exterminator's* Crew

THE PAST DOESN'T GO ANYWHERE; IT IS ALWAYS WITH US. THE TROUBLE is, how do you find it? Discovering anything about people who died seven decades ago is a daunting task. People back then didn't self-document their lives the way we do today. Many of the boys who served during World War II were in their late teens and early twenties and hadn't developed any talent for journal keeping or letter writing.

The best direct sources for learning about the Hammer Field boys are photographs, letters, and newspaper clippings kept by families of the boys. Next best are subscription-based online sites like newspaper archives.com and ancestry.com—useful for genealogy and finding surviving relatives. At the Laws Railroad Museum near Bishop, California, are the newspaper morgues from the *Inyo Register* that documented the loss of 463, its search and discovery, the army divers, and also information about other B-24s lost around the same time.

The United States military conducts an investigation for every member of the armed forces who dies, whether it be by accident, disease, natural causes, or combat. These Individual Deceased Personnel Files (IDPF), which can be anywhere from a page or two to hundreds of pages, are kept in the files of whichever branch of service the man or woman was assigned to. Family members can request the IDPF of their loved one. Researchers with legitimate reasons also have access to IDPFs through the Freedom of Information Act.

IDPF files for all of the 463 and *Exterminator* crewmen are available, although missing IDPFs are not unusual. IDPFs for Turvey, Hester, and Mayo weren't located until August, 2016, whereas files for the other boys had been found and made available over two years earlier. Reasons for lost files include that original paper folders may have been requested in the past and misfiled or not returned. They could have been lost or inadvertently destroyed. Many (not all) have been digitalized from microfiche or hard copy, which makes search, retrieval, copying, and distribution less onerous for family and researchers (and the military) than in the past.

For some of the Hammer Field boys there are huge amounts of biographical information, but for others, hardly anything. Tragic examples of the paucity of knowledge come from Turvey and Hester's radio operator on 463 and the navigator of *Exterminator*. Examples of a surfeit come from the copilot, navigator, and flight engineer of 463 and two of the gunners from *Exterminator*. Of the other boys, they all fall somewhere between the extremes of knowing and not knowing.

⌐⌐⌐

2nd Lt. Samuel J. Schlosser was born on March 6, 1918, in Manhattan, New York, to Pauline Mett and Max Schlosser. His mother was a native of Odessa, Russia, and had emigrated to the United States in 1917. His father emigrated to the United States from Austria in 1907, and was a native speaker of Polish. When Samuel Schlosser enlisted in the army on April 3, 1942, he was 147 pounds and 5 feet, 5 inches tall. He was unmarried, had completed four years of college, and worked as a commercial artist.

On October 15, 1946, Mrs. Rae M. Schlosser made an inquiry to the National Jewish Welfare Board, probably about a death benefit for Samuel J. Schlosser. On a 3-by-5-inch index card Rae is listed as "wife" and living at 1014 Avenue J in Brooklyn, New York. Not unlike many boys facing an uncertain future as a combat soldier, at some point between his enlistment and his death on December 6, 1943, Samuel had married.

Samuel Schlosser's IDPF demonstrates the crucial disconnect between what newspapers in 1955 reported when *Exterminator*'s crew was recovered and what was actually found. The September 26, 1955, issue of *Stars and Stripes* reported, "The remains of two of the wartime airmen were recovered from a section of the fuselage late Friday. Two other bodies were pulled from the tail and nose sections Thursday." Other newspapers marveled at the pristine condition of the bodies. What the IDPF for Schlosser shows is the difference between "remains" and "bodies."

Inside Schlosser's IDPF are all the pertinent data about Samuel J. Schlosser since he joined the army. Between his enlistment and a physical examination on October 5, 1943, Schlosser's weight had gone up 19 pounds and he'd grown 1.25 inches. His build is described as "stocky," his frame, changed from "medium" to "heavy," and his hair color as brown.

There is also an exploded diagram of a skeleton with all the uncollected remains of Samuel J. Schlosser blacked out. Disturbingly, the only part of his remains not blacked out is Schlosser's skull. His remains, what little there are of them, could only have been identified by dental charts. Except there are dental charts for his compatriots but none for Schlosser. So he was identified not by data, but by the lack of data.

A few items of interest from Samuel Schlosser's IDPF help to round out all we know about him. His middle name was "Jack," and he had a brother named Herbert Schlosser, who lived in East Meadow, Long Island. He also had a daughter, Sandra. After Samuel's death, his wife, Rae Schlosser, remarried. This was common

Samuel Schlosser's grave at Long Island National Cemetery. PHOTO BY GLENN R. PIWOWAR

during and after the war. It was difficult for a single woman with a child to support herself.

If all this information about Schlosser sounds like a lot, it isn't. It's only data. There is nothing to show what the man was like as a person. There are no personal accounts, no letters, and no photographs.

S/Sgt. Franklin Clark Nyswonger, flight engineer on *Exterminator*, was born on February 23, 1922, the third of six children, to Emory Edmund Nyswonger, a locomotive fireman, and Etta Marguerite Gowans, from Green Bay, Wisconsin. Mrs. Nyswonger apparently never used her first name; documents either refer to her as Marguerite or Margaret. The parents divorced (date unknown), with Marguerite being awarded custody of the children. Emory remarried in 1942.

Franklin was known as Clark in the family. He was a short and slight 5-foot-3 and 115 pounds. He had completed four years of high school (i.e., grades nine through twelve) and, incongruously, his enlistment record says he was working as an actor when he joined up as a private in the Army Air Corps on Thursday, June 19, 1941, in Milwaukee, Wisconsin. That would have been immediately following high school graduation, which makes it seem that

S/Sgt. Franklin Clark Nyswonger. PHOTO IN AUTHOR'S COLLECTION, COURTESY OF BIG CREEK SCHOOL 4TH GRADE PROJECT

Clark was anxious to get out of the house. Whether it was economic need or something else, this need to leave home was shared by at least two of Clark's siblings.

There is a sad note in Clark's IDPF. In a telegram dated November 15, 1955, Mrs. Nyswonger is told, "Due to the nature of the airplane crash and the condition of the remains, it is impossible to identify remains of S/Sgt. Nyswonger from remains of one other individual in the crew. Remains of your late son and remains of the other crew member will be

Headstone at Fort Snelling National Cemetery for Franklin Clark Nyswonger and Donald Vande Plasch, 1955. PHOTO BY LEE VANDER PLASCH WATTS. COURTESY OSCAR TRACZEWITZ AND VANDER PLASCH FAMILY

interred in one grave in Fort Snelling National Cemetery." Although her son had been found, he was essentially buried as an unknown soldier with one other boy. The remains of both boys were escorted from Oakland, California, by SFC Marion L. Solomon to the cemetery at Fort Snelling, Minnesota. Interment in Grave 8439, Section C, was at 10:00 a.m. on November 28, 1955. A photograph of the headstone was sent to Mrs. Nyswonger on May 28, 1956, by the cemetery operations officer.

<hr />

The boy whose remains could not be separated from Franklin Clark Nyswonger was **S/Sgt. Donald C. Vande Plasch** from Wauwatosa, Wisconsin. The 5-foot-9, 160-pound staff sergeant was a gunner on *Exterminator*. Born on May 29, 1913, Vande Plasch was the oldest of the twelve boys from the two missing B-24 crews, had enlisted on October 28, 1942, and was a married man. He and Leona "Lee" Traczewitz had tied the knot on December 6, 1941. The December 9, 1941, issue of the *Milwaukee Journal* described the wedding party at the First Congregational Church of Wauwatosa: "The bride wore a princess gown of ivory satin and a tiara which held a fingertip veil. She carried a crescent-shaped bouquet of white camellias, carnations, and snapdragons." Her three bridesmaids wore "rust velvet gowns and carried dubonnet and pink carnations and shell-pink snapdragons." The groom's brother, Melvin, served as best man. In wedding photos the bride is beaming and radiant as only a newlywed can be.

Prostrated by grief at the news of her husband, Lee Vande Plasch wrote to her younger brother, Oscar Traczewitz, a twenty-six-year-old ensign in the naval reserve. Oscar's reply shows a young man with an incredibly good head on his shoulders consoling his older sister. "Even your sorrows and woes, they interest me just as much as anything else that concerns you, and that's a very great deal."

Oscar's love for his sister is writ large across the page and gives some kind of indication of how deep Lee's love was for her husband. "Happenings like yours, Lee, are going on all over the world. Many of them have that terrible quality and mixture of doubt and hope and despair that you must feel—I'm sure that certainty [of Don's fate] would bring relief of some sort. Until that certainty comes we must bear up under a terrific strain which eats our hearts out." Here we see what tore Lee up the most: knowing that her husband was dead and gone, but not knowing what happened or where he could be. There is a need in all of us to bury our dead, and Lee Vande Plasch hadn't been able to do so. Until she did, there could be no closure.

Like her husband, Lee was thirty years old in 1943, and upon news of his death must have felt that her life

Aviation cadet Donald Vande Plasch. COURTESY OSCAR TRACZEWITZ

was now over, her best years behind her. Her brother disagreed. "Don't think yourself at the end of the road. You are young, younger than your age. You haven't even begun to near the top of the hill in that road of life, which, for some people, never descends." And to deal with her grief Oscar wrote, "You have so much to live for, so much to strive for, so much to do in this world. It's the people with drive and energy that keep the world moving in its path of progress. You are part of that group."

Finally, acknowledging his sister's despair, Oscar ends his letter with the only thing possible a person can share in such times. "I wish I could be home with you now," and he signs it, "Your loving brother," and his nickname, "Bud."

Lee Vande Plasch was remarried in 1946 to Maurice Gale Watts. The couple never had children. Lee's nephew, Oscar Traczewitz II, says, "She would have made a great mom. Aunty Lee was a sweet person; she was a real special lady."

On November 15, 1955, the parents of Donald Vande Plasch received the same telegram sent to Mrs. Marguerite Nyswonger. "Due to the nature of the airplane crash and the condition of the remains . . ."

The interment was a small affair. The Nyswongers were there, and the Vande Plasch family too. So was Leona Traczewitz Vande Plasch Watts and her second husband. They had traveled eight hours by train from Wauwatosa, spending the nights of November 27 and 28, 1955, at the Hotel St. Paul in St. Paul, Minnesota. All so she could say her final good-bye. Lee's husband, Maurice Gale Watts, must have been quite a guy to be there, too.

~

Lt. Culos Marion Settle, copilot on *Exterminator*'s final flight, was born on July 3, 1917. Between 1936 and 1940, Settle moved 40 miles away from his home in Wilkesboro, North Carolina, to attend Appalachian State University, where he graduated with a major in mathematics and a minor in history. During his time in university, Settle belonged to Alpha Lambda Sigma, and was active in the Math Club, YMCA, and Student Council. Upon graduation he began teaching at Hildebran High School, an hour south of Wilkesboro. He also got married in 1940 to Annie Mae Beard. They would go on to have three children.

Settle's draft registration card from 1940 reinforces George Barulic's description of a slightly built young man. At the age of twenty-three Culos (pronounced *Q-liss*) Settle was 5 feet, 11 inches, and weighed 140 pounds. His eyes were gray, his hair, black, and his complexion, light brown.

Settle was awarded the Distinguished Flying Cross for his participation in the July 15, 1944, raid in Romania where over six hundred B-17 Flying Fortresses and B-24 Liberators bombed four oil refineries in the Ploesti area and the Teleajenul pumping station. After surviving a combat tour with the 15th Air Force in Italy, Settle died young, of a heart attack, on April 26, 1957. His parents were no strangers to tragedy, having outlived five of their ten children.

Lt. Culos Marion Settle. COURTESY WILLIAM ROOT AND CULOS MARION SETTLE FAMILY

Capt. William Howard Union Darden was born on June 28, 1918, and graduated from Churchland High School in Portsmouth, Virginia, before enrolling at Virginia Military Institute in 1936. At VMI Darden studied civil engineering and field artillery, was an active equestrian, worked as a photography editor for the student newspaper, *Cadet*, and was known to his best friends as "Dimitri," and as "Billy" to his family. Darden left VMI to enlist in the Army Air Corps on July 26, 1940, with less than one credit remaining before graduation. At that time Darden was 5-foot-8 and a slightly built 141 pounds.

On Sunday, March 16, 1941, Darden married Barbara Thomas Lathrum in Montgomery, Alabama, where Billy was serving as a lieutenant in the US Army Air Corps Reserve. They had one daughter, also named Barbara, born while Billy was stationed in Mississippi. He spent March through August of 1943 in Texas and Idaho, getting flight instruction, before being transferred in August to the 461st Bomb Group as the squadron commander of the 766th Bomb Squadron at Hammer Field in California.

Billy Darden's father, Blount, was editor for the *Portsmouth Star* in Portsmouth, Virginia, and kept his son's career, and then his memory, alive in that newspaper until his own death in 1957. In Darden's file at VMI are newspaper clippings that document the son's career, death, and the eventual recovery of his remains.

At the time of his death, Billy Darden had just separated from his wife, though there is every indication it was an amicable separation.

Captain Darden was well regarded by his peers and subordinates—an opinion supported by his radio operator, George Barulic, and expressed in official paperwork of the 461st Bomb Group after *Exterminator* was lost. "The 461st Bombardment Group lost a fine gentleman and an outstanding squadron commander. He was truly an outstanding leader of men. Small but wiry, he was, nevertheless, highly intelligent and extremely resourceful. This little bundle of ceaseless energy was probably the best known, best liked, and the most inspiring officer in the 461st Group."

Sgt. Richard Lee Spangle, gunner on *Exterminator*, was born on February 13, 1924, the second of three children, to Sherman Lewis and Merle Leah Burns Spangle. They lived in the house Sherman bought in 1936 for $200 in the tiny settlement of Gazelle, on the far outskirts of Weed, California. The simple two-story house is still there, flanked by two large cottonwood trees that were old when the Spangle kids were growing up. Richard's younger brother, Tom, now lives there with his wife, Audria.

Ten years his junior, Tom Spangle remembers his nineteen-year-old brother, Richard, as a hunter and angler, and a kid that wanted to be a pilot. An automobile accident during high school scotched that plan. Richard was the passenger in a friend's car when they missed a turn in the even smaller hamlet of Grenada, a couple of miles north of Gazelle. Interstate 5 has changed the roads around there quite a bit, but the turn Tom and his buddy missed by driving too fast is still there, part of what is now Old Highway 99.

Richard's physical examination for flying as an aviation cadet at the Santa Ana Army Air Forces Base in southern California gives the particulars of his disqualification for pilot training. On March 1, 1942, he required three weeks of hospitalization for a compression fracture in his fifth cervical vertebrae. The three

Richard Spangle with his younger brother, Tom. COURTESY TOM AND AUDRIA SPANGLE

medical examiners who reviewed Richard's case concluded, "The physical condition ... is likely to result in permanent, partial, or complete physical disability." Despite what the doctors said, Spangle was still "qualified for general service." So, like many other cadets who washed out, Richard was directed elsewhere: He became a gunner—which probably pleased a country boy like him, who liked to shoot.

When he enlisted two days after Independence Day, 1942, eighteen-year-old Richard Spangle was 5 feet, 10 inches, and 130 pounds—what they used to call a "tall drink of water." The army was a good place for a lot of boys to bulk up, what with all the drill and exercise they were required to do; that, and three large meals a day. A physical exam on March 31, 1943, listed Richard's weight at 137 pounds, and by another exam on November 29, 1943 (a week before his death), he'd gained another 3 pounds.

After Richard Spangle's B-24 went missing, his mother, Merle, was so bereft by grief she simply closed the door to his bedroom and never opened it again. As his brother Tom recalls, "Ever since he went down, she [their mother] hung the flag in the window with the blue star. Had it there for *years*. They never touched his room until they found him in 1955." Displaying the blue star, rather than a gold star, meant Mrs. Spangle remained hopeful her son was still alive.

Tom Spangle's daughter, Lori, remembers, "It was like that forever. We could not go in there when we were kids. It was just like it was when he was a teenager, when Richard died." Tom's wife, Audria, understood what it was like to live with unanswered questions and without closure. Her uncle was lost in combat during the war and his remains never found. "My grandma always thought he was alive. She never gave up hope. Never gave up hope."

Losing her husband was pretty tough for nineteen-year-old Mary Dumble Spangle. She was visiting Richard in Fresno, to celebrate their first anniversary, when *Exterminator* went down. "When he left that morning he told her, 'If you wait for me tonight, I'll take you to dinner.'" She waited all that night and all the next day. And the next day.

Not knowing how to contact her husband at Hammer Field, she sent a telegram to the base. "And that night I was sitting, writing him a letter, and felt this knock on the door and it was three real young officers. They came in and told me, what? I don't remember." What she can remember all these years later is holding on to the end of the bed. "I noticed my knuckles were white and I wondered if I could even unclench my hands off of the end of that bed."

One of the other girls staying at the hotel volunteered to sit with Mary Spangle. The officers went back to the base and someone else returned with sedatives that knocked her out. "I don't remember going to bed. I don't remember much of anything." When she awoke the following morning, "My mother was in bed with me."

The next few days were horrible. Richard's parents drove down from Weed to Fresno with their son-in-law. Mr. Spangle spoke to some people at Hammer Field, but to no avail. Mary can remember visiting Hammer Field and talking to somebody and being told no divers were available to explore Huntington Lake, and the reservoir couldn't be lowered because the electricity the dam provided was too essential for the war effort.

This wasn't the life Mary had imagined when she and Richard were married. It had all been so whirlwind, so spontaneous—so much fun. They knew each other in high school, and although they hadn't gone out together then, she had caught his eye. In his address book, which was filled with plenty of girl's names, under the entry for Mary Dumble he'd written, "The Best." And it's underlined, too.

Weed was a bustling lumber town in those days, with a population of eight thousand. "It was a good place to grow up in. The thing to do then, after graduation, was to go work in the [lumber] mill," which was running seven days a week. That's where Mary and Richard met up again and began to go out. It got pretty serious pretty fast.

In early July of 1942, Mary was visiting her sister in Sacramento and Richard came south to visit her. That's when he told her about enlisting. "We got the smart idea that if we went to Reno and got married, I could go visit him wherever he was stationed." So they did it—ran off and got married. They had six weeks of living together in Weed before Richard was called up. Mary went back home to live with her parents.

In 1946 Mary married Dee Witt Condo and together they have raised a family, living in the Sacramento area ever since. She hasn't

Grave of Richard Lee Spangle at the Presidio, in San Francisco, California. PHOTO BY PETER STEKEL

forgotten Richard Spangle, though her memories are clothed in melancholy. Like many people who grew up during the Depression, "Richard never really had anything." They weren't married long enough for them to make future plans. All Mary can say so many years from when it happened was that Richard wasn't interested in driving a truck or working in a sawmill for the rest of his life. Richard had his sights set on doing something in Sacramento after the war. Mary doesn't know what their life together would have been like.

On November 14, 1955, Richard Lee Spangle's remains departed the Oakland Army Terminal in a hearse at 1:00 p.m., escorted by SFC Marion L. Solomon. Later that afternoon, attended by his family, Richard was interred at San Francisco National Cemetery, Section NAWS, Site 618-B.

The war affected Weed as much as any other small town. The community suffered and bore its losses. Reflecting upon that, and her own history of loss, Mary Condo says, "I think Richard's death was the first one I can remember that happened that people thought about. There were a few others. But that came along later."

Before he enlisted in the US Army on October 8, 1942, **Sgt. Dick Erwin Mayo** was going to be a lawyer. He attended college for four years, beginning his undergraduate career at Washington and Lee University in Lexington, Virginia. He finished at the University of Kentucky's College of Law, where he is listed on the World War II Honor Roll for the class of 1943. Mayo began law school without finishing his bachelor's degree.

An issue of the *Floyd County Times* reports on Dick's disappearance. "Sgt. Mayo volunteered for air service while a law student at the University of Kentucky." The article describes Mayo as a graduate of Prestonsburg High School, where he was "prominent in athletics," going on to say that "he was one of the town's finest young men."

His brothers were no less gifted, no less accomplished. Older brother Louis Harkey Mayo, known as "Harkey" to the family, attended the US Naval Academy. Once war was declared he served in all theaters, including the Pacific, where he won the Bronze Star for courage during the Battle of Leyte Gulf. After the war he was a distinguished lawyer, professor of jurisprudence and constitutional law, dean of the law school, and vice president at George Washington University.

Younger brother Walker Porter Mayo also served in the navy. After obtaining his medical degree in 1946 he did respiratory physiology research, and later, general and thoracic surgery. After a thirty-year medical career Walker Mayo returned to school to earn a PhD in history from the University of Kentucky, devoting the rest of his life to writing about the history of medicine.

Born on July 20, 1920, Dick Erwin Mayo was the adventurous and well-adjusted middle child of Walker P. Mayo, an attorney in Prestonsburg, Kentucky, and Reba Harkey Mayo. According to his nephew, David Mayo, Dick was named in honor of either his grandfather, John Dick Mayo, his uncle (sharing the same name), or both. In any event, Dick was never known in his family as "Richard." That use seems to have appeared for the first time in 1943, with official documents relating to the loss of *Exterminator*.

At the time of Dick's enlistment, to become a pilot a boy still needed to complete at least two years of higher education. Dick decided he would do his part, but he would do it his way. His two brothers had chosen the navy and the officer corps. With his background and education,

Dick could have done the same. He didn't have to choose the ranks, but that was his decision.

Begun four days after his enlistment and ending on November 15, 1943, Dick Mayo's diary provides a snapshot not only of his character but his state of mind across the next thirteen months. His excitement about a grand adventure is palpable, but so too is his boredom with "the long hours of routine moving and mass handling which is necessary in an army." Throughout, Dick expresses his nervousness and uncertainty about the future, along with occasional periods of self-doubt.

In the beginning he's quite pleased with himself. Dick does so well on all his army classification tests that he's given his choice of his course of study. He opts for mechanics school. He keeps hoping to be sent

Pvt. Dick Mayo, all bundled up for the cold. New York City, January 1943. COURTESY DICK MAYO FAMILY

south, where it's warm. He keeps being sent north, starting with Atlantic City in mid-November, followed by relocation to New York City, where "the weather is even colder . . . and the language a little more foreign."

To his diary he admits enjoying every day of being in the army, recognizing that "it is doing me a world of good," though he also admits, "The army is not an easy life and can get mighty lonesome at times." But the adventurous nature of his new experience keeps him in good spirits. That, and a goodly supply of letters from back home, which, "I appreciate very much."

The school in New York is pretty posh by army standards.

"Our barracks is a new apartment building and is a great setup for a soldier." There are maids who clean the soldiers' rooms and "No K.P. duty." The classes are "as hard as any I ever had in college," but "a little more interesting."

Some of the loneliness Dick feels, and the desire for something familiar, comes out in a November 22 diary entry when he writes about going to church for the first time since entering the army. "For the last several days I have had a strong desire to attend church service. I can't explain why, but I wanted to go to church and that is what I did." He can't find a Methodist church close by, and ends up attending an Episcopal service, which he finds, "very different," but enjoyable. Best of all, "the people were very nice to me."

A good Southern boy, Dick is still having trouble acclimatizing to the weather in the Northeast. One of his buddies wants to set him up with a date, but, "If the girls are as cold as the weather, I think I'll stay home and read." A month later his social life has picked up nicely after meeting a girl from his hometown. "New York seems like a much better city when there is someone to go places with."

Christmas is coming up soon, and he's not looking forward to spending it alone—his lady friend having returned home for the holidays. Good luck finds Dick when he and another Southern boy, John Waites, are invited by a South Carolinian family to Christmas dinner. Waites is from Alabama, and Dick tells his diary that Waites "is the first boy I've met since I've been in the Army that I would like to develop into a close friend. He is a good clean boy whom I'm sure I would enjoy running around with." Probably reflecting his own mood, Dick writes, "Boy, was he [Waites] homesick [on] Xmas."

With the new year comes new challenges, worries, and decisions to make. Dick will finish airplane mechanic's school at the end of February, and he's going to have to figure out what to do next. He *could* apply for officer's training. The thing is, Dick likes the work he is doing, believing it a "great future" for after the war—apparently, for the time being, not considering a return to law school. "There is a better chance for me to see action if I continue with this than if I go to officer's school," he tells his diary. But then, "There is the question of prestige and other things which an officer's uniform carries with it." He finishes the entry with what really worries him the most about going the officer route: "I'm also afraid I would want to get married if I got the commission." Not that there are any potential wives on the horizon. The Prestonsburg girl seems no longer even a memory.

At first glance it appears odd that Dick is so sanguine about throwing away his career in law for that of an aircraft mechanic. But that kind of wavering makes sense in the context of the totality of Dick's diary, where he continually returns to several serious themes: his certitude the war will not be a short one; a desire to get into the thick of it sooner rather than later; a longing not only for home, but a home of his own, preferably married life on a farm. Despite an occasional grouse here and there, Dick Mayo is relentlessly upbeat. Every change of duty station brings effusive comments of how beautiful the place is. Even the brown, flat plains of San Antonio, Texas, elicit a rapturous description as "the first country I've seen that compares favorably with Kentucky."

Dick's entries, which read more like an extended letter to himself, are often broken by several weeks of inactivity. And it isn't as if he is too busy, as he admits from time to time. No, Dick Mayo comes across as not an occasional jotter of ephemerata but an inwardly drawn young man thinking deeply about his subject. He appreciated the clarity that comes from seeing thoughts committed to paper.

So, Dick hems and haws about whether officer's candidate school is a better idea than remaining in the ranks. Being an officer means more prestige—which will impress the girls. But for a boy who is itching to get into the action, leaving aircraft mechanics behind for aerial gunnery school is much more attractive. And that's the path he chooses to follow.

The other boys in the mechanics' shop must have thought college-educated Dick Mayo was out of place. The same thoughts surely swirled around Dick's head, too, because he writes, "The boys are calling me 'Squire' now because of my big cigars, horn-rimmed glasses, and legal status. They come to me about their income taxes, divorces, and letter writing." He professes to himself that he doesn't know the reason for his popularity, but that "I like to help them, and they have built up some confidence in me."

Otherwise the boys might have considered Dick a "stick in the mud." On a hitchhiking ramble to Matamoros in Mexico from gunnery school in Harlingen, at the southern tip of Texas, "Most of the boys headed straight for the red-light district or the bars, but I managed to stay away." With wry humor he adds, "They are all worried this week about having a venereal disease."

Mexico amazes Dick. Visiting the country has been a "lifelong desire," and he discovers, like many boys then and since, "The Rio Grande River is the greatest dividing line I ever saw." He isn't pleased with the filth of Matamoros, but finds the central market in town "the most interesting place," where, "everything imaginable is sold."

In late September, with his promotion to sergeant in hand, Dick moves from Texas to Boise, Idaho. He likes it there because it's "clean and very well equipped for entertainment," though he rues, "If I could have just one good date I would give anything. It's been so long since I've been out with a girl, I feel like a hermit." Lack of an entertaining partner means he can send some money home for after the war. "If I can keep it up until I get out, I may have enough to start building that house up at the farm and raise some real grapes and horses."

From Boise, Dick is soon on his way to Wendover, Utah, for five more weeks of gunnery training. Wendover is the only place in Mayo's travels where he has nothing nice to say. "We are 110 miles from Salt Lake City and there is nothing between here and there except salt flats. There is not a tree in 75 miles. There is a scarcity of water here, and it's all cold." The official history of the 461st Bomb Group paints an even bleaker picture. "As far as the eye can carry not a tree or a blade of grass can be found. From the air one can see nothing but mountains to the west and north, and nothing but ditches of water running through the salt flats to the east and south."

At Wendover, Dick met Don Vande Plasch and Richard Spangle. On November 2, 1943, they all moved to Fresno, California, and Hammer Field. After the "hell hole" of Wendover, Dick loves Fresno. "The weather is nice; feels just like spring back in Kentucky." A week later the crew met their pilots for the first time.

Hammer Field was the last station for the boys before heading off to war with the coming of the new year, though it doesn't sound as if they are ready. "We have been scheduled for eight hours of flying every other day, but due to the faulty condition of the planes, we have spent most of the time on the ground." The boys on *Exterminator* didn't really know each other very well because they hadn't spent much time together as a crew. Dick's diary makes it sound that as of November 15, 1943, they had made only one flight together. It may be that the flight they took on December 6, looking for 463, was either their second or third.

—◆—

Sgt. George Barulic was born on April 13, 1922, in Croatia, and emigrated to the United States on July 29, 1927, with his parents, Nick and Mary, and his younger brother, John. They settled in New Jersey, where George had a tough childhood. But nothing like his family had in the Old Country. "I've had a lot of tragedy in my life. My grandfather was killed, murdered. My uncle was assassinated. And my cousin was assassinated." This was all in Europe, where political involvement could be fatal when you held the wrong views.

"When I was a little kid I just couldn't get over adventure stories." When Barulic was drafted on October 16, 1942, and found himself in the Army Air Forces, he was in heaven. "God! It was the most wonderful thing in my life." He grew up on Zane Grey novels and other adventure stories. "The first time I went out west and saw a cowboy, I went out of my head. It's probably the lowest-rated occupation in the United States, chasing cows. To me, it was a great experience, seeing a cowboy. These are my heroes."

Barulic ended up as a radio operator for the army because he studied radio in high school and already knew Morse code. He was in training at Fort Dix when the army found out about his ability, because he did so well on an aptitude test. "Hell! I *knew* it! It's nothing about aptitude," he says with a laugh. He knew Morse code well enough that the other fellows who were flunking the course would have Barulic take their tests for them. He would walk in with the other boy's dog tags and that was that.

Late in life George Barulic still retained respect not only for his pilot, Culos Settle, but for their commander, Lt. Col. Frederick Glantzberg. "He was a super guy." Flying in combat with the colonel, "He could make you feel like you're at home sitting with a cup of coffee. The . . . coolest guy [I] ever saw. When he spoke he made everyone feel great." After surviving the trauma over Huntington Lake, Colonel Glantzberg told Barulic he would be willing to take him permanently off flying status. "He talked to me like he was my father." Barulic wasn't interested. He replied, "Why can't we have me and Settle get together and have a sergeant and crew and move overseas?" Barulic and Settle eventually flew fifty-two missions together. They had a few close calls, but they made it back alive, and in one piece.

George Barulic died at the age of ninety-two, on June 22, 2014, at his home in West Palm Beach, Florida.

CHAPTER 10

Finding the Hammer Field Boys—
463's Crew

S/SGT. HOWARD A. WANDTKE, RADIO OPERATOR ON 463, WAS BORN ON November 30, 1923, which means he celebrated his twentieth birthday less than a week before he died. According to a summary of his enlistment record, Wandtke was from Lucas County, Ohio, and had enlisted as a private in the Army Air Corps at the US Army post at Camp Perry in Lacarne, Ohio, nearly one year to the day, December 8, 1942, before his death. He was 5-foot-8 and weighed 157 pounds. Wandtke graduated in 1941 from Toledo's Macomber Vocational High School, where he studied plumbing and refrigeration. Howard's senior photo shows a handsome boy with a slightly crooked smile. His hair is pomaded into a pompadour with a prominent widow's peak.

Howard had an older sister, Dorothy. Their parents were Arnold E. and Sophia Wandtke, who were married in 1915. At some unknown time after her husband Arnold's death in 1938, Sophia Wandtke was remarried to David Valentine, of Toledo, Ohio. In an August 4, 1960, account in the *Tucson Daily Citizen* about the recent discovery of 463, Howard Wandtke is identified in the article by Mrs. Elizabeth Shanks as the brother-in-law of her son, W. E. (Winfield) Shanks. This would make Winfield the husband of Howard's sister, Dorothy.

Elizabeth Shanks reports that "His [Howard Wandtke's] crew was in training at Fresno for night fighting in the South Pacific and flew here to receive promotions to staff sergeants." Part of that statement might be true, but they weren't training for any kind of night flying in the South Pacific; their unit eventually went first to North Africa and then to Italy with the 15th Air Force. Also, the boys were already staff sergeants.

One last word about Howard Wandtke. Very little that we possess truly belongs to us. Material objects are temporal; like people, they get old and wear out or lose their ability to satisfy and please us. One thing that does remain our own from birth to death is our name and our identity. Given how little we know of Howard Wandtke,

Howard Wandtke, circa 1943. PHOTO IN AUTHOR'S COLLECTION

it's a shame how often his name is misspelled, both in official reports and in the books and articles covering the loss of 463. Wandtke's name usually appears in print as "Wamptke," but other variations occur as well.

Little of the life of **2nd Lt. Charles Willis Turvey Jr.**, pilot of 463, can be pieced together except for some letters written by Turvey's mother to Clint Hester, which show her appreciation for Clint's dogged search for the boys on 463.

Charles Turvey Jr. was born on July 23, 1921, to Charles Sr. and Margaret White Turvey. The family lived in Reesville, Ohio. Also in the home was an older sister and two younger brothers. Charles attended Reesville schools and played on the high school basketball team. After graduation, he

2nd Lt. Charles W. Turvey. PHOTO IN AUTHOR'S COLLECTION, COURTESY OF BIG CREEK SCHOOL 4TH GRADE PROJECT

attended Wilmington College for two years, followed by his enlistment in the US Army Air Corps in 1940. Turvey was a big man, 6 feet tall and 192 pounds, when he enlisted as a private in the air corps on June 30, 1942, at Patterson Field in Fairfield, Ohio.

～

Born on June 12, 1916, **2nd Lt. Ellis Homer Fish** was the oldest of the boys on 463. He was a stocky 5-foot-6 tall and 169 pounds, with black, curly hair and a smile as wide as the Great Plains. He made the trip from his home in La Crosse, Wisconsin, to Fort Snelling, Minnesota, on February 24, 1942, to enlist as a private in the Army Air Corps. At the time, Ellis had completed one year of college and was working at a retail

store. Like any other aviation cadet at the time, he had begun in pilot training, washed out, and was redirected to bombardier training. On August 21, 1943, he was commissioned a second lieutenant.

Ellis had a younger brother, Carroll, who worked as a machinist on the railroad, and an adopted sister, Arlene. Their parents were Lyle and Susan Fish.

All of the IDPF files for the boys on 463 and *Exterminator* are interesting, not only for what they contain, but for what they often don't contain. There is

Aviation cadet Ellis Fish. COURTESY DEBBIE COULTER

a lot of duplication of telegrams, letters, official documents, and memos. Medical reports centered around dental charts and identifying remains range from extensive to nonexistent, depending upon which of the boy's files you are looking at. What makes the IDPF for Ellis so interesting is the volume of documentation covering (the impression is "justifying") the family's expenses for attending his funeral at Arlington National Cemetery. Unfortunately, all of this paperwork doesn't tell us anything about Ellis Fish; rather, it reveals how administrative nitpicking can suck the life out of a family's grieving.

Mileage expenses, at five cents per mile, was computed by "the most direct rail mileage." Carroll Fish used his private automobile to transport himself, Susan Fish, and Arlene Granberg. One check, each was sent to Susan and Arlene on October 20, 1960, for $108.00, representing 2,160 miles, round-trip from Winona, Minnesota, to Arlington, Virginia. No per diem to pay for hotel or meals was authorized. Carroll was reimbursed at seven cents per mile, because it was his car, for a total of $151.20. The interment costs for Ellis H. Fish were $75.00.

S/Sgt. Robert Oakley Bursey was born on December 17, 1921, in Rutland, Vermont. His father, William Bursey, worked on locomotives for the railroad as a machinist. Bob's mother, Ida May Bursey, worked as a seamstress. There were two other children besides Bob, Rena Mary and Reta Mary (pronounced *Rita*). The girls were fraternal twins. William and Ida May were married in 1917, but William Bursey had been married once before. His first wife, Rosa Douglas Bursey, had died in 1916, at age forty-three, probably in childbirth. The baby, Joseph, named for Rosa's father, was stillborn.

Living next door to the Bursey family in Rutland was Carroll James (CJ) Hill. He and Rena Bursey were married on February 17, 1942, and had four children. David Hill is convinced it was his father, CJ, who inspired Bob to enlist. "Uncle Bob emulated my father because he was like [the] big brother Bob didn't have." Both boys were talented "shade tree" mechanics, and bonded together while working on cars in the yard. CJ also owned and operated a filling station where Bob would often

Robert Bursey in uniform. COURTESY DAVID HILL AND
THE BURSEY FAMILY

hang out. In 1942, CJ enlisted in the army and tested into the pilot program. "The story goes that Uncle Bob wanted to follow my father into the air force." Bad eyesight and other health issues defeated that dream.

It's strange that Bob Bursey ended up flying on 463. At the bottom of his September 12, 1942, enlistment physical it says, "UNDERWEIGHT— LIMITED SERVICE." Bursey's slender 5-foot-9 frame supported a scant 126 pounds, but he also suffered from *pes planus* (flat feet) and *genu varum* (bowed legs). There was a scar on his neck where Bursey's cervical lymph nodes had been removed. His vision is described as "defective." Six of his teeth were missing, and two were misplaced either inward or outward. Eight other of his teeth had cavities and required serious dental work to repair. A year later all of the work had yet to be completed. And he smoked like a chimney.

Bob's other sister, Reta, married Richard Allen on August 23, 1943. Bob and Dick were the best of friends, and the last time any of the family saw Bob was when he returned to Rutland for the wedding. On the seventh of that month Bob had completed his course in aerial gunnery at Laredo

Army Field in Texas. The timing was fortuitous for arranging a furlough—Uncle Sam's graduation gift for a job well done. Once in Rutland Bob posed for numerous photos with everyone; there are some humorous snaps of the girls shouldering Bob's parachute.

When it was time to move on, Bob left most of his personal belongings behind in Rutland—the possessions he would have normally wanted close by. It's almost like he had a premonition of an ill wind. The last anybody heard from Bursey was a phone call to CJ, shortly before Bob's death. Something happened that frightened Bob Bursey half to death. Bob begged his friend and brother-in-law to do anything he could to get Bob out of there, to get him a

Robert Bursey's sister, Reta Allen, with his parachute, 1943. COURTESY DAVID HILL AND THE BURSEY FAMILY

transfer. Pilots were so revered in those days, it isn't too much of a stretch to see Bob thinking his brother-in-law held sway with the brass. But what could CJ do? He was a lowly first lieutenant flight instructor.

What was so scary to Bob? According to Dick Mayo's diary, by December 5, 1943, Hammer Field flight crews had been constituted for a month. They hadn't had much practical experience in the air, though—at least by November 15. "We have been scheduled for eight hours of flying every other day," Dick wrote, "but due to the faulty condition of the planes, we have spent most of the time on the ground." As a mechanic and flight engineer, Bob Bursey would have been fully aware of faulty engine and aircraft conditions at Hammer Field. Perhaps it was a lack of confidence in the B-24 Liberators that scared him so. Prior to the disappearance of 463 there had been several aircraft mishaps due to mechanical issues. Or could it have been a lack of confidence in his crew because of a previous navigational problem?

Only one letter from Bob survives, and it's a love letter to his mother that arrived with his wings. The note is written on a piece of torn foolscap. It's an amazing and wonderful letter for its unabashed affection and sentimentality. In it he asks her to please wear his wings, because, "I went through hell to get them, and I am sure proud to have you wear them for me. Please keep them shined up well. God bless you all, and please don't worry."

Robert Bursey graduated from Mount Saint Joseph Academy, a Catholic high school in Rutland, in 1940. Between June 13 and November 12, 1941, he was enrolled at the Frederic Duclos Barstow Memorial School in nearby Chittenden, where he attained a certificate in machine shop practice after a 210-hour course of study. From there he quickly moved to a $68.00 per week job at Ford Motor Company's Astoria, Long Island, aircraft plant, working in the sensitive drill department. Foreman F. Austinat later remembered the young man as "a conscientious worker; if I'd had a shop full like him, there'd be no production problem. Everybody liked him."

Bob's nephew, David Hill, says the family always knew his uncle's remains were not complete when they were brought home. Of the boys on 463, at least Bob's remains were identifiable. This didn't make the knowledge any more acceptable or understandable. Losing Bob tore up his sister, Reta, and she never recovered from the shock. It was made worse nearly seventeen years later when Bob's remains were recovered, because it felt like dealing with the death a second time. Closure is wonderful; but it's also awful, horrible, terrible when you have old wounds gouged and ripped open.

The United States of America, Office of the Quartermaster General, Memorial Division, conveyed Robert Oakley Bursey's earthly remains to the Clifford Funeral Home at 2 Washington Street, in Rutland, Vermont, accompanied by Sgt. Joseph Oresik. Mrs. Bursey called the sergeant "a very fine gentleman," who she was proud to receive in her home. In appreciation of Oresik's service to this hometown boy, a grateful Rutland citizen presented the sergeant with the latest in 1960s technology: a black-and-white television set.

Robert Oakley Bursey's remains were then committed to God and eternity in the Bursey family section of Rutland's St. Joseph Cemetery. A solemn requiem Mass was conducted by the Right Reverend Monsignor Alfred L. Desautels from the Immaculate Heart of Mary Church, with full military honors provided by the Air Force 380th Combat Group from Plattsburgh, New York. Bob is at rest in this cemetery along with his parents, his sister Reta, and her husband Dick Allen.

On October 6, 1960, Mrs. Ida May Bursey, a still-grieving yet appreciative mother, wrote to Donald L. Wardle, lieutenant colonel with the army's memorial division, to express her gratitude for everything the army had done to finally bring her boy home. "We will always cherish

David Hill and the grave of his uncle, Robert O. Bursey, in Rutland, Vermont.
PHOTO BY PETER STEKEL

and hold in grateful remembrance your kindness, courtesy, and sympathy, shown to us, in your long journey to our home. God bless you, Colonel Wardle, with a long and happy life. May God reign in our home and hearts forever."

——◆——

By December of 1943, a lot of American boys were dying over European skies. But luck, if you believed in it, was equally poor for British boys. And the Germans, for that matter. You were more likely to die in airplanes than anywhere else. Germany's air casualties during the war numbered 80,588; British air casualties were 78,287. And the United States suffered 79,625 air casualties.

How bad was it, really? The only thing Truman Smith could recall from the address at the graduation of his pilot class was, "Only 3 percent of us were expected to survive the war." That represented 291 killed out of a class of 300. Until the spring of 1944, 8th Air Force boys were expected to complete twenty-five missions before coming home, though the statisticians had computed that this was an impossible task. Because replacement crews couldn't be trained fast enough, the requirement was bumped up to thirty missions. Later, it was bumped up again, to thirty-five missions. Crews working in the Mediterranean had to complete fifty missions before going home. In the Pacific they kept flying until the war ended.

Who survived had nothing to do with courage, though it took lots of it to face aerial combat. Mostly it took a load of luck. And woe betide him who does not realize that the difference between the hero and the dead is naught but for luck. The boys who faced combat may have been ignorant during training about what they would face, but they sure knew it midway through their first mission. George Barulic recalls his first combat mission: "We lost two planes. They were excited in formation and one bumped into the other one and there was a collision and they lost the planes." The reason? "The first mission you're nervous. Everybody is excited."

You could, maybe, almost, beat the odds. It helped to have a tight crew: nine boys on a bomber with a skipper, all who knew their jobs and how to do them. A team like no other team you can imagine. Everybody working together, everybody covering everybody. That's what training was calculated to accomplish. Except, the war didn't give boys much time to build a team. Sometimes it happened quickly, a miracle of good luck. Sometimes it came late, and a crew felt themselves fortunate, if not lucky, to pull through with a minimum of grief—injuries or death. And sometimes the luck didn't come at all. In which case the crew was doomed.

Consider the famous bad luck boys of *Lady Be Good* #41-24301. They were with the 376th Bomb Group, on their first bombing mission over Naples on April 4, 1943. They had arrived one week before, as well-trained and prepared as the crews on 463 and *Exterminator* would have been. Unable to complete their mission, and lost in a sandstorm, they overflew their base and were never heard from again. Despite desperate attempts to locate them, their B-24 wasn't discovered until November 9, 1958. The remains of all but one of the boys were recovered fifteen months later.

Everybody on board a bomber was important. But the navigator was the guy who got you there and back. Where Charles Lindbergh may have crossed the Atlantic with years of flight and navigation experience, World War II navigators were loaded up with plenty of book learning but precious little real-life experience. Many flyboys wrote memoirs decades later proclaiming their joy, relief, and surprise to reach Hawaii or Ireland or the Azores on their first open-water crossing from North America. As for the boys who never succeeded, we will never know. Some were confident and lucky. Others were only confident.

2nd Lt. William Thomas Cronin, a resident of Olean in Upstate New York, was the second child of Patrick J. Cronin, a native of the Irish Free State, and his wife, Katherine. Both were immigrants, and both, naturalized citizens of the United States of America. Their first child was Harold, who would eventually become a lieutenant colonel in the US Air Force. In addition to the boys were three sisters, Lillian, Mildred, and Eileen.

William Cronin. The patch on his shoulder is for General Headquarters, and was in use from 1937 to 1941. COURTESY RON WELCH JR. AND WILLIAM CRONIN FAMILY

William Thomas Cronin was born on October 15, 1919, and enlisted in the US Army Air Corps on July 3, 1941. He attended St. Bonaventure's College in nearby Allegany, New York. Because of his enlistment, Bill never graduated. Years later, one of Bill's professors remembered, "He used to walk the three miles from his house to the university. He was taking classes there before the war. I remember him well."

Bill's little sister, Eileen Cronin Welch, remembers Bill not walking to class, but *running*—both ways! Those miles of open fields and farms Bill ran through are now paved streets with residences, corner malls, hotels, and other commercial properties. The Cronin family owned a house at 416 North Ninth Street, a two-story affair covered with deep front porches on both levels that ran the width of the building. Eileen says, to this day, when she thinks of her brother, "I can see him in the kitchen. Oh! And I can see him and [our] brother, walking up the street."

Mr. Cronin insisted the children go to church every Sunday. Bill and Harold would be out to all hours on Saturday night, coming home when the roosters crowed. Mr. Cronin would hear them come in the house and would say, "Okay! Time to go to Mass." All these years later, Eileen is still amused. "They didn't want to go to church! Father would say, 'You were up all night, and you're going to go to church.' So they'd go to twelve o'clock Mass and sit up in the choir and, I'm not sure, but probably to sleep. But they went!"

Bill Cronin was a popular guy with the girls in town. "He could do so much. Good at sports. Handsome. Smart. Personable. Well-liked." Charlotte Yahn Murphy knew Bill back in Olean. She was two years his junior, but Eileen Welch remembers that Bill was sweet on Charlotte, who was the "pick of the crop" of women who were interested in Bill. In turn, Charlotte Murphy remembers, "We were good friends. What can I say? I know that I liked him and he liked me! He was a very nice young man." Like everyone else in Olean, Charlotte was shocked and devastated by Bill's death.

Bill and his brother, Harold, were as close as two peas in a pod. They did everything together. To the south of Olean is a turtleback-shaped peak known as Mount Herman. The boys built a cabin up there during high school that became their retreat, and stayed that way when the boys entered college. Bill spent time up there on his last visit home in 1943.

Eileen Welch was fourteen years old when her brother's airplane went missing, and it took a lifetime for her to be able to talk about those dark days and confront the past. Memories can be sweet and they can be terrible, and given the situation, either kind of memory can be painful to remember. Then something happens. For Eileen it was the physical process of taking all the family memorabilia about Bill—letters, photos, and papers—and mailing them off to her son, Ron. She kept them all in a box, "where I stored all my memories of that time many years ago." For the longest time, "I just couldn't open that folder."

It broke Eileen Welch's heart when her brother disappeared. It broke her heart again the following year, when the army shipped all of Bill's belongings back home in a duffel. "We didn't have any place to store it, so a lot of it, like his uniforms and stuff . . ." She lowered her voice to a whisper, and with deep sadness in her voice, said, "We just threw it all away."

CHAPTER 11

The Plane in the Lake

THE ARMY SEARCHED FOR SIGNS OF *EXTERMINATOR* FROM DECEMBER 6, 1943, through January 7, 1944, before abandoning the effort. Nothing was accomplished. The search effort for the airplane and its crew failed completely in the face of extreme winter weather.

Telegrams were dispatched to the families telling them of this failure to find any trace of their boys. Nothing hopeful was expressed about the crew being found alive, except a promise to "keep you informed on progress of searching parties." Internal memos suggest that administrators at Hammer Field were initially confident the crew and the wrecked airplane would be found quickly.

Judging by the amount of flotsam collected from the reservoir, Hammer Field was convinced *Exterminator* was in Huntington Lake. It could be no other place. Debris collected along the shore included badly damaged oxygen cylinders, parts of a cruise-control chart, parts of the aircraft's nose section, Sgt. Franklin Nyswonger's jacket, pages from the navigator's and radio operator's logbooks, bits of radio equipment, first-aid kits, and an engine tag identifying the aircraft as #42-7674: *Exterminator*.

Pilots from Hammer Field searched the forest around Huntington Lake and the surface of the reservoir from the air in 80-mile-long strips, 3 miles wide, "in case personnel bailed out of [the] aircraft." All they found was an oil slick—more evidence the plane was in the reservoir.

By the next day Hammer Field personnel knew that the reservoir was currently between 50 to 150 feet deep. Col. Frederic E. Glantzberg, com-

Huntington Lake reservoir, looking east. *Exterminator* crash site is on the right, near the far point of land. PHOTO BY PETER STEKEL

manding officer of the 461st Bomb Group at Hammer Field, requested from army headquarters in Winston-Salem, North Carolina, that "[the] base furnish men and equipment to remove bodies from aircraft in lake." A week later the magnitude of the task of locating *Exterminator* was sinking in. Results from using radar were negative. No sign of the boys was found on the ground, either.

Colonel Glantzberg wrote a long letter to Dick Mayo's mother, Reba, on December 14 to explain what had happened and what was being done. The colonel had been writing many letters the past few days. To Mrs. Mayo, Colonel Glantzberg wrote of how unpleasant a task it was to send such terrible news. "The loss of this crew has been keenly felt throughout the entire group."

Beginning December 15, verbiage in daily reports from Hammer Field to Headquarters becomes redundant: "Search for wreckage of B-24 42-7674 being continued in Huntington Lake and surrounding area

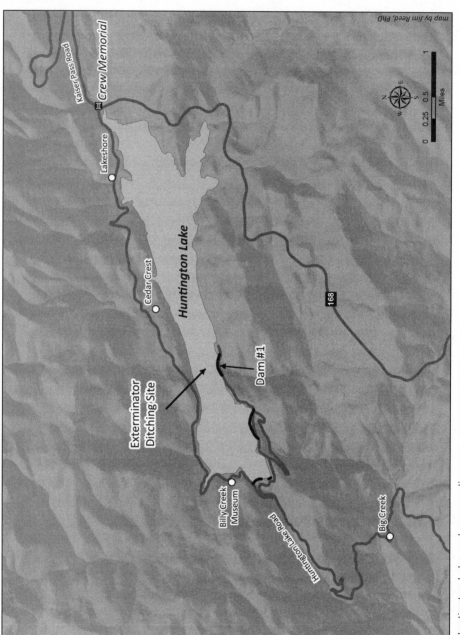

Huntington Lake and surrounding area. CARTOGRAPHY BY JIM REED PH.D.

with negative results." The repetition of the daily reports coincided with another spate of letters from Hammer Field to parents of the boys. In one of his first duties after replacing squadron commander Capt. William Darden, Capt. James C. Dooley wrote to Mr. and Mrs. Mayo on December 17: "I regret very much that I must now inform you that your son, Sergeant Mayo, who has been declared missing, is now presumed to be dead."

On Christmas Day, Hammer Field informed Army Headquarters that Huntington Lake was being intensively dragged in hopes of snagging onto some piece of wreckage. Divers would then be used to investigate any found objects. Beyond this, nowhere in the official accident report does it give a glimmer of how the search was being conducted.

However, the scope of the search can be gleaned from a December 8, 1943, issue of the *Oakland Tribune*. "Some 36 men under Second Lieutenant Douglas D. Rappley are making the search in the lake." Also with the search team were a dozen forest rangers and a large number of employees of the Southern California Edison Power Company. The searchers were focusing on a 1-square-mile area, but half a hundred men and then some is a pittance when terrain, a large body of water, high elevation, and a primeval forest are factored into the equation. And then there was the weather.

It is possible to picture what the conditions were for the searchers. According to data kept with the National Oceanic and Atmospheric Administration, Huntington Lake's temperature the morning *Exterminator* flew on December 6 was 18 degrees Fahrenheit. The temperature that day would eventually climb to a high of 48 degrees. Five inches of snow and ice lay on the ground. The sky was CAVU—clear above, visibility unlimited.

The days continued warm, with freezing nights, until December 18, when the nights began to warm—signaling a change for the worse in the weather. First it began to rain, just a little, but on December 20, it started snowing. Within twenty-four hours, 6 inches of snow had fallen, and temperatures dropped into the low 20s. Another 2.5 inches of snow fell the next day. After a week of cold and mostly clear weather, it began to snow again on December 28. During the next ten days 36.5 inches of snow fell at Huntington Lake. Daytime temperatures hovered around freezing. One day it got as high as 39 degrees. Nighttime temperatures ranged between 10 and 28.

Pity the poor thirty-six army boys searching the area around the lake. For one thing, they were camping out. In canvas-wall tents. Sleeping in blankets on cots, no doubt, and without insulating pads. The cold night air could circulate freely all around the sleeping soldiers, keeping them nice and frosty. During the day, lacking winter gear, they had to posthole and stomp around the forest and lakeshore through ever-increasing depths of snow in their loafers or combat boots, if they had them. Gloves or mittens would have been makeshift. Winter jackets, nonexistent. At the end of the day they would return to camp and attempt to cook a hot dinner over a campfire.

Since the army was certain *Exterminator* had ended up in the reservoir, the boys conducting the search would have spent most of their time either along the shore, searching for debris (and bodies), or in boats, engaged in dragging the bottom of the lake. The entire bottom of Huntington Lake was once forest, and the trees hadn't been logged until the reservoir began to fill. The lake bottom was a pincushion of stumps, short,

These are the tree stumps on the bottom of Huntington Lake that made dragging the reservoir for *Exterminator*'s wreckage so difficult. PHOTO BY PETE ELLIS

tall, and taller. That meant there was plenty for the searcher's grappling hooks to glom onto other than an airplane.

A partial financial accounting of the search for *Exterminator* can be found in IDPFs for the boys. Civilian laborer Eric Bergh, of Big Creek (the company town near the reservoir, operated by Southern California Edison), was paid $1.00 per hour for sixteen hours' work. A motorboat and engine, owned by A. M. Sinner of Fresno, had been used, and ruined. The cost of an engine overhaul was $25.00. The State Department of Public Works was reimbursed $416.30 for labor and equipment rental. Jack Bennett, of Oakland, had been hired as a diver. He was paid $1,329.20 on March 20, 1944, for his time, tender, and gear, and another $922.73 six months later. Paperwork all so very neat and tidy, but nothing concrete had come from all the effort.

In the middle of the army's search, Richard Spangle's father, Sherman, drove down from his home in Weed to see if he could lend a hand. With him were his wife and son-in-law. Given a staff car, some soldiers, and Lt. Culos Settle as a guide, Sherman Spangle made four circuits around the reservoir and found nothing.

These days it's a fairly easy and unexciting six-hour freeway drive from Weed to Fresno, and then another two-hour drive on a solid two-lane state highway to Huntington Lake. Not so in 1943. True, State Route 99 between Weed and Fresno was the major north-south route in the Sacramento Valley, but the two-lane blacktop in no way compares to the modern roadbed. Also, the Sacramento Valley wasn't as populated then as it is today, and filling stations were few and far between. Automobile reliability in those days doesn't compare with today, either. You could wait a long time for help if your car broke down. Finally, winter driving in snowy conditions was not to be taken lightly. But if Sherman Spangle thought about these things, he didn't let them dissuade him.

At Hammer Field, Mr. Spangle met someone he refers to as Mr. Harkey. This was either Dick Mayo's cousin, Paul Harkey Jr., or possibly his uncle, Byron Harkey. Both were in the navy during the war and could have been on the West Coast. At Mr. Harkey's suggestion, Mr. Spangle wrote to Porter and Reba Mayo. There are four letters from Mr. Spangle preserved in the Mayo family archives. Each missive is an example of the formalities people of the World War II generation adhered to. For instance, never are the letters addressed to Porter and Reba, always to Mr. and Mrs. Mayo, though the final letter, from March 15, 1944, is addressed to "Friends." Each letter is filled with manly restraint. And every line is heartbreaking, as Mr. Spangle reaches out to the only people who can understand his state of mind or comprehend his loss.

In his first letter, December 22, 1943, Mr. Spangle reviews the basic reason for the mission, *Exterminator*'s engine trouble, and Captain Darden's order to bail out. "They all had a chance to jump but preferred to stay with the ship, as they say they have a good chance to crash on the water without exploding, as they carried bombs, etc., which reduced their chance to [crash] on land." *Exterminator* wasn't carrying bombs. Mr. Spangle must be alluding to when a bomber during a combat mission has to ditch in open water or set down on dry land with a full load of bombs.

Putting on a good "game face," Mr. Spangle informs the Mayos, "The weather is such that it's useless to search further on land at the present." He promises to return to the reservoir next March, as the water level should be at its lowest point at that time, and conduct another search. "I have been 20 years becoming attached to our boy and I am a hard loser, and I am sure you are too, as Mr. Harkey told me you would have been here [but] for serious illness."

On December 31, 1943, the 461st Bomb Group left California for their overseas assignment at Torretta Field in Italy, and within the week the nature of *Exterminator*'s search changed. The weather had been terrible the previous week, and on January 5, 1944, Hammer Field reported to Headquarters, "Approximately 43 inches of snow and considerable quantities of ice on lake. No progress today. Extreme difficulties encountered maintaining supply road to Huntington Lake camp due to weather conditions mentioned above." Two days later the search was suspended and the searchers' campsite was abandoned.

Being unable to come west hadn't stopped Mrs. Mayo from writing prodding letters to Southern California Edison and the US Army to get on with it and find her boy. Return letters to her from both organizations in early January of 1944 are not encouraging. "As you know, Huntington Lake is at the 7,000 ft. elevation, and we have 40 inches of snow at the present time," wrote H. M. Beemer, special agent for the Edison Company.

Col. Guy Kirksey wrote to the Mayos to say the search was abandoned "temporarily" due to "inclement weather," but would be resumed in late March, "at which time the lake level will have been lowered by approximately 40 feet. Everyone is hoping a shallower reservoir will ease the search effort; perhaps they will even be able to see the Liberator on the lake bottom." Kirksey concludes, "I have every confidence that we will be successful when searching operations are resumed, and you may rest assured that you will be informed of our progress at that time."

Following on the heels of these discouraging letters was a new message from Mr. Spangle to the Mayos. He begins by reinforcing what the Mayos have already been told, before moving to their shared grief. "If we only knew if they are in the plane we could eliminate the ground search." Culos Settle told Mr. Spangle, "They all had time to put on their chutes and bail out, but he thinks they didn't have altitude to survive if they had jumped." Responding to a comment from Mrs. Mayo's previous letter, Mr. Spangle writes, "We too find it hard to believe they are dead, and it will be a relief to find the bodies at least." This is the kind of agonizing uncertainty that will follow thousands of families when their children or spouses do not come home from the war. What happened to them, and where are their remains buried?

In the same letter, Mr. Spangle reports getting a letter from "the young wife of Sergeant Vande Plasch," rear gunner on *Exterminator*. He also acknowledges the work being done at Hammer Field by Capt. Whitney Newton, and how H. M. Beemer, from the Edison Company, "was the one to conduct a search the day of the crash and lent us assistance, and we are very grateful to him." Mr. Spangle ends with, "It hurts me to be so helpless. I wish I could do more to locate them."

Not even a week later, on January 20, 1944, Sherman Spangle writes again to Mr. and Mrs. Mayo. Captain Newton has corresponded with Mr. Spangle to report the search for the boys has been temporarily halted due to snow and ice. The timing of these last letters is interesting, since the official record is that Hammer Field called off the search on January 8. The Edison Company representative, H. M. Beemer, apprised the Mayos of this in a January 10 letter, followed by a letter from Colonel Kirksey on January 13. It's a week after that when the Spangle family hears of the suspension—and not from Kirksey, but from this other officer, Newton. Absent correspondence from any of the other families, there is no way to know when, or even if, they found out about this important information or were kept perpetually in the dark.

Mr. and Mrs. Mayo were not sitting idly by at home in Prestonsburg, Kentucky. They constantly wrote letters and sent telegrams to Hammer Field, asking for information on when the search would be resumed and whether they could accompany it. Citing the large snowpack at the reservoir and impassable roads, on February 29, 1944, Colonel Kirksey advised against coming to California. This was reiterated in another letter from Hammer Field on April 20. Meanwhile, word came to the Mayos from Sherman Spangle on March 15 that "We have had bad weather here for some time, and [it's] still quite cold. The last report from the Lake also was that the lake had gone down to its lowest level. I do hope the weather will permit a thorough search while it is down." Winter was not about to cave in to a family's grief.

At the beginning of June, Mr. and Mrs. Mayo finally made it to Huntington Lake, and were not only able to observe the search for their boy, but also to attend a service for him at the lake, conducted by chaplain John W. Knoble from Hammer Field. That's probably where the Mayos first met H. M. Beemer in person, the special agent employed by the Southern California Edison Company.

After returning home, Mrs. Mayo was advised by personnel at Hammer Field on July 11, 1944, that the search had been terminated. "With the exception of several weeks when snow and the weather conditions made it impossible to continue searching operations, there has been an almost continual organized search."

In a July 15, 1944, letter, the Edison Company's H. M. Beemer gave Mr. Mayo an earful on how poorly that "almost continual organized search" was conducted. "After you left here June 6, the men and the search for the plane relaxed and didn't make much of an attempt to locate it. I was very disgusted with the way they were searching, as I don't believe they wanted to find it." This poor performance by the army was in addition to the month of May being wasted by searching, "in an area that is most unlikely for the plane to be in," because that part of the lake "was dry all winter and had been searched by my men, who made several trips up there during the winter and early spring." Beemer conveyed his feelings to the powers that be at Hammer Field, and they requested that he assume supervision of the operation, which he did on June 27, along with a new crew.

The army was using three amphibious trucks known as "Ducks" to search the lake. On the stern end was attached a "magnetic box" which they hoped would locate metal in the airplane. The previous crew had ruined or lost two of these boxes, which meant only one of the Ducks could be used. Beemer had a better idea. Procuring another box from Hammer Field, he attached two magnetic boxes to a spreader bar and then attached the spreader bar to a 14-foot Chris-Craft launch. Now, instead of a huge crew to operate the Duck *and* conduct the search, Beemer only needed three men on the launch and one man onshore. With the increased efficiency of this setup, Beemer was convinced that in thirty days he could survey the entire reservoir.

The army thought differently, and on June 28, one day after authorizing Beemer's supervision, informed him to discontinue the search. Beemer remained at Huntington Lake, hoping for authorization to begin again. By the time he wrote to the Mayos in July, Beemer had been told, unofficially, that "the army is finished."

Another reason Beemer wrote to the Mayos was to inquire if they were interested in continuing the search on their own hook. Beemer was willing to find the gear and organize the men. He felt certain Edison would release him for the necessary time. "If you can come out here I will be glad to work with you and help all I can." There is no indication that the Mayos took Beemer up on his offer.

Walker Porter Mayo was a knowledgeable and experienced lawyer. Professionally, he must have recognized the futility of pushing against bureaucratic intransigence, but, personally, he kept at it. Two years had passed since the crash and World War II was over. He wrote to Hammer Field on December 13, 1945, after receiving notice from the previously helpful Maj. Whitney Newton, that the Edison Company had lowered the reservoir to work on the dam. The search was on again for Dick Mayo and his crewmates.

The news was not good. Lt. Col. Frank G. Millard replied how a small boat and a detail of men was sent up to the reservoir from the first of November to the tenth of December, when the lake's minimum level of 53 feet was reached. Not a thing was seen. Nothing discovered. Millard dismissively concluded, "We feel that everything has been done that could be done up to this time, and it is now questionable in our minds whether or not the airplane is in the lake. We assure you that we have done everything in our power to find this airplane." How galling to read Millard's opinion that the airplane wasn't in the lake, when all the evidence from past years pointed to that fact.

A major part of the Big Creek Hydroelectric Project, construction of Huntington Lake had been completed in 1912 and was named for Henry Edwards Huntington. The project includes the company town of Big

Dam #1. Huntington Lake is impounded by four dams, is 14 miles long, and has a surface area of over 1,400 acres. PHOTO BY PETER STEKEL

Creek and a system of reservoirs (including Shaver Lake), tunnels, steel penstocks, and powerhouses. Huntington Lake is impounded by four dams, is 14 miles long, and has a surface area of over 1,400 acres. It is a big place to search for such a small airplane. Such a daunting search area might explain why succeeding commandants at Hammer Field weren't enthusiastic about looking for *Exterminator*.

On November 14, 1946, Porter Mayo passed away. "His heart could hold out no longer," Reba Mayo wrote to Sherman Spangle. "I feel now that you are my only connection concerning anything about our interests at Huntington Lake. You can imagine that I am terribly forlorn."

Despite losing her husband, "while in the full participation of an active life," Reba Mayo was made of stern stuff, and she carried on the fight, pelting Hammer Field with letters, always asking for an update on the search for her boy. Mrs. Mayo's logic is unassailable, as in a 1947 letter to the Hammer Field commanding general. "In view of the fact that we are bringing the war dead [home] from the South Pacific, surely we may search for the boys who were lost in their own homeland." To abandon the search was simply untenable. "It seems too terrible that we should have to let them go, just go, as a piece of wood, without finding them." To drive home her point as only a mother can, Mrs. Mayo concluded with, "My awareness and concern, and grief for Dick are so constant and so alive, that I fear that something must be done, JUST MUST BE DONE."

When nothing was done, Mrs. Mayo wrote to the Secretary of War, requesting that the lake be drained sufficiently, "to make a complete search for the plane." And she repeats her argument of how right it is to do so. "I do not think I am asking too much of the War Department, in view of the fact that we are bringing [home] the remains of our men from overseas. I feel that we could do something about the remains of our men here on our own soil."

And that's where the story lay for years until two young boys, walking along the shore of the Huntington Lake reservoir, chanced upon some airplane wreckage.

Nine-year-old Don Ekhoff and his friend, thirteen-year-old Bill Disterdick, were campers with their families at Huntington Lake during the summer of 1955. Beginning on the July 4 holiday, Southern California Edison had been drawing down the reservoir's level so the power company could frost-proof the dams and perform other preventative maintenance work. Don and Bill would get up early every morning to walk the shore, looking for what might present itself in the retreating water. Mostly they were finding fishing lures and things lost overboard from boats. One morning in early August the boys were walking the shoreline near the largest of Huntington's dams. Don Ekhoff was in front, and he saw what appeared to be a small ladies' purse. He picked it up and read the bold print: "In case of emergency, pull flap." On the next line was "Dye Marker."

Bill Disterdick ran to his friend's side to see what he had found. "I handed it to him just as I spotted something else about 15 feet away." It was an uninflated military life vest, what the flyboys used to call a "Mae West." Don and Bill reported their discoveries to their parents, and the boy's fathers drove them to the local post office, where they told their story again. Alerted by Don and Bill's discoveries, local Big Creek diver, Ronald White, tried to locate the aircraft, but was defeated by deep water and poor visibility.

Meanwhile, divers associated with the volunteer Alameda County Sheriff's Underwater Rescue Unit got word of a B-24 lying on the bottom of Huntington Lake, and resolved to find it. Ten divers with the unit planned their expedition for September 17–18, which they were told would coincide with the lowest water level of the reservoir due to the Edison Company's drawdown. The divers' plan was blown out of the water when a local fisherman contacted the Fresno County Sheriff's Department to report seeing the tail section of an airplane sticking out 2 feet above the reservoir's surface, north of Dam #1.

This was news indeed, and the army was inspired to do something about it. Unfortunately, they fell down on the job when it came to notifying the families. All of them found out about *Exterminator*'s discovery by reading the newspaper and seeing their boys' names printed there in black and white.

On September 2, 1955, Mrs. Merle Spangle writes to Mrs. Reba Mayo, having seen an article in her local newspaper about "the plane in which our boys were lost." She adds, "We have had no official word, and I presume you have had none either." As in 1944, Mr. Spangle has "offered his assistance" in the search. "So far we have not heard from any one, and all we know is what we have seen in the papers." Having seen a similar newspaper story as the Spangles, but in ill health due to a ruptured disk, Mrs. Mayo doesn't respond until September 21. She informs the Spangles that her son, Dr. Porter Mayo, has already written the Fresno sheriff for more information, but "I don't think he has received anything."

Herbert Schlosser writes to the Casualty Branch, Director of Military Personnel, in Washington, DC, on September 29, 1955, enclosing a recent newspaper article about *Exterminator*'s discovery, revealing, "Three days of diving in partially drained Huntington Lake have already brought up two bodies." He's disturbed because his brother is named in the story. "While reading the *New York World Telegram* dated September 24th I came across an article which is of urgent interest to me. I am the brother of Second Lt. Samuel J. Schlosser. Although I am not listed as the Beneficiary, I am the only blood relative remaining." Herbert Schlosser ends his brief letter with, "I would very much appreciate any information that could be forwarded to me upon any additional developments in this case." No reply from the army resides in Samuel Schlosser's IDPF.

The Nyswonger family also learns about the discovery of *Exterminator* from the newspaper. Annoyed, and feeling forgotten by the army, they go directly to their congressman, John W. Byrnes. The congressman's office pens a letter on October 14, 1955, to the air force liaison at the House of Representatives, requesting information on Franklin Nyswonger, saying that, "sometime between August 28 and September 15, 1955, bodies of at least some of the crew were found." The letter works its way through air force and army bureaucracy before landing on the desk of somebody at the Decedent Branch, Memorial Division, on November 4.

Meanwhile, Melvin Vande Plasch writes to National Air Force Headquarters in Washington, DC, on October 3, 1955, saying, "I would like to get some information concerning my brother who was killed in an airplane in December 1943 at Huntington Lake near Fresno, California." Melvin has seen an article about *Exterminator* in the September 24 *Milwaukee Journal* that reports how "The bodies of four of six crewmen who died . . . were recovered Friday by army divers." Donald Vande Plasch is identified in the article. "I would like an answer within the next 10 days, as this news has made my mother and dad very ill, as they have received no information from the Air Force about this." Angry at the military's behavior, Melvin Vande Plasch ends his letter with, "If we do not hear from you within that time, I am writing to our Senator Wiley to see if he can get some information concerning my brother."

Melvin Vande Plasch contacts Congressman Clement Zablocki instead. An October 28 memo to Congressman Zablocki from the army's Decedent Branch reviews the situation. "We believe all the remains have been recovered, but that it is necessary that they be processed by identification specialists and anthropologists before individual identification is released in individual cases." There is nothing in the letter about recovered "bodies," as mentioned in newspaper reports; only of "remains." The memo offers an apology to the congressman for not informing the family, because, "We did not previously have the name and address of the parents." By November 2 they are still trying to locate Mr. and Mrs. Vande Plasch, informing Melvin by telegram, "Concerning the remains of your late brother Sgt. Donald C. Vande Plasch. Efforts are presently being made to locate legal next of kin."

On November 5, Mr. Vande Plasch finally receives a telegram. "Due to the nature of the airplane crash and the condition of the remains of one other individual in the crew, remains of your late son and remains of the other crew member will be interred in one grave in Fort Snelling National Cemetery. This cemetery was selected because it is nearest to next of kin of both deceased." Congressman Zablocki gets a similar telegram on November 14, and Melvin Vande Plasch receives a letter to that effect on November 17, 1955. No apology or explanation is given for the delay in delivering notice, and nothing is said about the amount of remains to be buried, because apparently, they consisted of very little.

A letter from the army dated October 5, 1955, was dispatched to the Mayos and Spangles, informing them that five or six weeks would be needed at Huntington Lake to complete their work. Mrs. Mayo writes to Mrs. Spangle on November 2, explaining how she received some newspaper clippings in mid-September from a young soldier in California, "with pictures of the plane showing, etc., but at that time, only four [sets of] remains had been found." She fears her son, being a turret gunner and stationed in the Liberator's middle, "was thrown clear of the plane, and that his was not one of the first four found."

The IDPF paper trail for William Darden, Samuel Schlosser, Franklin Nyswonger, Richard Spangle, and Donald Vande Plasch makes clear that as early as August 18, the army and air force had settled their minds on who would be responsible, "should remains be recovered." They agreed that the disposition of remains belonged to the army for military personnel, "Whose deaths occurred prior to 18 September 1947 [date on which air force was established as a separate department]."

Other papers show requests for dental charts, enlistment records, and physical examination records to aid in any identifications, and contact data for next of kin. Extensive memoranda cover the actual recovery of the crew, where the remains were taken, and how easily / not easily the boys were identified. There is also an extensive accounting of the recovery costs and, in each individual boy's IDPF, further accounting for casketing, the cost of transporting the boy home, and the expense of his funeral. It's unknown why the authorities took so long to tell the families their children had been found.

While the army was mum, newspapers continued covering the Huntington Lake operation. One of them in late September wrote of a four-man diving crew at work in the lake, and graphically reports, "The badly decomposed remains of two of the wartime airmen were recovered from a section of the fuselage late yesterday. Two other bodies were pulled from the tail and nose sections Thursday." The gruesome story goes on to quote the coroner as saying, "little more than bones remained after the long exposure in the murky waters of the lake, and that identification at the crash scene was impossible."

A letter from Sherman Spangle to Mrs. Mayo contradicts the newspaper report—at least in one instance. Mr. Spangle was at Huntington Lake with his youngest son, Tom, during the recovery. He wrote, "Your boy's body was the first recovered and the only one identified at the lake. His body was intact, still in his sheepskin flying suit, in his position as tail turret gunner. This tail section was broken off at the bomb bay and about

450 feet from the other section." He goes on to say that the other five boys were found in the cockpit at the time of the crash, and "most of the remains were recovered." The IDPFs for the boys contradict Mr. Spangle on this point and support the newspaper account.

The divers working in Huntington Lake were from the 561st Engineer Company, the same group that would be flown to Hester Lake five years later. Utilization of the 561st was approved as a training mission as long as the minimum number of personnel were used. The divers and support team were billeted in the nearby resort communities of Lakeshore and Cedar Crest Lodge.

The divers were probably S/Sgt. Henry M. Waskavitch and his brother-in-law, Sgt. Douglas McCoy, the same two who would work at Hester Lake five years later. In stories told to Paul McCoy by his father and uncle, he remembers, "There were a couple of them [crewmen] in the plane itself," and, "for as many years as they'd been in there, they looked awful fresh." This sounds more like the Huntington Lake Liberator than the Hester Lake plane, and perhaps the McCoy family story became blended over the years. This interpretation also supports what Sherman Spangle wrote to Mrs. Mayo about her son, as well as the condition of Captain Darden's remains.

The broken aircraft lay in about 20 feet of water. Twenty-two-year-old Tom Spangle, observing the recovery operation from the shore, remembers the mud below the reservoir's retreating waters being around waist-deep. It frustrated the divers' efforts because they couldn't do anything without causing a roiling mess of silt to envelop them and the objects of their search.

Then, someone had the idea of pulling the wreckage out of the water. A cable was wrapped around the Liberator and a winch began pulling *Exterminator* onto shore. They quickly ran into the same problem experienced by crews dragging the lake in 1943 and 1944: 10-foot-tall stumps of trees left over from when Huntington Lake was first built. Tom Spangle says the aircraft would snag on a tree stump, "and they would just pull it through." If *Exterminator* was already a wreck, dragging it across the reservoir destroyed the rest of it. "But they got most of it up on the bank," recalls Spangle, "so they could get to it out of the water."

When the army was done and all the remains they could collect were collected, Sherman Spangle explained to Mrs. Mayo that the aircraft was "tied down with steel cables, and will remain there under 125 to 200 feet of water forever."

Finally recovering his son's remains filled Mr. Spangle with both satisfaction and melancholy. In one way, he and his wife at last had the closure they had longed for, but, in another way, just like Robert Bursey's sister would express five years later, any grieving that had settled upon them in the past had to be gone through all over again. You can tell from his final letter to Mrs. Mayo on December 19, 1955, how Mr. Spangle is already beginning to work through this renewed grief when he writes, "I know you feel relieved that all is over, and all we have left is the precious memories they have left us." It must have been a bittersweet Christmas that year.

❧

In June of 1980, John Marion was spending his honeymoon at Huntington Lake, staying in the cabin his grandmother had bought in 1925. Marion and his wife had ringside seats to observe the spectacle involving the next chapter in *Exterminator*'s story.

Since April of that year, Sherman Spangle's twenty-five year old prediction that *Exterminator* would remain underwater forever had been tested by a salvage operation led by twenty-eight-year-old Gene Forte. With the knowledge of at least one of *Exterminator*'s families, Forte's idea was to lift the Liberator from the bottom of Huntington Lake, reassemble all the pieces, and put it on display in a museum in Prather, a small Sierra Nevada foothill town midway between the reservoir and Fresno.

It sounded like a fantasy; an impossible undertaking. Everyone around the reservoir knew about the "plane in the lake," the pincushion of tree stumps, and the 1955 recovery when the B-24 had been ripped apart as the army had dragged it to shore. A local historian by the name of Charlie Hill had kept the story alive for residents and visitors with his evening programs at the Huntington Lake Lodge. Hill even had photos from 1944 when the army had dragged the lake.

Gene Forte's salvage operation elicited quite a bit of interest with local residents, and spectators were commonly in attendance, watching the work progress. Media of the day were interested too. George Barulic, the only living survivor of the crash, was interviewed and confessed he hadn't heard of the bomber being found in 1955, and "some of the bodies recovered."

Historical confusion was heaped onto the story from newspapers reporting how after the plane was discovered in 1955, "the bodies of three crewmen were recovered in what scientists described as remarkably well-preserved conditions." The intimation was that more bodies would be recovered, and "Fresno County sheriff's deputies are waiting to see what is found, since they will be charged with notifying next of kin."

At least one spectator had doubts that anything of value would be brought up from the lake bottom. Walter Ullmann, a longtime Huntington Lake resident, reminded the *Fresno Bee* how low water in 1964 had exposed the bomber. "I know a lot of pieces have been taken off by divers and other people. It's been stripped of so much equipment, it will be impossible to restore."

The project moved forward. Dutra Construction Company in Rio Vista, California, was hired by Forte to do the difficult and dangerous work of salvaging the wrecked B-24. Led by Dan Webb, four divers used a 100-million-candlepower light to spot the wreckage lying in the dark waters over 100 feet below the surface. Even with such powerful illumination, visibility was limited to 10 feet. The water was a frigid 33 degrees. Unlike during the 1960 army dive operation at Hester Lake, Dutra brought in a decompression chamber for the safety of the divers, and only allowed the men to work fifty minutes per day.

Why nobody involved in this 1980 effort bothered to contact the army or ask the families what had been accomplished back in 1955 is unknown. Chances are that some would have found this private salvage operation to be an offensive desecration. One family member did know about the project and he was there to watch the work: Tom Spangle, whose older brother had been killed in the crash. Perhaps thinking of how the Liberator would be displayed as a museum memorial, Spangle told a reporter, "I think the recovery of the plane is great, but it still brings a lot of memories." He planned on remaining to watch the salvage work until pieces of the plane were recovered or the effort abandoned.

Spangle was also there to keep his eye on an investment he'd made. To raise money for the wreckage recovery operation, Gene Forte formed a limited partnership, Salvage II, and subscribed units (shares) of $2,500 each. Spangle and his wife had purchased two of the units. The subscription agreement stipulated that "in the event this subscription is not accepted, or all 20 units of the limited partnership are not sold by Salvage II, my investment will be returned."

With such extreme diving conditions it took many weeks to bring anything up from the lake bottom. Using a 30-ton crane, they eventually managed to pull a couple of engines and a section of wing up onto either of two large barges.

One Saturday evening John Marion, his wife, his parents, and brother, boated across the reservoir to check on the operation. "They had pulled the wing section up and sunk it by the side of the dock," in 4 feet of water. "You could drift over it and look at it. The landing gear was stowed and the tire was inflated and the de-icing caps on the side of the wing appeared to be inflated still."

Money problems precluded the completion of Salvage II's goals. Through his limited partnership, Forte had anticipated raising $50,000, but he announced in early July that "a backer had lied about contributing to the salvage operation." Suddenly Forte was $50,000 short. Forte was paying $1,000 per day for the divers, and had racked up another $5,053 in back rent. With no money to pay for the operation, Dutra Construction stopped work and promised they wouldn't begin again until Gene Forte came up with $10,000 cash, and $40,000 in guaranteed pledges.

From there, lawyers took over. Forte sued Dutra. GTY Investment Planning sued Forte for back rent plus damages. The engines already recovered were pushed off the barges and sank back down into deeper water. The wing section was left in the shallows where John Marion had seen it.

Gene Forte's operation was neither the final salvage attempt nor the last to be interested in the plane in the lake. Unknown to any of the families involved, in 1989 two dozen members of the US Navy Reserve Mobile Diving Salvage Unit spent time at Huntington Lake at the behest of Castle Air Museum in Atwater, California. The museum was restoring a B-24 and hoped *Exterminator* could be cannibalized to provide parts. They were not successful.

In the early 1990s a private salvage effort was quickly abandoned. In 2008 Matt Finnegan and a crew of divers went looking for the wreck in hopes of filming it, but were unsuccessful in finding any pieces.

In 2013 a short video was produced by a group of explorers led by Dan Zurcher and his daughter Rachel. An area local, Zurcher grew up with stories about the plane in the lake. He finally decided to learn something about those stories. With his team, Zurcher plumbed the depths of Huntington Lake, searching for signs of *Exterminator*. They were there to learn something about their home around the reservoir and to understand its history. Diving to the bottom of Huntington Lake they found plenty of wreckage strewn about but Zurcher believes the site should remain undisturbed because it's as sacred as any other cemetery.

———

As World War II slips into our past, a small museum at Billy Creek on the northwestern shore of Huntington Lake reminds visitors of *Exterminator* and her crew. Located in an old Forest Service guard station, inside the museum you'll find a tiny room dedicated to the plane in the lake. There are some photos on the wall, a few artifacts, yellowed newspaper clippings in a display case, and a framed portrait of *Exterminator*.

———

One final story about *Exterminator* and her crew remains to be told. In 1991, a fourth-grade student at Big Creek School (the Southern California Edison company town just downstream of the reservoir) saw a newspaper article about the Edison Company's plans to lower the reservoir level so they could work on the dam. The plane in the lake was mentioned, along with the exciting comment that it might be visible as the shoreline was exposed. The student brought the article to school one day and her teacher, Bob Crider, recognized his student's interest in the story. The crash became an unprecedented class research project, "the likes of which he [had] not experienced in twenty years in the classroom."

During the next four months, under Crider's direction, the fourth graders pushed everything aside to focus on the plane in the lake. "They are acquiring writing and language skills far above the fourth-grade level," their teacher reported. "It's really turned the kids on to education." Working in pairs, the students researched the history of *Exterminator*, her crew, and the 461st Bomb Group at Hammer Field. They succeeded in contacting most of the airmen's families, too. On multiple field trips they visited the crash site and the wreckage, visible that winter as the reservoir level dropped to a historic level. They even made the long journey to Castle Air Museum where they got to see a B-24 Liberator on display.

The Big Creek School students also raised money to fund a memorial to *Exterminator*'s crew and their mission. On December 6, 1991, they dedicated a monument with a large brass plaque containing the names of the eight boys and an image of a B-24 Liberator. Also part of the project

Big Creek School (1990–1991) fourth-grade class, with their teacher, Mr. Robert Crider. PHOTO IN AUTHOR'S COLLECTION, COURTESY OF BIG CREEK SCHOOL 4TH GRADE PROJECT

Dedication of the Big Creek School fourth graders' memorial to the crew of *Exterminator*. December 6, 1991. PHOTO IN AUTHOR'S COLLECTION, COURTESY OF BIG CREEK SCHOOL 4TH GRADE PROJECT

was a portrait of *Exterminator*, painted by Mike Rasmussen. The artist eventually completed two canvases: One shows *Exterminator* flying over snowy mountains, and the other one shows the Liberator flying low over Huntington Lake.

The first portrait was commissioned by Bob Crider and hung at the Fresno Air Terminal (former site of Hammer Field) for several years. Eventually this portrait was returned to Crider and was later donated around 2012 by his widow to the Billy Creek Museum. There is some confusion about the second portrait, and even the artist is unsure about who asked for it to be painted.

The Big Creek School class project continued the next year with thirteen more fourth graders. Broadening the field, this second class researched the Hester Lake story, since it was the boys on that Liberator the Huntington Lake boys had been looking for. And to round things off, the class also found out all they could about three other boys from Hammer Field's 461st Bomb Squadron who were killed during training. They published their research in a seventeen-page booklet, dedicated to the memory of the sixteen Hammer Field boys from the 461st Bomb Group who died between 1943 and 1944. Winnie Mason, sister of Capt. William Darden, was one of the family members the students were able to reach. She was overjoyed to hear about the project and sent the students a portrait of her brother and a photograph of his grave marker at the Olive Branch Cemetery in Portsmouth, Virginia. In a letter of appreciation she wrote, "This Memorial Day weekend when I visit Bill's grave will be the first time

Capt. William Darden's headstone at Olive Branch Cemetery in Darden's hometown of Portsmouth, Virginia. PHOTO BY STEVE POOLE

that I have ever felt that anyone cared, except the family, that he gave his life for his country. I will convey this message to him in prayer. Another Hero laid to rest."

CHAPTER 12

The Searchers

IT ISN'T EASY REACHING HESTER LAKE. YET, EVEN IF IT'S ONLY TWO OR three people a year, somebody is always trying to get there. Most are turned away by the Notch—that 300-foot rock climb through a crack in the granite wall far below the lake. Motivations for visiting are hard to pin down. Some come because it's adventurous. There are those Sierra Nevada mountaineers who revel in visiting hard-to-reach places. There is no other reason for them to be there because Hester Lake gives no access to any significant peak for climbing.

What drives others to make the long and difficult trek? Some come because Hester Lake is a historic place to visit. The plane in the lake is a strong draw to people who like their history tangible; something they can touch or someplace where something important happened.

In spite of any danger, some come for history spiced with adventure. Many have tried to reach Hester Lake with their scuba tanks. They want to touch 463, and by doing so, touch history. And they come to photograph and document the wreckage in a site still as sacred as any cemetery. In recent years these searchers have been joined by scientists who come to explore with tiny submersibles called remotely operated vehicles (ROVs).

There are no recorded visitors to Hester Lake after the army divers departed in 1960, until August 9, 1972, when Brother William McCall from Chaminade Preparatory School in Canoga Park, California, visited the area with Boy Scouts from Explorer Post #288. In a letter written

Hester Lake basin from Dusy Basin. A) LeConte Canyon Ranger Station. B) The Notch. C) Peak 12,483. D) Hester Lake (vicinity). PHOTO BY PETER STEKEL

to Sequoia & Kings Canyon National Parks, Brother McCall describes ascending the forested slope above the LeConte Canyon Ranger Station until confronted by a "granite friction face." Rather than climb through the Notch, McCall took his Boy Scouts up this more difficult route. They used a rope, "for morale and safety purposes." Of the danger he added, "An experienced climber probably would not need one, but he had better not fall!"

The Scouts camped that night near the 10,800-foot level near the top of the Notch, alongside Hester Creek. The next morning they made their way to the lake. Unfamiliar with the plane in the lake story, Brother McCall was surprised by what they found. There was airplane wreckage "of a service aircraft scattered along the N.E. shore." He assumed the aircraft must be in the lake, because the Scouts found "an old-style diving suit on the shore—evidently left behind when they had sent in a search or salvage party."

Brother McCall jumped to some conclusions after discovering other historic artifacts. "I found an old weathered cosmetics kit. Inside, preserved over the years by two gradually melting ChapSticks, I found a perfectly preserved Swiss Army Knife." Because there were "feminine articles in the kit," McCall surmised the aircraft accounting for the wreckage around the lake must have been a single-seat aircraft flown by a "woman ferry pilot many years ago." One of the boys in his group disabused him of that notion by informing him that "it was a B-17, or possibly a transport." To state such a hypothesis the Scouts must have come across significant, diagnostic pieces of wreckage to suggest a very large aircraft.

⌒⌒

Keeping the Hester Lake story alive was S. Samuel Boghosian in a June 1979 article in *Air Classics*. Boghosian previously wrote about *Exterminator* in a September 1976 issue of the magazine. That article contained the first mention of the oft-repeated story of Captain Darden attempting a landing on Huntington Lake reservoir, thinking the lake was a snow-covered field while flying "hopelessly lost in a blinding snowstorm."

The snow-covered lake claim has always been a head-scratcher for Huntington Lake residents, because "the lake doesn't freeze over that early in the winter." During John Marion's boat trip to examine the 1980 salvage attempt, he observed that the landing gear was stowed. This is positive proof that Captain Darden had intended to ditch *Exterminator* and knew a reservoir was beneath him and not a snow-covered meadow.

Boghosian was using the best information available to him at the time, but unfortunately his *Air Classics* articles contain errors that would be repeated over the years. Searchers intrigued by the two lost B-24s would return again and again to Boghosian's stories, as well as to other writers who built on his work, looking for clues as to what happened to the aircraft and crews in 1943.

In his Hester Lake article of 1979, as with his previous story about the Huntington Lake Liberator, Boghosian did not have access to the accident reports for the two B-24s. Otherwise there would have been no mention of a blinding snowstorm in either article. Lieutenant Settle and

Sergeant Barulic, the two surviving crew members of *Exterminator*, make no mention of a storm, and neither do either of the accident reports. Boghosian also separates the two aircraft losses from each other, failing to make the connection that Captain Darden, his crew, and *Exterminator* were lost while looking for 463 and the Turvey-Hester crew. After reviewing Clint Hester's long quest to find his son, Boghosian tells the tale of how 463 was found, his account paralleling 1960 newspaper accounts.

Lumped in with all the newspaper accounts written over the years about the two B-24s and another magazine story published in 1978 by *Air Classics*, the Boghosian articles demonstrate difficulties researchers have with teasing out the truth from published "facts" that can be more supposition and conjecture than anything else. Over time, with repetition, these "facts" *do* replace the truth. Eventually, all that remains is the story. And the story is what continues to captivate people's imagination, leading them to haunt the waters beneath Hester and Huntington Lakes.

In 1986, Randy Morgenson, that year's LeConte Canyon ranger, made a very late summer trip to Hester Lake. On September 22 Morgenson arrived to have a look around at the behest of his supervisor at park headquarters, Paul Fodor. Morgenson was asked to survey the area and report back on the amount of visible aircraft debris. The park service knew there was aircraft wreckage at the lake, but they didn't know how much, or where it was located.

Unlike the Explorer Scouts in 1972, Morgenson didn't find anything that would suggest a large aircraft. That evening he made an entry into the official logbook for the ranger station. "Found about enough aluminum (NE shore) to fill a backpack if it's stomped on." With an eye toward removing all traces of the aircraft, he wrote, "Surely more could be found w/a search. Biggest, [approximately] 3 feet." Due to snow and ice in "the gulch" (i.e., the Notch), Morgenson elected to take a much longer route home by climbing higher in the basin, then talus-hopping for several miles to the John Muir Trail, high up in LeConte Canyon.

Morgenson had to wait until the following year before following up on his proposed Hester Lake cleanup project. On August 31, 1987, he was back at the lake for the first of two visits. "Gathered up pieces of the old bomber (found considerably more than I found last year), and filled a backpack. Left a pile representing another trip or two. I think most of the pieces scattered on the shore have been found and there aren't any large pieces. It's simply a ranger job carrying that stuff down. What's needed is a wet suit to get into the lake. There's a lot of stuff along the shore in water 10 feet or less."

Like everyone else who has succeeded in reaching Hester Lake, Morgenson was not only intrigued by the story, but also speculated on what had caused the big bomber to come down in the first place. What bothered him most was, "How did that plane crash into the lake and not leave debris on the ridges along its approach? Were the motors, wheels, large body sections ever found?" He surmises, as did everybody in 1960, "Appears like it hit the lake and skidded into the rocks on the NNE shore."

On September 20 Morgenson returned and "Carried last load of B-24 from Hester Lake." Still trying to puzzle out the cause of the crash and why the wreckage was distributed as it was, he asked himself, "How did that hit the peak to SW and splatter all over NE shore?" He sums up his janitorial project thus: "That's all I've found, but likely more will come to light. Need a wet suit for lots [of aircraft debris] in water." Morgenson's total haul of debris in 1987 was three bags of parts, collected and removed from the site as garbage.

Randy Morgenson was the LeConte ranger the next year, 1988, but didn't return to Hester Lake. On July 26 of that year, just as Morgenson was preparing to depart on patrol, he was visited by somebody from the "the deep past": Leroy Brock. In the ranger station journal, Morgenson wrote, "Rest of the day and into the night with stories of the early days, including the real story of Hester Lake."

The next searchers came in July of 1989 when Stephen DeSalvo and his brother hiked to Hester Lake. They carried wet suits and snorkeling gear to make an assessment of whether it would be feasible to bring scuba gear in by helicopter. They could see remains of the airplane that appeared to be in about 60 feet of water. The brothers decided diving the wreck would be justified, and on August 7, 1989, DeSalvo wrote to the park service to formally request permission to "enter the park via helicopter mid-week, either late August or early September, 1989, [bringing] the appropriate scuba-diving and photographic equipment necessary for a proper survey of the B-24E." His intent was "to verify the current condition of B-24E and evaluate for recovery."

It's unlikely that a private party would be allowed a personal flight into the Kings Canyon wilderness today, but in 1989, the park service was more concerned with determining who owned the wreckage of the plane in the lake: the army, the park, or . . . ?

Before responding to DeSalvo's request, acting superintendent of Sequoia & Kings Canyon National Parks, William L. Bancroft, con-tacted the claims and litigation staff in aviation and admiralty law with the US Air Force. In an August 9 letter Superintendent Bancroft briefly outlined the history of 463, erroneously adding that "Much of the wreck-age was removed" in 1960 when the B-24 was initially discovered. But he also said that wreckage remained in the lake. He then inquired "as to the procedure the National Park Service needs to pursue permission to remove the remaining wreckage." There was no mention that a private party was interested in doing the removing.

Without receiving a reply from the air force, Superintendent Ban-croft dispatched a letter to DeSalvo on August 17, stating, "Sequoia and Kings Canyon National Park authorizes you to use a helicopter to fly into and land at Hester Lake to inspect the B-24E wreckage." Stipulations are given. The flight can occur that year, but only after September 4. Flights must be kept to "an absolute minimum." The flight must be a direct line from departure point to arrival; no side trips and no sightseeing. Most importantly, nothing could be removed without pending permission from the air force. "This authorization must be granted by the Air Force before you can remove the wreckage," and "once you start to remove the wreckage, you will have to remove all of the wreckage and not just the valuable portion."

The letter gives no indication of the enormity of the task involved, or the expense involved in removing the wreckage of one of the largest aircraft from World War II from an alpine lake tens of miles away from the nearest highway. Even if "much of the wreckage was removed," in 1960, the sheer impossibility of a couple of scuba divers salvaging anything 60 or more feet underwater had to be a complete nonstarter.

Tying removal of valuable items to removing everything else as well was reasonable in the minds of park administrators. If somebody wanted one part of wreckage, they should take the whole thing and leave nothing behind. The parks didn't want salvagers "high-grading" for parts and leaving the rest behind. At the time anything man-made lying on the ground or in the water that was less than fifty years old was not considered historic. That made the airplane in the lake garbage, not a relict.

Speaking about the private flight nearly thirty years later, John Kraushaar, one of the rangers involved in approving the project, suggests, "He [DeSalvo] probably made a proposal to the park to fly in and get the airplane out." Since the park service wanted the wreckage removed, the deal became, "If we let you fly in to find it, if you find it, you'll have to be willing to get it all out." Kraushaar suspects, "We either didn't have the money or didn't want to spend the money. It was easier for us to require somebody else to fly it out. If they wanted the good stuff, they had to take all of it."

Kraushaar also remembers, "Previously, when airplanes crashed, both private and military, the wreckage was left in place, or oftentimes only the valuable components were removed." Based on Kraushaar's recommendations, the park service developed a policy of working with private insurance carriers and the military to remove wreckage and restore wilderness sites to their natural conditions. To encourage responsible parties to perform this cleanup, the park sometimes gave permission to individuals or companies to take what they wanted in exchange for cleaning up the sites.

Park administrators needn't have worried about permission to remove lake wreckage, because the air force didn't care. In an August 24, 1989, letter, after some bureaucratic hemming and hawing and term and non-term definitions, the rangers were told, "There is no interest in preserving the wreckage for any purpose . . . and as far as the Air Force is concerned, you may remove the remaining wreckage."

As with divers and salvagers at Huntington Lake, no consideration was given to what the Turvey, Hester, Fish, Cronin, Bursey, and Wandtke families would think about anyone exploring the wreckage at the bottom of Hester Lake. IDPFs for the boys make it plain that most of the crew's remains were still entombed either in the lake or within the aircraft. For anybody who cared to think of such things, this effectively made Hester Lake a cemetery and anyone poking around the wreckage looking to salvage it, a grave robber.

However, the information within the IDPFs for the boys was still classified and unavailable to everybody except the military. As far as the families and anybody else knew, all six of the boys had been found and their remains recovered by army divers in 1960. One of the boys had been buried in his home town and the other five interred at Arlington National Cemetery.

The DeSalvos were flown by privately contracted helicopter to Hester Lake in September of 1989. Diving to the airplane they found it was in "fabulous shape." They felt that the Liberator was completely preserved. "The aluminum is shiny and the paint is clean. We saw a leather shoe and it is soft and supple and the parachutes were still white." There was a lot to see, but not much to interest a salvager. "The wreck was scattered over quite a [large area]. But it looks like the whole plane is there. Engines, instruments, radios. It's all there. It's all in the lake." The problem, however, was that it was a "big tangled mess." This is plainly seen in a video DeSalvo shot.

An unsigned memo in the Sequoia & Kings Canyon National Parks archives makes the park's next communication with DeSalvo interesting, but contradictory. It is now one year later and the hand-written memo, dated October 24, 1990, appears to be a summation of a telephone conversation between DeSalvo and somebody in the park. The memo's author outlines in bullet points the gist of a conversation. DeSalvo is not interested in pursuing a salvage effort with the plane in the lake because it is 100 percent destroyed, "except the landing gear," which is complete but "smashed up." The wreckage is concentrated in

Diver holds a shoe found in Hester Lake. IMAGE CAPTURE FROM VIDEO SHOT BY STEPHEN DESALVO. COURTESY STEPHEN DESALVO

"50–60 feet of water, with some scattered debris to 120 feet in depth." Also, "there are large yellow oxygen bottles and wooden flooring on the lake bottom."

The contradictory part is a letter from DeSalvo to Paul Fodor, Sierra District ranger, on September 13, 1990—that is, over a month before the unsigned memo. In it, DeSalvo discusses his passing interest in another airplane crash—several, actually—from October 24, 1941, when a squadron of P-40s were forced down in bad weather around the Sierra Nevada. Three of the craft crashed in southern Kings Canyon National Park. DeSalvo relates in his letter that he had seen debris from two of the planes the previous month in the backcountry, before the wreckage was removed, and is skeptical of plans to salvage and restore the P-40s, provided by somebody named Fourtner.

Seeing the P-40 wreckage has rekindled DeSalvo's interest in recovering and restoring the Hester Lake B-24. "After all, it is in better condition, and 100 percent complete." He has shown his videotape from last year's dive to "various metal fabricators and machinists," and their opinion is "that it is a monumental task, but not impossible." Therefore, he asks Paul Fodor for information on how to proceed with obtaining permission to proceed from the army or air force. Evidently DeSalvo was never told the content of the August 24, 1989, letter from the aviation and admiralty's law department of the air force.

Fodor's reply comes six months later, with apologies. Without letting on that the answer to DeSalvo's question has been known for two years, the district ranger tells him that the military "essentially said that they are not interested in any of the old airplane wrecks in the Parks." All DeSalvo will need is a "written permit from the Park Superintendent." DeSalvo never followed up on this.

The next searcher inquired about 463 and Hester Lake in 1993, with salvage and recovery once again the basis for interest. Christopher Thomas had a gentleman's agreement with the Yankee Air Museum in Willow Run, Michigan, former site of the enormous World War II Ford Motor Company aircraft assembly plant for the B-24 Liberator. According to Thomas, "They wanted to have a B-24 on display at Willow Run, where they were built. Their stumbling block was the main wing spar." If the museum could procure one they could build a restoration around it.

On October 22, 1993, Christopher Thomas wrote to the Sequoia & Kings Canyon National Parks superintendent inquiring about "procedure and requirements to recover this wreck" in Hester Lake. He promised, "Neither I nor anyone associated with this project would personally profit from this recovery."

Nearly four months later Superintendent J. Thomas Ritter responded to Christopher Thomas. Superintendent Ritter dredged up the unsigned, handwritten memo from October 24, 1990, and his letter essentially repeated the bullet-point list. The wreckage is in 50 to 60 feet of water with scattered debris to 120 feet deep. Large yellow oxygen bottles and wooden flooring are on the lake bottom. The aircraft is destroyed and not recognizable as a B-24. While there is no single part completely intact, certain components appear to be in good condition. Park staff have contacted Stephen DeSalvo, who has agreed to provide Thomas with additional information and a copy of his dive video. All he need do is call. Thomas is also referred to the new Sierra District ranger, Randy Coffman, if he wishes to pursue a salvage operation.

Accompanied by four friends, Thomas hiked over Bishop Pass in the summer of 1994. At LeConte Canyon, two remained behind to tend their camp and two made the arduous trip to the lake with Thomas. They found the route up to be challenging, especially the Notch. "We completely underestimated that climb up." All were convinced, "If we get back down to camp without breaking our necks, we'll count ourselves lucky." They had initially decided on making multiple day trips to the lake rather than camping there. The first day would be a survey on land and in the water. Once at the lake they realized how poor an idea that was. None of them wanted to return to Hester Lake; the lake approach was simply over their heads. Knowing they wouldn't return again to the lake, they made the best of their time.

The three adventurers brought wet suits, snorkeling gear, and flippers, and paddled around the lake. They also did some free-diving down to "interesting" pieces of wreckage. They had hauled up an underwater video camera to the lake but ended up not using it. Like the army divers from 1960, they were stymied by Hester Lake's silt. "You'd kick in any one area and it would billow up," erasing any visibility.

Thomas and his buddies had done their homework before the trip and this allowed them to identify much of the wreckage they saw under-water. "Up on the ridge above the lake (i.e., the area below Peak 12,483), was the ram for the aircraft's skid bumper." Located between the waist gun positions, the bumper protected the bottom of the fuselage in case the airplane accidentally tilted back during takeoff or landing. Finding the "severely mangled" skid bumper on the ridge above the lake below Peak 12,483 reinforces previous hypotheses that 463 was heading north-east before hitting close to the summit of the peak.

The three searchers made another important discovery. "One engine that we found was turning at impact. One engine we found was feath-ered," the non-rotating blades turned on edge to reduce drag. One engine wasn't feathered but wasn't turning on impact. And the fourth engine, we couldn't find. It was in a deep part of the lake and we couldn't find it in the time that we had." The condition of 463's engines is significant. Two of the three engines Thomas found were not operating at the time Turvey and Hester crashed.

A deployed B-24 Liberator tail skid bumper similar to the one found by Christopher Thomas in 1994, above Hester Lake. PHOTO BY PETER STEKEL

Obviously, Turvey and Hester crashed because they flew too low through mountainous terrain. But Thomas's evidence demonstrates that the boys were flying with a severe handicap not known to the writers of the 1943 accident report and subsequent visitors to the lake. According to the accident report, Turvey and Hester were flying an aircraft with a faulty radio compass. They were also flying into a quartering wind which pushed them to the eastern side of the Sierra Nevada when they should have been on the western side. A properly functioning compass would have helped tell them this. With his constant course-checking, navigator Bill Cronin would eventually discover they were not where they expected to be.

Being away from the coast, Owens Valley would not have been in blackout conditions, but to the boys aboard 463 it would have appeared pretty much that way. Even today Owens Valley is a dark place at night, and there are but four bright constellations of light: the towns of Lone Pine, Independence, Big Pine, and Bishop, with lots of empty and dark ground between them. Their last radioed position was in the Mojave Desert near Muroc, another dark area. Flying at night, the lightly populated San Joaquin Valley between Bakersfield and Fresno—the route they were supposed to be on—would have appeared dark to aviators in 1943. Given this, it's reasonable that Bill Cronin needed time to positively ascertain where 463 was after his last radioed position if he was navigating by pilotage and dead reckoning.

When the boys on 463 finally figured out their position, why didn't they radio this to Hammer Field? Were Turvey and Hester embarrassed to be lost? Perhaps. But that in and of itself is no reason they wouldn't have called home to say they were going to be late. Could the reason be that they were flying on two engines and losing altitude, and the boys in the cockpit were too busy flying the aircraft?

Christopher Thomas stumbled on the answer to this question by accident. When Thomas began his Hester Lake investigations in 1991, many of the players, both integral and peripheral, to the story were still alive. "One of the gentlemen I talked to who was up there in the late sixties, he had the VHF antenna reel unit [from 463]. It had the meter that shows how much of the antenna is let out. It's set to zero." This means that "At impact they didn't have their long-range antenna out." The boys in the cockpit may have believed that Sergeant Wandtke, their radio operator, was sending a signal out to Hammer Field with their new position. But that signal was going nowhere.

Like previous searchers at Hester Lake, Christopher Thomas thinks the debris field both in the lake and onshore indicates that 463 was heading northeast. They were not heading west, across the Sierra Nevada, toward Hammer Field. With engine trouble as they crossed the mountains the pilots were either in the process of turning east, toward Bishop, when they hit Peak 12,483, or they had already completed the turn. Their maps showed an auxiliary field located close by in Bishop. Maybe they were heading there.

"They made a bad decision," says Thomas. It wasn't one thing that caused them to crash. "It was turning, poor navigation, led by the poor decision to cross the Sierra Nevada in winter." Looking at what happened he's certain that "They had a mechanical failure," and, "Once they started to do that, they made the decision, as far as we can tell, to turn back toward the closest place that he [pilot Lieutenant Turvey] knew." Surrounded by mountains and losing power and altitude, "he ran out of time and space."

Philip Ardery flew Liberators and served as a B-24 instructor. According to him, with practice, you could fly the airplane on two engines. "But once you put your landing gear and flaps down and start an approach for a landing, the airplane is coming down." This could have been the case with 463—two engines out, and the pilots believing they were either on approach to Hammer Field or making an emergency approach to the field in Bishop.

Christopher Thomas and his friends were unsuccessful in their quest for the Yankee Museum. They could plainly see that "The main wing spar was gone. The outer portion [of the spar] that we could see, on one end, was completely destroyed. Everything was twisted, mangled, and not flyable." And so, they went home.

⌒⌒

In 2001 Kevin Neal completed a diving trip to Tinian and Saipan, exploring a sunken B-29. While researching that project he came across an aviation archaeologist named Craig Fuller. They got to talking about sunken aircraft in the United States, and the Hester Lake B-24 came up. People from Neal's Tinian/Saipan trip were interested, so plans were made for a 2002 expedition to the lake.

One of the participants, Paul Sweinhagen, wrote an article about it for a limited-release dive magazine. He called it "The Jackass Expedition"—not pejoratively (as some have supposed), but for the manner of getting all their gear up the trail. Mules were enlisted to carry tanks, rebreathers, dry suits, "and all the little stuff, plus carne asada for burritos, a hibachi, and boxed wine."

This first of a planned two-part article reviews the Hester Lake story accurately, and in depth, before concluding with an indication of the difficulties encountered by the expedition. "At the trailhead, the team was optimistic." That changed with every footstep, growing "tiresome by early afternoon, and ended painfully with the group seriously strung out." With a time schedule requiring 15 miles of hiking this first day, they pushed on, the lake seemingly "a mythical entity."

Their second day out was supposed to be a diving day, but no one was in any shape to make the final push to Hester Lake except Sweinhagen. He went alone, promising to survey the lake basin for a return trip the next year. His memory of the trip is fuzzy, but he does remember seeing large pieces of airplane wreckage. "It looked like they could have been wing spars or something to that effect. They were only 10 or 12 feet underwater, but you could make it out pretty well."

The expedition's lack of success was due to unrealistic expectations. "They were the right guys to do it, but unfortunately they were more dive types than mountain types. They didn't take into account how strenuous it was going to be getting up there." Sweinhagen never returned to Hester Lake and he never wrote a second part to his article. But expedition leader Kevin Neal came back older and wiser the following year.

Neal's 2003 Hester Lake trip, under the banner of Marine Expeditions International, was much better prepared, much better organized, differently outfitted, and comprised of people better able to handle life on the trail as well as in the water. There were nine participants. They all rode horses, with ten mules carrying the gear, considerably lightened from the previous year. Neal was adamant that everyone travel with the minimum amount of gear for camping and diving. There would be no repeat of 2002 when the crew groaned under the weight of their equipment. Estimated costs ran at more than $1,200 per person.

Despite their heightened level of preparedness the expedition was plagued with bad luck. Kevin Neal recalls, "We had injury. We had death." The mules were tied together and on the switchbacks below Bishop Pass the last mule in the string lost its footing and went crashing down, dragging several other animals with it. One mule was killed. Also dragged down was a horse and rider. The rider had to jump from the horse to save his life and suffered a broken rib and a hairline hip fracture. Taking a rest from riding, one of the other participants blew out his knee, hiking down the west side of Bishop Pass.

According to plan they reached LeConte Canyon in late afternoon and began to shuttle their gear to their base camp in the meadow below the Notch. The following day they shuttled diving gear to the lake. Bad luck dogged them. When the three divers hooked up their scuba tanks, the air "tasted funny," and, fearing contamination, they elected to not use them.

Using weights and their dive suits they were able to swim around and see things in the water, finding lots of wreckage along the shoreline. "It was hard with buoyancy suits to go much deeper" than 20 feet. Neal went out to the middle of the lake with weights and dove as far as he could. "I could barely see the bottom. There's still a lot of wreckage at the bottom."

After spending the day at Hester Lake they packed up their gear and shuttled it back down to base camp. Neal found it humbling to be on the site where the boys were killed. "It's a touch of human tragedy in the midst of a war where so many people were lost. Not much attention was paid to them." Having visited the crash site, Neal now comprehends the deep allure of the story. "I love history and I like diving and exploration," he says. When he heard about Hester Lake for the first time and realized there had been only one dive attempt since 1960, he knew it would be an interesting trip. So what if it didn't go according to plan? "Not many people had been to the lake; it was pristine." That was enough.

David Hill is the nephew of Robert Bursey, flight engineer on 463. In early September of 2003, a week before Kevin Neal's second Hester Lake expedition, Hill was guided over Bishop Pass, through Dusy Basin, and into LeConte Canyon by three Salinas, California, police officers. Their leader, Mike Groves, had a personal connection to the story: A friend of his father-in-law had met Clint Hester repeatedly in the backcountry during the 1950s.

Assisting Groves were his two friends, Ben Draeger and Andy Miller. The trip proved a tough one. The amount of gear each man carried totaled about 70 pounds, and included a two-man raft, underwater video camera gear, and 100 feet of cord in order to lower the camera into the water and obtain footage of the wreckage. Then, like so many others, they were stymied by the Notch. Only Groves continued on to Hester Lake.

Once he'd arrived, Groves shed his hiking clothes. Donning swim goggles he entered the lake, instantly impressed by what he saw. From the surface, there was one of 463's engines. "I saw it. I knew what it was. That's how clear the water is!" He dove down to the engine, still in awe. He figures the engine sat in water no more than 20 feet deep, "if that." Being so close to the engine figuratively and literally took his breath away. "It's so funny because *it is so out of place.*"

Although Ben Draeger didn't make it to Hester Lake, he still considered the trip successful. A backpacker his entire life, he says this was a different kind of trip. By bringing a relative of a crew member to the lake, "It was like we were going up there to do them some honor." He was also impressed with David Hill, who had never backpacked before. "I could tell how much it meant to him. Pushing himself the way he was to get up there was very motivating to everyone else involved."

David Hill was deeply moved by the experience. There was much to amaze and provoke awe. "As we came nearer the crash site, my overriding impression was one of isolation: the craggy high peaks, devoid of any life, contrasted starkly [with] the lush, tree-covered mountains back home. As a Vermonter, I couldn't imagine a more terrible resting place. I was also struck by the irony that here I was in California with a handful of strangers, much as my uncle had been so many years ago."

When Hill returned home he had a DVD of photos and video from the trip put together by Mike Groves, which he shared with his mother. "She was just so pleased that we would honor the memory of her brother," and "was very impressed that these three good guys, these police officers from Salinas, would take time out of their schedule, and day, and lives, to honor a flight crew of soldiers they didn't know." David Hill's commitment to this uncle springs from the belief that a person *never* be forgotten. Throughout his life, Hill says, "My uncle Bob was always a constant presence. My older brother was named for him. Our family always seemed to have pictures of Uncle Bob in his uniform somewhere in our houses."

People interested in telling the underwater story of 463 still visit Hester Lake. Martin McClellan, with New Millennium Dive Expeditions, was drawn to the story in 2004–2005 after being unable to solicit community support around Huntington Lake for a documentary film about *Exterminator*. "They were really up in arms. They didn't want anything to do with us." McClellan figures, "They'd been beaten and battered" in the past by salvagers who wanted to exploit *Exterminator* and her crew.

McClellan's biggest challenge with making a Hester Lake documentary film was obtaining approval from the park service to use helicopters to fly in personnel and equipment. He spent time between 2009–2011 on the project, but gave up the idea after he couldn't secure permission from the park service to use helicopters.

The alternative to helicopters was to use pack animals—a repeat of Kevin Neal's expedition—and McClellan wasn't interested. "Horses are limited to 80 pounds per animal," which meant at least thirteen horses to meet expedition equipment needs. And they would still have to haul everything up on their backs from LeConte Canyon to the lake. McClellan figured, "That would be [gear from] two or three horses" for each person on the trip. With projected expenses already penciled in at $10,000 per dive, New Millennium decided to give Hester Lake a pass.

Another set of searchers continues to express interest in Hester Lake. Divers and underwater film documentarians Peter and Trevor Fulks have been interested in producing a film about the Hester Lake B-24, and are currently seeking funding.

The latest attempt to explore below the surface of Hester Lake eliminates the need for diving equipment and a huge support staff by utilizing a remotely operated vehicle (ROV). These lunch-box-size, battery-operated submersibles weigh 5 pounds each and are tethered to an operator onshore. ROVs contain lights, an electric motor, and a movie and still camera. Video is transmitted to the operator via a 100 Mb RJ-45 Ethernet cable using a laptop computer.

In late summer of 2015, Walt Holm and Eric Stackpole visited Hester Lake with an ROV. They were joined by Craig Fuller, who ini-

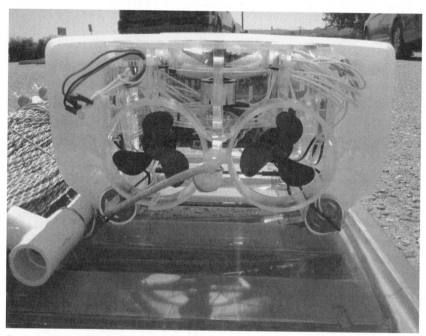

An example of a remotely operated vehicle (ROV). PHOTO BY PETER STEKEL, ROV COURTESY OF WALT HOLM AND OPENROV

tially got Kevin Neal interested in Hester Lake, along with three others. Fuller explored the lakeside and plotted a debris field on land. The team performed transects of the lake bottom and mapped the distribution of wreckage. The deepest part of the lake was about 115 feet, though the primary distribution of debris lies in water between 35 and 60 feet deep. With their ROV Holm and Stackpole saw everything visible in the video shot by Stephen DeSalvo in 1989. "The main body of wreckage, if you look at what's actually there," says Holm, "is basically the center of the fuselage and the wings from the inboard engines, inward." Essentially all that is visible is "the central core of the airplane."

David Hill is not the only family member to attempt Hester Lake. Bob Hester's daughter, Diane Coombes, and her husband were guided there on September 11, 1990. Coombes was unperturbed by climbing through the Notch, lacking any experience to tell her to be afraid or concerned.

Diane and Robert Coombes at Hester Lake, September 11, 1990.
COURTESY DIANE COOMBES

The entire climb from LeConte Canyon was tiring, though, and at times Coombes wondered if she would make it. What drove her was knowing she would be at the lake where her father's plane had crashed. Reaching the lake Diane Coombes was overcome by a sense of calmness and peace.

Coombes is not only happy she made the trip, but proud of it too. If she could not have a childhood with her father, at least she could see the place where he died. Being there was "one of the things I needed for closure." When she thinks of Hester Lake she remembers, "You hear that wind up there. It's as desolate as desolate can be."

CHAPTER 13

What They Faced

WHEN THEY ENLISTED, THE BOYS HAD NO REAL IDEA OF WHAT THEY would face in the aerial war over Europe and the South Pacific. Absolute numbers vary with the sources but nobody disagrees that deaths within the Army Air Forces were horrendous. According to Dr. Sheila E. Widnall, US Air Force Secretary between 1993–1997, over 52,000 airmen were killed in action during the war. Over 40,000 of those airmen killed served with the 8th and 15th Air Forces in Europe; losses greater than the total worldwide losses suffered by the US Navy and Marine Corps. Those who served came from all walks of life—from homes and farms and factories—and "were asked to become pilots and bombardiers, gunners and radio operators, typists and teachers, mechanics and engineers." All were asked to put their lives on hold. All hoped to come home at the end of the war, older, maybe wiser, but mostly they wanted to return whole and alive.

Figuring out why the Hammer Field boys found themselves flying over California in B-24s in December of 1943 is a complex matter. With historical hindsight it's easy to assume the boys rushed to enlist following Pearl Harbor. But the boys didn't rush at all. If they had, all six on 463 and eight on *Exterminator* would have enlisted by the closing of the day, December 8, 1941. They didn't. That makes figuring out what motivated the boys to enlist a difficult question to answer.

Only two of the boys had joined up before the war. William Darden enlisted on July 26, 1940, and Franklin Clark Nyswonger, on June 19, 1941. There's no explanation for Darden dropping out of college with less than one credit remaining for graduation. It wasn't impending marriage; that was nearly a year away.

Nyswonger's motivation for enlisting seems easier to explain. For whatever reason, Clark and all of the Nyswonger children were anxious to leave the family home as soon after high school graduation as possible. Clark Nyswonger was in the army one year after leaving high school.

Of the other boys, Ellis Fish enlisted for flight training the soonest following Pearl Harbor. But he still waited until February 24, 1942—nearly three months.

Samuel Schlosser enlisted on April 3, 1942, as a single man with no dependents. By his death twenty months later he was married, with a daughter. Being Jewish, and the son of refugee parents who lived in Poland, Austria, and Russia, Schlosser had the closest of all the boys to personal reasons for wanting to go to war.

Robert Hester enlisted on May 18, 1942. The requirement to complete two years of college in order to qualify for flight school had been dropped the previous January. All Bob needed to qualify for the program was to pass a rigorous proficiency test—no big deal for a boy who already had a civilian pilot's license and probably Civilian Pilot Training Program experience. When the college requirement was dropped, so too was the minimum age for officer candidates. You no longer needed to be twenty years old; eighteen was plenty. Voluntary enlistments were terminated, making it possible for draftees to join the air forces.

When he enlisted on May 26, 1942, Culos Settle was out of college, had been married eighteen months, and was teaching high school math in a small town close by to where he grew up, in Wilkesboro, North Carolina.

Charles Turvey enlisted on June 30, 1942, at the end of the school year, having completed two years of college. Any reasons for Charlie to not enlist in flight school had certainly evaporated when the two-year college requirement and minimum age requirements were rescinded.

Reasons for Richard Spangle's delay in enlisting are unknown, but his Monday, July 6, 1942, enlistment is too close to Independence Day to rule out spontaneity. He'd been married six weeks at the time.

Robert Bursey waited nine months after Pearl Harbor before enlisting on September 12, 1942. He had a skilled job in a critical defense-related factory and would have been exempt from the draft. There isn't any reason he had to enlist, or should have enlisted, except for wanting to follow in the footsteps of his Army Air Forces aviator brother-in-law.

Three members of *Exterminator*, from disparate sections of the country, enlisted within weeks of each other in October of 1942. Dick Mayo signed up on October 8, 1942. He could have easily stayed in school to finish his law degree, but was itching to get in the fight before the war was over. Seeking adventure, George Barulic enlisted on October 16, 1942. The oldest of any of the boys, thirty-year-old Donald Vande Plasch, was married the day before Pearl Harbor. He enlisted eleven months later, on October 28, 1942. Howard Wandtke waited an entire year after Pearl Harbor before enlisting on December 8, 1942. William Cronin waited fourteen months after Pearl Harbor, and was the last of the boys to enlist, on February 6, 1943.

We do know why some boys enlisted from the memoirs they wrote after the war. Army reservist Philip Ardery always wanted to learn to fly. He'd taken a few private lessons, but couldn't afford to go on. While lying in a tent in the July Wisconsin rain and mud during army practice maneuvers, "It crept into the back of my mind that I might learn to fly at government expense and at the same time break clear of the Infantry." He liked the idea that fliers weren't required to stand out in the rain all day, and they got to return to warm beds and hot meals, "if they got back at all."

John Boeman's reasons for enlisting were directly related to the Japanese attack on Pearl Harbor. "From that day there was no question in my mind. I would enter military service." Boeman had been reading the newspapers for the past two years and was convinced United States involvement in the Europe and the Pacific wars was not a question of "if," but of "when." Enlisting therefore gave him a choice of how to serve that being drafted would not.

Samuel Hynes was a marine dive-bomber pilot in the Pacific. In his memoir, *Flights of Passage*, he writes, "In the thirties airports were romantic, and drew boys to them." No one ever expected to fly. All that interested young boys like Hynes was being close to the romance.

As a small boy Hynes joined his chums to explore the nearby Naval Reserve Air Station hangar. He recalls the light inside, "soft and unfocused from the high ceiling, and the soft cries of the swallows that nested in the roof beams." There was always present the fragrance of hydraulic fuel and oil. Sounds within the hangar were soft and muted, giving the effect of a "careful quietness, as though the hangar were a church, and the mechanics priests engaged in some ritual that we were too young, and too earthbound, to understand." Not even in his imagination did Hynes see himself as a pilot, but, "I was a true believer in the religion of flight."

Leaving civilian life behind for the military required accepting huge changes in a boy's life. Many of them had never slept anywhere but in their own beds, and they experienced homesickness. Edgar J. Allen wrote of "a tearful parting all around as my family saw me off on the all-night train ride," from his home in the flatlands of Kansas. "The long journey did nothing to alleviate my sorrow. My family had always been central to me; and now, I had no idea when I would see them again."

Frighteningly, Allen recognized his life was no longer his own. "I had to relinquish control. Somebody else owned me completely, not just at that moment but indefinitely." Congruently came an awful realization. "There would be people out there who would be very serious about killing me."

Our involvement in the European and South Pacific wars was a great shock to most Americans. From the close of the Great War to the Japanese attack on Pearl Harbor, the United States was an isolationist nation. Pacifism in the 1920s and 1930s was not "merely a state of mind." It was a "powerful movement to be reckoned with." In its May 1931 issue, the popular church magazine, *The World Tomorrow*, reported the results of a poll that would startle Americans today. Nearly twenty thousand Protestant clergymen were asked whether their congregations should go on record and refuse to sanction or support any future war; 62 percent responded in the affirmative.

The Japanese attack on Pearl Harbor completely changed Americans' view, pacifists and isolationists included. And where obstruction in

Congress to military appropriations once existed, all barriers were broken down. Chief of staff since 1939, General George C. Marshall, who once begged for defensive and offensive weapons and was refused money, now got whatever he wanted.

If patriotism could be an element to why the Hammer Field boys enlisted, there was also romance. Airplanes during the 1930s held the same fascination for boys and girls that computers possessed in the 1990s, and electronic devices hold today. Aircraft were the most sophisticated and challenging machines of the age, and an endless source of inspiration for creative energies. Airplanes brought color, fun, and excitement to life. Winners of various air races or long-distance races were held up as heroes. Who *didn't* want to fly?

Boys read pulp magazines like *Air Trails* and *Flying Aces*. They read aviation novels situated during the Great War or in exploration, with titles like *Racing Around the World, Tom Swift and His Sky Train*, or *Airplane Boys in the Black Woods*. There were also the "Ted Scott Flying Stories," like *Flying to the Rescue* or *Over the Ocean to Paris*, which featured a front-cover aircraft similar to *The Spirit of St. Louis*.

They also went to movie houses to see popular pictures such as *The Dawn Patrol* and *Hells Angels*. As fascism swept across Europe and the Empire of Japan expanded across China, there were movies for older boys and their parents, such as *Captains of the Clouds, Dive Bomber, Test Pilot, Wings of the Navy, I Wanted Wings*, and *Spitfire*, Leslie Howard's inspiring drama about the iconic warbird's designer.

Growing up during an era of high unemployment and economic depression meant there was also a monetary reason behind wanting to fly. Aviation cadets were on a fast track to being commissioned officers as pilots, navigators, and bombardiers. From Preflight to Advanced training, the boys could become second lieutenants in less than twelve months, drawing a salary of $1,800 per year, with a 50 percent supplement for flight pay. In comparison, four-star generals were paid $8,000 per year.

After finishing flight training most boys were directed to bombers because that's where the need existed. Many were disappointed in the assignment because they knew nothing about bombers. They gravitated toward fighters, because that's all they saw in movies and read about in books and magazines. Dogfights looked exciting, hang the danger! Heavy bombers weren't in development until the 1930s, so there's no reason to think the boys knew anything about them. "Bombing was certainly no less dangerous than dogfighting; indeed, it may have been even more so, but it lacked the panache of the fighters."

Some bombing occurred during the Great War, and it was a shock to civilians. Germany dropped 9,000 bombs, for a total of 280 tons, on England. Slightly more than a hundred raids killed about 1,400 people and wounded 3,400 more, resulting in an "inordinate effect on people who had habitually regarded war as something visited upon someone else." Due to the long peace in Europe prior to 1914, there was a population that had never witnessed war firsthand.

To appreciate aerial war during World War II it's essential to understand the revulsion people felt against the trench warfare of 1914–1918. For the British, the military and political inclination toward bombing also derived from "the realization that Britain could never win a Continental war unless her adversary were first fatally weakened by some indirect means." This meant by blockade, intervention of a powerful Continental ally, or by bombing.

The genesis of this "bomber dream" was the work of Gen. Giulio Douhet, an Italian air commander. General Billy Mitchell, seen today as America's airpower savant, was an early adopter of Douhet's assumptions of airpower. Both men were Great War veterans and believed the next war could be shortened by abandoning fixed defensive positions in favor of pushing the offensive. And that meant airpower. Douhet believed future wars "would be won from the skies with vast fleets of long-range bombers, with the winning side the one that attacked first and without cease," obliterating an enemy's "airbases, communications, and centers of production." During the 1936–1939 Spanish Civil War, Germany, with its Italian allies, experimented successfully with terrorizing civilians along with attacking military targets from the air.

Once an enemy's ability to fight back was annihilated and air superiority achieved, the bombers would return to pound civilian populations without mercy. This "strategic bombing" was designed to destroy morale so civilians would either revolt or pressure their government to sue for peace before the need to commit large land forces to battle.

Douhet and Mitchell were convinced their tactics would be successful because they believed that "civilians lack the fortitude to stand up to vertical warfare waged with high explosives, incendiaries, and poisonous gases." Paradoxically they believed by making war more terrible, "warfare would actually become more humane," because the quick wars they envisioned would obviate the killing fields they'd seen during the Great War. Mitchell went so far as to write that terrorizing populations with "a few gas bombs" was preferable to "the present methods of blowing people to bits by cannon projectiles or butchering them with bayonets."

According to fighter pilot and ace General Adolf Galland, Hitler disagreed with Douhet and Mitchell's thesis. As early as 1942 Galland says Hitler knew strategic bombing wouldn't result in citizen uprisings or pressure on governments to end any war. Reichsmarschall Hermann Göring told Galland, "Don't talk to me about a possible internal collapse of the Bolshevist regime. The Führer regards such a possibility as absolutely out of the question. Even in Germany any action by subversive elements would be a hopeless undertaking. In the Soviet Union, a regime twenty years older than ours, it would be madness and suicide to try a *coup d'état* to overthrow the government."

After the war, the United States made a comprehensive study of German wartime morale, which has since been buttressed by recent research in Germany. The study's stark conclusions were that bombing had serious psychological effects, such as "defeatism, fear, hopelessness, fatalism, and apathy. War weariness, willingness to surrender, loss of hope in German victory, distrust of leaders, feelings of disunity, and demoralizing fear were all more common among bombed than among unbombed people." Yet, German society did not collapse, nor did the populace pressure their government to sue for peace.

The number of Great War dead is mind-numbing, but the statistics serve as avenues to discovery in explaining the thinking of post–Great War military planners. Over 35 percent of German men between the ages of nineteen and twenty-two when the fighting broke out were killed in the next four and a half years. Fifty percent of all Frenchmen between twenty and thirty-two at the war's outbreak were dead when it was over. Over one million British soldiers died. In Belgium there were still British stonemasons carving the names of the missing onto memorials when the Germans invaded in 1940. Total numbers of wounded were twenty-one million. By 1918, 70 percent of the British economy was supported by the war. By its end, the Great War had become the most deadly catastrophe to strike Europe since the Black Death.

While nations grappled with their Great War legacy, militaries did what militaries always do when not at war: They planned and prepared. Bombing appealed to planners because they felt the risks to their soldiers in airplanes was slight compared to risks facing ground troops. Sustaining this "bomber dream" throughout the war, "The Royal Air Force alone dropped a million tons of bombs on enemy territory," hitting 131 towns and cities. Some were attacked once and others repeatedly, with many nearly entirely flattened to the point of bombing the rubble. The apotheosis of this type of thinking led to England and America's January, 1943, Casablanca Directive. It called for "A sustained and unremitting air offensive against Germany and Italy," hitting precision targets, breaking German morale, and wearing down and destroying enemy fighter strength. This would be the job of the Hammer Field boys, their heavy bombers, and the Norden bombsight.

The Americans maintained that the Norden bombsight was so accurate, a bombardier at 20,000 feet flying over 200 miles per hour could drop a bomb into a pickle barrel. The British demurred. Around 1942, General Sir Arthur Harris, of Bomber Command, pointed out the Norden bombsight's disadvantages. "Its only tests thus far had taken place under ideal circumstances: during practice missions in the sunny, cloudless—and flak-less—skies of the US Southwest."

As the English knew already, and the Americans would soon discover, skies over Europe were seldom clear of cloud cover. If you're going to hit a pickle barrel from 20,000 feet you're going to have to first see it. Some of the boys liked to joke that when their bombs went astray, "There must not have been any pickle barrels on the ground that day." During clear weather, the Norden could direct 20 percent of an aircraft's bombs within a thousand feet of the target. The experience of the US Navy at the Battle of Midway is telling. A squadron of B-17s during the battle "could not claim a single hit on the large Japanese fleet, in perfect weather conditions."

If daylight and clear-weather bombing was 20 percent accurate, night bombing was a disaster. Therefore, to accomplish their goal of a sustained and unremitting air offensive, the bomber boys were committed to daylight attacks. Generals believed in daylight bombing because they believed "the bombers will always get through." This was predicated on the firepower of the B-17s and B-24s, which provided formidable defense against German pursuit aircraft. But on-board firepower of the bombers could not counter the offensive power of ground-based anti-aircraft flak. Lots of the boys would recount in their memoirs how flak made them feel like sitting ducks on their bomb runs when they had to fly a set course, set altitude, and set speed without deviation.

In 1943 RAF Air Chief Marshall Arthur Harris began living up to his nickname, "Bomber" Harris. He started the year with a list of sixty enemy cities he intended to obliterate, and "persisted despite intense pressure from his boss, Chief of the Air Staff Charles Portal, to concentrate on the top Allied bombing priorities, oil and communications—targets whose destruction was paying far greater dividends to the Allied cause than were being gained by the wholesale onslaught on the cities." Harris had other priorities. Effectiveness by 1945, not morality, became the watchword.

It wasn't only "Bomber" Harris who expressed little compunction when it came to dropping bombs on civilians—especially if it resulted in a competitive advantage. Contrary to his Führer's beliefs, Joseph Goebbels wrote in his diary for September 11, 1940, about the certainty that aerial bombings from Operation Blitz in London, Coventry, Birmingham, Manchester, and other English cities "would be decisive in forcing the British government to surrender."

The Japanese also placed faith in the "bomber dream." They had been bombing indiscriminately beginning with the January 1932 attack on civilians on Shanghai. "Thereafter, Japanese bombers targeted civilians in Nanjing, Wuhan, Chongqing, and other cities." Chongqing was targeted "in more than 200 air raids over three years from the end of 1938, bringing the total death toll up to 12,000."

The effect of RAF bombing led to about 600,000 German civilians falling victim to the air raids. "Three and a half million homes were destroyed, while at the end of the war seven and a half million people were left homeless." In one town, Pforzheim, a third of its 60,000 residents were lost in one night when it was bombed on February 22, 1945. Out of a population of twenty-five million, at least another 800,000 Germans were injured. Most casualties were women, children under the age of five, and the elderly. All others had either been evacuated to the country or were at the front.

The 8th Air Force's staggering losses demonstrate how horrible daylight bombing was for aircrews. There were 26,000 to 28,000 deaths, which is about 10 percent of the Americans who died during World War II. This number also represents 12.3 to 13.3 percent of the 210,000 combat crewmen in the 8th Air Force. A further 28,000 boys were shot down and were either prisoners of war or among the missing. Another 18,000 men were wounded. Taken all together (26,000 dead + 28,000 POWs/missing + 18,000 wounded = 72,000), 34.3 percent of those in combat with the 8th Air Force (210,000/72,000) were killed, wounded, or captured. Only submariners, with deaths reaching as high as 70 percent, had a higher fatality rate than 8th Air Force crews flying over Europe.

The boys flying in the South Pacific had one more worry added to the rigors of combat: the dangers of mechanical breakdown and the frightening chance of running out of fuel. An airplane flying over open ocean has no safe place to go when the pilot has to get out of the sky *right now*. For instance, during the Battle of the Philippine Sea on June 19 and 20, 1944, 425 Japanese aircraft were shot down in a battle known as the "Great Marianas Turkey Shoot." Of the 125 planes lost by the United States, "two-thirds of them [were lost] as a result of running out of fuel while returning in the dark from the long chase."

As for the boys, romantic notions of aerial combat and notions of the cleanliness of the air war were not to be. World War II aircrews escaped dirty deaths in trenches, but "The redemptive quality of aerial heroism was in the minds of journalists who had never pulled a charred corpse out of the wreckage."

One of the few boys who wrote of such things was Guy Gibson, an RAF pilot who actually published his memoirs during the war. Gibson's account of one such fiery loss is particularly gut-wrenching. One stormy, snowy night, a Wellington was returning from a bombing mission. "For some reason or other something went wrong and the great Wimpy crashed into a field and burnt up." With a friend, Gibson was the first to examine the wreck the following morning. Approaching the still smoldering bomber, "We could see quite clearly the pilot sitting still at his controls burnt to a frazzle, with his goggles gently swaying in the wind hanging from one hand." Without a word, "We began to retreat and were back in our operations hut within a few minutes." Each of them could easily imagine themselves in the cockpit being peered at by a friend.

John L. Stewart tells a similar story from his time in England. In thick ground fog Stewart and another pilot in his squadron were lined up for takeoff. Visibility was so reduced that both pilots blindly taxied off the runway and out of line. The first four Liberators in front of them took off, crashed, and burned. At last, the mission was scrubbed. "Later that day, one could see (and smell) rows of blackened bodies collected on a grassy knoll." Who knows whether these deaths were considered killed in action or accidental?

Aircrews suffered appalling losses throughout 1942 and into 1943. What makes the famous B-17 *Memphis Belle* so famous is that on May 17, 1943, the crew survived their twenty-fifth mission. At the time the feat was statistically nearly an impossible accomplishment. By January of 1943 mounting losses had exceeded replacements. On the August 17, 1943, raid on Schweinfurt and Regensburg, the loss rate was an unacceptable 19 percent. Then, to the horror of crews working out of England, in August of 1944 the number of missions was raised to 35, because commanders had decided "individual missions appeared less hazardous."

German, Japanese, Russian, and British crews flew, fought, and died with no end in sight. At least the British pilots were rotated out of combat for periodic rest or to serve as flight instructors. German pilots flew until they were either too wounded for combat or they were dead. American crews working out of North Africa had to fly at least fifty missions before being sent home to the "Zone of the Interior." In the South Pacific, US crews flew 500 to 600 combat hours before being sent home. It could take over twelve months to do so. The whole idea of a combat tour applied only to flight crews. "I was aware of the fairness of complaints from the ground forces that there was no combat tour for them. But only a very small number of the combat people from my old group lived to the end of such a tour."

Chances of survival for heavy bomber crews during World War II were grim. Looking certain death in the face, it took a special breed of man to enlist in a service branch that guaranteed one out of every three of your buddies wouldn't make it back home. These were the Hammer Field boys—boys like the crews of 463 and *Exterminator*. They saw what they were doing as simply doing their job. Those who survived the war would go home and pick up the lives lived before they answered the call to duty.

It's not enough to know these twelve boys from 463 and *Exterminator* died while serving their country. That they died "over here" in accidents rather than "over there" in combat doesn't matter. Given the grim odds of surviving aerial combat during World War II, there is a very real chance some or all of them would have been killed anyway. It's amazing that Lt. Culos Settle and Sgt. George Barulic made it back home unscathed.

After over seven decades it would be unfair for us to ascribe motivations to the Hammer Field boys for their enlistments and for their timing. Laying it all out to a country at war is too simplistic. Each boy had his reasons for wanting and waiting to get into the fight. We know how they fought, but we don't know why. At this late date, all we can say is they did what they did. That should be enough.

CHAPTER 14

Accidents: Why There Were So Many

Lt. Thomas Selfridge holds two aviation records that will never be broken. He was the first military officer from the United States to solo in a modern powered airplane. The date was May 19, 1908. The distance traveled was 100 feet. Serving as an observer, with Orville Wright as pilot, four months later the twenty-six-year-old Selfridge earned his other aviation record. On September 17, he became the first fatality from a powered aircraft accident.

The unprecedented buildup of the US Army Air Forces (USAAF or AAF) during World War II led to equally unprecedented numbers of aircraft accidents. Following the war the AAF compiled a statistical digest of accident numbers, rates per 100,000 flying hours, aircraft wrecked, and fatalities. They discovered 47,462 accidents, of which 5,533 led to fatalities, with 13,621 killed and 12,506 aircraft wrecked.

Recent research by Anthony Mireles has revised these data. Combing through all the accident reports he could find, Mireles came up with 6,350 fatal accidents and 15,530 pilots, crew, and ground personnel killed.

For his doctorate in history at Kansas State University, Marlyn Pierce studied accidents and fatalities in the AAF during World War II flight training. Pierce has calculated that there were, on average, ten deaths and almost forty fatal or nonfatal accidents each day of the war. The year 1943 was especially bad, with 2,268 fatal accidents leading to 5,600 deaths and destruction of over 2,500 aircraft. Though a drop in fatal accidents and fatalities occurred in 1944, the numbers were still high—nearly 2,000 fatal accidents, and the deaths of 5,000 pilots and crew.

There were plenty of reasons for accidents, fatal or not, during training. Some kind of mistake by the pilot was the biggest cause, but poor aircraft design and manufacturing and aircraft maintenance contributed. After all, ground crews during the war had just about as much experience working on military aircraft as the pilots did who flew them. The same is true with the people working in the airplane factories.

The number of aviation accidents grew as airpower grew. At the start of America's involvement in the Great War in April 1917, "the Air Service consisted of fifty-two officers and eleven hundred enlisted men." There were fifty-five aircraft; none of them combat types.

The Air Service became the Army Air Corps in 1926, and over the next fourteen years it remained about 10 percent of army strength. On September 1, 1939, the day Germany invaded Poland, starting World War II, the Army Air Corps was a small, almost fraternal, organization of 26,000 men, with 2,200 aircraft. During the 1920s and 1930s this smaller US air corps averaged fifty-one fatalities per year. That's an impressive number for an era when high admittance standards meant the "number of cadets in training never exceeded 500 for Primary and 270 for Advanced training."

As war with Germany and Japan became inevitable, the number of people serving in the air corps began to rise. In 1940 there were 51,185 serving in the air corps, and in 1941, corps strength was 152,125. The Army Air Corps became the Army Air Forces on March 9, 1942, and by 1944 consisted of 2.4 million personnel, representing 31 percent of the army's strength. By the end of the war the AAF had almost 80,000 aircraft and had trained nearly 200,000 pilots. An additional 124,000 who entered the pilot training program were either washed out or killed during training.

It's a simple equation. With America's entry into the war there were lots more people learning to fly, and this meant more accidents. Multiple institutional and administrative issues contributed to the numbers. Early in the war the army had trouble rounding up enough qualified flight instructors and finding enough qualified ground school teachers. These shortages led to the use of contracted private aviation schools to teach the boys how to fly. Embry-Riddle in Florida and Ryan Aeronautical in California were two of the larger, more-established schools, but there were others as well.

A shortage of qualified instructors meant that "Often, in the early part of the war, the instructors were themselves recent graduates of the flight program. Later, the majority of them were combat veterans." But using combat veterans didn't always work out well. Marlyn Pierce tells the story of one combat veteran, now an instructor, so bored from flying in circuits for gunnery practice that he experimented with flying his B-24 with all four engines feathered. "The resulting crash killed the pilot and several gunnery cadets."

Training accidents were random; they happened any time, any- and everywhere. Student pilots, navigators, and bombardiers, all known as aviation cadets, quickly learned that while there may be routine flights, there are no uneventful flights. "Man is out of his element in the air. Every flight, from takeoff to landing, is a series of events. The first of those events for which the pilot is unprepared ends the routine."

Throughout the war the Army Air Forces prided itself on being an organization with competent and confident pilots. While tacitly acknowledging that accidents were inevitable, the philosophy at the top of army command equated accidents with cadets doing something they shouldn't have done. There was an acceptance that cadets should suffer the consequences of not being good pilots. "Pilot error" is the term they used, but "human error" is more descriptive.

Errors are a natural feature of being human and can provide a learning environment. As B-17 pilot Truman Smith writes in *The Wrong Stuff*, "It is the mistakes and not the successes that give us wisdom to cope with the complexities of life." We shouldn't be robbed of our "right to make mistakes."

Not so, according to Chuck Yeager, who contemptuously dismissed these "weak sisters" killed in training accidents as likely being the first to die in combat. He recalls the sky over Nevada during training was "filled with green pilots practicing night landings, dogfighting, and strafing, so accidents were inevitable." In six months, thirteen pilots were killed, "And in nearly every case, the worst pilots died by their own stupidity—making a low-altitude turn that dropped them into the ground, or waiting too long to come out of a dive. Guys snapped wings off their planes doing crazy power dives, or buzzed into the side of a hill." It was a "gruesome weeding-out process."

Accidents directly attributable to pilot error occurred at all periods of flight, from taxiing for takeoff to landing and taxiing back to the hangar. Aviation cadets not only collided with each other in the air, they collided with each other on the ground. They also hit trees, buildings, telephone poles and wires, and ran into mountains. They hit the ground too hard while landing, overshot runways, and made wheels-up landings. They became lost and were never heard from again. They ground-looped. They also stalled and couldn't recover, or spun out of control and into the ground. Cadets even forgot to put on their oxygen masks and died of anoxia.

There were stupid mistakes caused by insufficient oversight by instructors coupled with youthful exuberance. Into this category would be "hot-dogging"—buzzing trains and cars, swooping down on houses, flying under bridges, flying too close to the ground, attempting aerobatics too low to the ground, and so forth. Sadly, poor fliers sometimes succeeded in not only killing themselves but their teachers as well.

Youth, inexperience, unfamiliarity with technology, technology that was imperfect or still in development, and a hastened training program that made mastering the skill of flying a difficult task all led to the inevitability that cadets would make mistakes, have accidents, and die.

In his memoir of the war, John L. Stewart writes of how the stress of flying combat missions actually began with the stresses introduced during training. The United States was a rural nation during World War II. The boys learning to fly were normally between nineteen and twenty-two years old, though occasionally older. Many had never been in any vehicle faster than a tractor or an automobile. They were people who had spent the majority of their lives as children. Now, after less than a year of training, most were flying multi-engine bombers at altitudes approaching 30,000 feet and at speeds over 200 miles per hour.

One way of dealing with stress during training, and then combat, was as endemic to boys of that age as it is to today's young men. When you're twenty years old, and embarked upon a great adventure, an adventure involving risk and the possibility of death, your first reaction to risk is denial. "Thoughts of getting killed were purged from the mind. Each of us younger flyers had the advantage of believing we were immune to harm."

In many memoirs or other books covering training during the war, it's rare to read about accidental injuries or deaths. Once the boys reached combat the accidents continued, even though mistakes and errors leading to those injuries and deaths are seldom discussed. Whether in combat or not, in their day-to-day flying the boys faced a high probability of being killed.

A paramount danger every time they went up day or night came from flying in formation. With formation flying planes were required to fly closely packed together. Flying in formation was developed to take advantage of the B-17 and B-24's defensive array of .50 caliber machine guns that provided overlapping firepower directed and focused on any fighter that attacked.

Joseph William Loftus, a second lieutenant and friend of Bob Hester's, was killed in combat due to a formation-flying accident during the 461st Bombardment Group's first combat mission. On April 2, 1944, Loftus was copilot of B-24H #41-29336. Another B-24H, #42-52388, flown by 1st Lt. William Zumsteg (who had crashed-landed a B-24 on December 5, 1943 at the Manzanar War Relocation airfield during training), had dropped out of his formation position. As they were trained to do, 2nd Lt. Sidney Wilson, piloting with Loftus, moved their Liberator into the spot vacated by Zumsteg. They made their bomb run over Bihac, Yugoslavia, and about three minutes after leaving the target, all hell broke loose.

Wilson and Loftus appeared to lose their position and, rising from below, Zumsteg moved his Liberator to fill the gap and reclaim his former position in the formation. In effect, he climbed under, and then collided with, Wilson and Loftus. Zumsteg's B-24 was nearly cut in half by the other Liberator's propellers and it went down with the loss of the entire crew of ten. Violently spinning out of control, Wilson ordered his crew to abandon ship and they all got out safely, except Joseph Loftus. Escaping through the top hatch of the cockpit, it appears Loftus was struck by the spinning Liberator as he tried to exit. His parachute did not open and Loftus fell to his death. The remaining nine boys were captured and sent to a POW camp.

Mastering formation flying was scary enough in clear weather, but the "pucker factor" in clouds was extreme. It was a tricky business in the best of conditions during the daytime, hell at night, and frequently fatal. "Sometimes the sky was bright with fire from a midair collision. Occasionally you might see the clouds light up, and you would know that some plane had hit something."

The army knew that "the accident rate for flying at night was two to four times greater than flying in daytime." The problem for the training program was when to teach such skills. Some thought them too difficult to learn until Advanced training, and others thought the skills so important that they needed to be taught at the very beginning. Many crews found themselves in Europe or the South Pacific and unable to fly combat missions because they lacked the requisite night-flying or weather skills, or because navigators couldn't navigate in poor conditions.

Getting lost due to poor navigation was another leading cause of accidents and death, and making it through training was no guarantee you wouldn't be killed in an accident overseas. Or that you would actually make it to combat. "Between 1943 and 1945, four hundred AAF crews were lost en route to their theaters." Given that there were ten men on each heavy bomber like the B-24 and B-17, there is the potential these losses could represent four thousand boys who never made it to combat.

It's easy to lose situational awareness and get lost when flying an airplane. This is especially true when flying in bad weather, and even more so when flying in combat. There is always a lot going on in the cockpit and, even with as much training as they received, the boys were always short on practical experience. That's why the crews on 463 and *Exterminator* were in Phase training to begin with, polishing their navigation and piloting skills on long practice flights.

A radio operator's ability or inability to learn Morse code was another factor leading to accidents. "There was a near unanimous agreement among all the cadets that the most difficult part of ground school was learning Morse code."

Inadequately lit airfields or aircraft that were not mechanically sound being cleared for takeoff also contributed to accidents. Which begs the question about 463: Why was it allowed to fly when at least one pilot (Lt. John K. Specht), and presumably many others, were aware of its faulty radio compass? That could have been one proximate cause for Turvey and Hester getting lost and crashing, leading to the deaths of all six crew members.

The men in charge of the Army Air Forces were not oblivious to the accidental death and destruction going on around them. In a 1944 report to the Army Air Forces, General Arnold expressed his awareness of the inherent dangers involved in training for aerial combat. "In these maneuvers a few are bound to be injured or killed, but the overwhelming proportion of men are better prepared to defeat the enemy." As the statistics rolled in, what they would not be able to comprehend until much later was the scale of the accidents and number of fatalities.

The AAF responded to the rise in accident numbers and deaths by creating a bureaucracy focused exclusively on safety. The Office of Flying Safety was founded in 1942 to combat the rise in accidents and seek solutions. The duty of the organization was to investigate each incident, analyze the data, and produce a written document with conclusions about what happened, why it happened, and suggest solutions or recommendations to ensure that it didn't happen again. More than half of their reports attributed accidents to pilot error. The remaining causes for training accidents were mechanical errors, supervisor errors, and instructor errors. During the first half of 1944, more than 1,100 accidents in the official accident report were attributed to instructors. As with 463, without survivors or witnesses to quiz, a large category of accidents fell under the heading of "Unknown."

Solutions to accidents included "transferring more experienced personnel to bases with higher accident rates," and updating training programs. Also, ensuring that "[r]eturning combat pilots [who served as instructors] understood their responsibilities in training command." "Accident officers" were assigned to squadrons to pound into the heads of aviation cadets the principles of safety. Achieving their goals involved posters, briefings, and a written exam for all pilots covering safety procedures.

Pilots should not be held responsible for accidents due to design flaws or imperfections and the inexperience of the people manufacturing the parts and assembling the airplanes. Though they represented the epitome of design and reliability for the era, World War II aircraft are antiquated and mechanically untrustworthy by today's standards. Many parts were defective because of poor design, poor manufacturing standards, or workers untrained in the manufacturing process. "Throughout the war, material failure was the primary contributing factor in more than 13,000 accidents," and included 5,500 powerplant failures, 4,400 landing-gear failures, and over 1,000 airframe failures.

The army system was designed to train pilots and crew, and train them quickly. After all, there was a war on. For the army to have an acceptable number of qualified pilots they had to recruit a large pool of candidates. The anticipated washout rate of students who entered the program was 50 percent. Most of these boys would wash out during Preflight training, which was strictly an academic program, with psycho-motor and psychological tests and physical education.

From there the boys went on to Primary, Basic, and Advanced training. Each level increased in difficulty, with larger, faster, and more-complex airplanes to fly. Cadets still washed out, but not so much for academic reasons or poor test results. Uncle Sam had invested quite a bit of money and resources in the students at this level, and increasingly needed something dramatic to cause a washout. Frequently this meant washing out for being involved in accidents, including the ultimate wash-out: getting killed.

The most dangerous time for pilot training was not at the very beginning, at Primary or Basic, but during Advanced. Or, as Turvey and Hester demonstrated, during Phase training. These were the times when pilot error became a huge factor in accidents. (See Table 1.) When an aviation cadet got behind the stick of a Stearman trainer during the Primary training level, he flew straight and true in an underpowered and slow-moving aircraft, without any fancy maneuvers. He also flew only in the daytime and in good weather.

Higher-performance aircraft during Advanced training were more complex to operate and less forgiving of errors committed by pilots. Pilot error in the form of too much confidence was a major cause of student accidents at the Advanced training level. As pilots moved from Advanced training to their final stage, Phase training, and were introduced to four-engine bombers or high-performance pursuit aircraft, there was another increase in accidents.

The issues were not only more engines, and/or more-powerful engines, but also more-complex instrument panels, and such seemingly simple things as having to make sure you raised and lowered retractable landing gear. It might seem intuitive to us today, but for boys who had never worked an automobile gas pedal, brake, and clutch, there were significant coordination issues to keep track of. A pithy 1943 army accident study neatly summed up problems faced by newbie pilots: "The planes are powerful and the training period short."

Darden, Settle, Turvey, and Hester probably thought of themselves as highly trained and experienced pilots. Reviewing again the accident report for *Exterminator*, we know that Darden had 1,453.05 hours gained over a period of about three years. The record is unclear regarding exactly when he got his wings, but does indicate that he served as a flight instructor from January through September of 1942, with 235.1 hours in the B-24, but only 128.3 in the previous ninety days. Darden had completed Transition training on July 1, 1943, so had been certified to fly Liberators for a total of six months, or 159 days. This means Captain Darden had, on average, 39.2 hours per month in the B-24. That's the equivalent of one long flight each week.

Turvey began Primary flight training on December 17, 1942, and had accumulated 613.2 total hours, with 259.3 in the Liberator. In the last ninety days Turvey had flown 150.3 B-24 hours.

The accident reports are mum on Settle or Hester's flying experience. It's safe to assume, though, that Settle would have had about the same level of experience in the air as Turvey; they were both pilot-rated at roughly the same time. Hester, on the other hand, as copilot on 463, would have been less experienced in the B-24, though his pre-Liberator experience would have been equal to that of Turvey and Settle.

Table 1. Airplane Accidents in Continental United States, by Principal Model of Airplane

Army Air Forces Statistical Digest World War II
Second Printing, December 1945, Page 310
Prepared by Office of Statistical Control
Table 214 -Airplane Accidents in Continental United States, by Principle Model of Airplane - Number and Rate: 1942-1945
(Rates are per 100,000 flying hours.)

Year	B-29	B-17	B-24	B-25	B-26	A-20	A-26	A-36	P-38	P-39	P-40
1941-1945 All Accidents											
All Accidents	272	1589	1713	921	739	728	181	226	1403	1934	3569
Rate	40	30	35	33	55	131	57	274	139	245	188
Fatal Accidents	63	284	490	233	223	167	29	24	337	369	324
Fatalities	461	1757	2796	936	993	303	77	24	379	395	350
Airplanes Wrecked	119	479	746	446	408	331	50	69	758	865	967
1942											
All Accidents	0	146	123	151	165	219	0	9	247	414	798
Rate	0	55	75	104	162	206	0	409	234	351	507
Fatal Accidents	0	28	31	39	52	47	0	2	67	80	78
Fatalities	0	183	165	185	249	88	0	2	76	83	94
Airplanes Wrecked	0	46	46	66	88	87	0	3	124	171	202
1943											
All Accidents	5	539	457	284	304	282	2	193	503	904	1070
Rate	72	39	39	44	65	155	<0.5	273	165	228	297
Fatal Accidents	3	120	157	85	85	65	1	20	112	186	108
Fatalities	46	789	1023	376	382	127	2	20	132	193	111
Airplanes Wrecked	3	182	240	139	159	134	1	56	267	403	285
1944											
All Accidents	88	638	779	239	195	182	44	23	467	590	1280
Rate	59	25	33	24	37	78	84	248	128	228	127
Fatal Accidents	21	105	233	62	66	44	9	2	111	99	102
Fatalities	150	598	1268	212	280	74	29	2	118	115	110
Airplanes Wrecked	41	203	359	123	123	92	14	10	258	278	360
1945											
All Accidents	179	266	354	247	75	45	135	1	186	26	421
Rate	34	23	29	24	31	127	51	<0.5	78	156	115
Fatal Accidents	39	31	69	47	20	11	19	0	47	4	36
Fatalities	265	187	340	163	82	14	46	0	53	4	35
Airplanes Wrecked	75	48	101	118	38	18	35	0	109	13	120

(From Table 214 *Army Air Forces Statistical Digest for World War II*)

P-47	P-51	P-63	F-4/5	F-6	C-46	C-47/53	C-54	Advanced Trainers	Basic Trainers	Primary Trainers	Communications	Totals
3049	824	251	223	14	145	604	22	13511	4881	8256	2407	47462
127	105	131	145	62	29	20	18	55	27	48	108	
404	131	39	48	2	19	109	4	943	825	333	133	5533
455	137	47	52	2	94	648	16	1888	1175	439	197	13621
1125	358	109	127	7	39	181	5	2227	1558	1032	500	12506
106	3	0	40	0	2	49	1	2835	1200	1788	618	8914
245	102	0	292	0	<0.5	26	<0.5	78	32	45	432	
13	1	0	10	0	0	14	0	210	193	91	42	998
14	1	0	10	0	0	93	0	363	275	122	65	2068
41	1	0	21	0	0	23	0	473	326	286	132	2136
958	186	2	54	0	24	212	1	4992	2262	4131	1202	18567
163	210	<0.5	218	0	59	31	38	64	31	54	130	
133	28	0	9	0	4	40	0	327	387	169	59	2098
145	30	0	9	0	12	266	0	679	541	226	88	5197
380	72	1	26	0	8	54	1	751	712	482	205	4561
1303	318	136	83	3	46	255	12	3964	1337	2086	477	14545
122	111	128	159	82	32	19	38	43	21	43	97	
183	52	25	16	0	5	41	2	292	219	68	26	1783
217	54	27	18	0	29	212	7	625	316	86	37	4584
474	137	69	46	2	11	78	2	739	473	232	120	4244
682	317	113	46	11	73	88	8	1720	82	251	110	5436
97	79	133	73	58	23	11	9	44	22	39	60	
75	50	14	13	2	10	14	2	114	26	5	6	654
79	52	20	15	2	53	77	9	221	43	5	7	1772
230	148	39	34	5	20	26	2	264	47	32	43	1565

Phase training came in two parts. The first part involved learning to operate the new plane. With the second part, the pilot was joined by his crew. Hester would have missed the first part. Therefore, subtracting Turvey's 259.3 hours in the Liberator from his total of 613.2 hours gives Hester at least around 353.9 hours from Primary to Basic to Advanced flight training, before he joined the crew of 463. But Hester also could have had as little as 271 hours' experience, along with no experience at all in the Liberator.

The losses military planners anticipated once war began helps to explain the rush to train as many crews as possible in as short a time as possible. Four months before the Pearl Harbor attack, planners were predicting that combat losses in an air war against Germany would be so great, the entire force would need replacing every five months! How would such losses affect the morale and psychological well-being of the boys who would be required to face such a horrendous rate of attrition? Where would the huge number of candidates come from, to apply, be screened, and then trained for such a distressing reality? Who would want to face such odds?

John Boeman was one of those boys expected to make up the difference, and he admits to being ignorant of it at the time. "I didn't know then, and did not learn for many years, that the Army Air Forces planners had in fact estimated that operational losses in combat would be 5 percent per mission, and that we who volunteered were expected to provide the manpower pool from which they would draw replacements to make up those losses."

American boys rose to the challenge probably because they didn't know what the challenge entailed in a practical life-and-death sense. "In FY 1941 nearly three times as many men, 9,272, applied for pilot training as in the proceeding eighteen years combined. However, the next year sixty times that number, over 550,000, would apply for flight training." In 1941, 26 percent of that 9,272 would be accepted. The need was so dire, and the pool of candidates so deep, that in 1942 there were 52 percent accepted. As General Arnold expressed it, to succeed in their goals, training of aircrews would have to be done no differently than assembling automobiles on Ford's mass-production assembly line. This philosophy would interject a base-level degree of error that contributed to airplane accidents.

As the war progressed training had to be reduced to its core principles. The army couldn't afford to take two years to train a pilot. Even the eventual one year it took was too long for some, especially the first Americans to join the fray in 1942. New crews were needed, not only as replacements to fill attrition, but also to build up the force to the levels required to assist and take pressure off the British. The need to prepare aircrews required a shortening of training programs, and this was reflected in simplifications that facilitated General Arnold's assembly-line metaphor.

A flying technique that resisted the instructional assembly-line model involved flying in bad weather. General Arnold insisted that pilots needed to learn how to fly in all conditions, and that meant flying in bad weather. At least one pilot had greater concerns. When Edgar Allen entered Phase training in mid-1943, "Weather conditions were the least of our concerns." Of more import was the fact that "[we] could never be certain of an airplane's condition," because the best planes were reserved for combat. "That left us with the dregs," and, "during our preflight inspections, we would sometimes find parts missing, even though the airplanes had been signed off by Engineering as 'ready to fly.'"

Nevertheless, weather took its toll. "Over 2,700 accidents during the war were attributed to bad weather conditions." Many weather-related accidents occurred because the pilot wasn't sufficiently trained in instrument flying. Instrument flying was another technique that did not lend itself to assembly-line training. "Even [General] Arnold noted the difficulty in mastering flying by instruments." He observed that it took between fifteen to thirty hours for *experienced* pilots to learn the skill. The accident report for *Exterminator* shows that after three years of flying and 1,453.05 hours in the air, William Darden had finally earned his instrument rating on October 9, 1943. Two months of experience before his final flight gave Darden a total of 39.55 hours on instruments, and a paltry 1.25 in the previous thirty days.

The accident report for 463 shows that on his final flight, Lt. Charles Turvey was flying at night, in bad weather, with 97.2 hours of instrument training (58.3 in the previous thirty days) and 37.3 hours of night flying (7.2 in the previous thirty days). That's anything but hot stuff, but significantly more than Captain Darden's experience.

Fighter pilots were especially prone to accidents during Phase training. Like their friends in the big bombers, this was where fighter pilots transitioned to the aircraft they would be flying in combat. Heavy bomber pilots were selected on the basis of their flying ability and leadership skills, since they would be captains of ships with nine men under them. For their Phase training in the big bombers, pilots could fly with an instructor. Fighter pilots were selected on the basis of their aggressiveness to drive home the attack. "The transition to single-seat fighters presented a unique challenge. Because of the lack of two-seat tactical combat fighters, a single-engine pilot's first transition flight was by necessity a solo flight."

There are a glaring number of fighter plane accidents seen in the Army Air Forces Statistical Digest *for World War II*, especially with the P-40 and P-47 (see Table 1). Theirs was a more risky type of flying than the bombers, but the number of fatalities in bombers was significantly higher. When a fighter pilot crashed and burned it was one person. When a B-24 or B-17 went down it could mean the deaths of ten people. There were 1,757 B-17 and 2,796 B-24 fatalities between 1941 and 1945. The greatest number of fighter aircraft fatalities was in the P-47 Thunderbolt, with 455—which also experienced 3,049 total accidents.

USAAF accident fatalities rose from 2,068 in 1942 to 5,197 in 1943, and dipped slightly in 1944 to 4,584 before dropping to 1,772 in 1945, according to the *Army Air Forces Statistical Digest for World War II*. (Totals from the *Statistical Digest* don't always jibe with other sources or books on the subject.)

Naval aviators suffered equally with their army counterparts, and total naval aviation deaths from all causes during the war was 12,133. Between December 7, 1941, and December 31, 1946, 3,618 navy and marine pilots died in enemy action, with 2,891 deaths being from air combat and 727 from "other action." Deaths from nonoperational (that is, noncombat) plane crashes numbered 3,257. Deaths from aviation accidents other than plane crashes or not under military jurisdiction were 155. Another 1,471 deaths were from accidents other than aviation, disease, or other causes. As can be seen, combat losses were actually fewer in number in the South Pacific than losses from accidents or non-operational causes. As for the number of aircraft involved, "In 1943 in the Pacific Oceans Areas theater . . . for every plane lost in combat, some six planes were lost in accidents. Over time, combat took a greater toll, but combat losses never overtook noncombat losses."

In his 1944 report, General Arnold is actually pleased with how low the rate of accidents compares with prewar numbers, even though prewar fatalities were on the magnitude of fifty per year. He justifies this attitude by saying that pilots "must receive training which will enable them to undertake their combat missions safely." To do this, "their own safety requires that they be trained in night and bad weather flying, which, of course, raises the accident rate here, but tremendously reduces the combat losses abroad." But combat losses didn't approach training losses, at least during the first thirty-two months of the war. During that time the Army Air Forces lost over 11,000 planes to accidents in the continental United States, and 7,700 in combat zones.

Investigators often didn't know what caused an accident because the pilot was killed or the airplane completely destroyed by fire or explosion. As Philip Ardery wrote after witnessing a fiery aerial collision, "By the time the fire reached the ground there was almost nothing left. The few bits that had not been consumed had fallen clear of the flames. Where the collision had occurred the sky was black with smoke." Two planes were involved with the loss of twenty men.

Aircraft accident sites for the uninitiated were a terrible reminder of where luck and skill ended. While waiting to be assigned to aviation cadet status, future congressman Jim Wright was asked to drive an officer to a mountainside crash site. "When we got there, the sight was sickening. The plane's fuselage seemed totally consumed, black from the carbon of the fire's toxic smoke. An acrid, dark cloud idled off, overhead and to the east. There was a noxious smell, like burning rubber. The medics were there with stretchers," carrying away cadavers, "burned crisp, blackened flesh covering lifeless bodies with trickles of red blood oozing out of little crevices here and there."

Accidental death numbers during military training were high and they were bad. But there's evidence the United States civilian population suffered greatly as well. According to the Bureau of Labor Statistics, between 1942 and 1945, "More than 75,000 Americans died or became permanently and totally disabled in industry during the war." Added to that were 378,000 Americans who suffered a permanent partial disability.

Naiveté, inexperience, and general lack of psychological readiness of the boys for the task at hand were also factors in the high accident rate. Pilots were confronted with "confounding situations" that continually cropped up, "one after another, from mission to mission, with little time and no expertise for resolving them," and they lacked training in such matters. What they did receive was a concept of blind obedience and discipline that some pilots felt conferred no insight into how they should command a bomber crew in combat. The training cadets did receive that did them good "had been concentrated almost entirely on learning how to fly an airplane."

In analyzing the safety record of the air forces, a postwar report concluded, "The heavy accident toll experienced during the hurried wartime expansion of the AAF was the price which had to be paid to achieve the airpower required for victory. That price was accepted as part of the cost of the war." When it came time to collect on that accepted price, the cost was borne by people like Charles Turvey, Robert Hester, William Cronin, Ellis Fish, Howard Wandtke, William Darden, Samuel Schlosser, Franklin Clark Nyswonger, Dick Mayo, Richard Spangle, and Donald Vande Plasch. What's amazing is not that so many pilots were killed and aircraft lost to training accidents within the United States during the war—it's that the numbers were so low.

CHAPTER 15

Some Were Unlucky

VISITORS HAVE HAUNTED HESTER LAKE AND HUNTINGTON LAKE IN the years since 463 and *Exterminator* were found. For whatever reason they visit, the question of what happened to the two B-24s always surfaces. The cause of 463's accident seems more evident than that of *Exterminator*; the Liberator hit an unnamed peak at 12,483 feet and crashed into Hester Lake. *Exterminator's* accident is more difficult to explain other than there was a mechanical issue the pilot felt would be fatal to the aircraft and crew. His decision to ditch the B-24 became a cruel and ironic self-fulfilling prophecy.

Anyone who studies the two airplane crashes brings an additional layer of interpretation to what was originally postulated from the 1943 accident investigations, the 1955 recovery of *Exterminator*, and 1960 discovery of 463 by James Moore, Frank Dodge, and Leroy Brock. The IDPF for Robert Bursey contains a tantalizing clue as to 463's last moments. Nevertheless, what happened to the two B-24 Liberators in December of 1943 will always remain a mystery.

—◦—

Accident investigation was a new and inexact discipline for the Army Air Forces during World War II. However, fixing the cause and laying blame for *Exterminator's* loss was rushed. In part this was because the entire bomb group that Darden and his crew belonged to, along with the accident investigation board, were four weeks away from being deployed to a combat zone, and some amount of administrative tidying up was undoubtedly desirable. Initially the accident was "100 percent undetermined," and due to a "collision in flight with [an] object." But the final report was changed to "50 percent pilot error, 50 percent unknown." Despite that 50/50 determination, the report submitted on December 27, 1943, by the Office of Flying Safety concludes, "It is the opinion of the Board that the accident is attributable to personnel error."

Lt. Culos Settle testified that *Exterminator* lost a propeller governor on the #2 engine just as they began to peel off (i.e., turn) north of Huntington Lake. Settle also testified how he checked the tachometer, looked at the propellers, obeyed Darden's order to reduce power to #2, and that the prop "sounded all right." They were losing altitude, and that's when Captain Darden gave the order for the crew to "get out of here." Then came Darden's order, countermanded, to the engineer to change some fuses—all the while ringing the bailout bell and ordering the crew to leave the aircraft. Given the emergency in the cockpit and the need for quick decision-making and getting his crew out of the Liberator, Darden can be excused for changing his mind about the fuses. The three examining officers decided to ignore any indicated mechanical difficulties with *Exterminator* and apparently interpreted Darden's actions as panic, perhaps leading to their conclusion of "personnel error."

Lieutenant Settle had trouble opening the bomb bay doors and they had to be opened manually by Sergeant Barulic. Curiously, Settle couldn't hear the bailout bell from the bomb bay. A warning horn sounded, which Settle interpreted as indicating the landing gear was being lowered. But the warning horn quit suddenly. Before exiting the plane, Lieutenant Settle looked forward from his position at the bomb bay and could see the instrument panel. "The engines were putting out 25 inches on all four engines," which would have been normal, given their altitude. Between 300 and 500 feet aboveground, Settle jumped. Barulic was close behind. It was about 09:50, December 6, 1943.

The weather forecast over the San Joaquin Valley that day was not the best: scattered and broken clouds from 5,000 to 6,000 feet, with a danger of icing, visibility 3 to 5 miles and increasing by 10:00 a.m., and low clouds obscuring the peaks in the Sierra Nevada. There was a possibility for rain or snow showers. Statements by Lieutenant Settle and Sergeant

Barulic make no mention of adverse weather the morning *Exterminator* was lost. The only thing Settle says remotely about the weather is that he saw a cloud, and they would have hit it in 2 miles had they not turned back after *Exterminator*'s problems began.

Yet, it is to the weather the investigation board turns to in order to justify their determination that Captain Darden was at fault. Referring to a comment made by Lieutenant Settle that "over the lake it [the wind] was blowing west," the board decided that "A strong wind from the southeast is believed to have caused a downdraft which confused the pilot momentarily." They decided on this because Settle told them the wind was "[p]retty strong, and later that afternoon I went over the lake

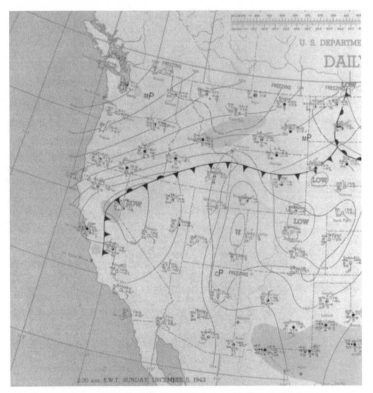

Weather map from December 5, 1943, shows a front moving through central California. UNITED STATES DEPARTMENT OF COMMERCE, WEATHER BUREAU

in a boat and the waves almost turned it over. Pretty strong wind. It was from the east. Blowing east to the west. Two high peaks just in front might create a downdraft."

The weather map for December 5, 1943, shows a front approaching Fresno and Hammer Field. By December 6 at 2:30 a.m. EWT (Eastern War Time), or 11:30 p.m., December 5 in Fresno, the front has passed and is located on a line between Santa Barbara on the west and Las Vegas in the east. Strong winds from the east across the Sierra Nevada crest could be expected due to the counterclockwise airflow associated with low pressure systems. There might also be a danger from atmospheric

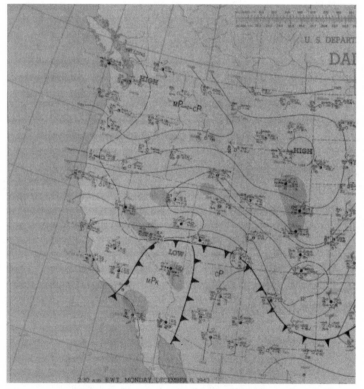

Weather map from December 6, 1943, shows the front has moved past central California, and there is clear weather around Huntington Lake. UNITED STATES DEPARTMENT OF COMMERCE, WEATHER BUREAU

rotors, extremely turbulent and circular movements of air that produce equally extreme up- and downdrafts.

The weather map for December 6 suggests the examiners may have been right in surmising a strong southeast wind caused a downdraft. A wind from the east would mean the lee side of the weather was on the ridges and peaks west of the Sierra Nevada crest. This is where downdrafts from "rotors," could be expected. Retired airline pilot Mike Tanksley has flown over the Sierra for years and has experienced its winds and its storms. "While it is less common for the wind to be from the east over the Sierra, it does happen when there is a stationary high pressure system sitting over the Great Basin, and occasionally when a slow-moving low goes south of the area in question." This condition is shown on the weather map for that day.

The board believed that "low altitude with reference to surrounding terrain and the pilot's lack of familiarity with the terrain caused him to commit himself to landing in the lake as an emergency procedure." Also, "He was apparently unable to maneuver so as to avoid a downwind landing." The board's final conclusion: "There is no definite evidence to show mechanical difficulties resulting in a lack of power."

The reason for there being "no definite evidence" is because the investigators were unable to examine the actual airplane. The Liberator was on the bottom of Huntington Lake. Why the investigators didn't consider mechanical problems with *Exterminator*'s loss is a conundrum. *Exterminator* was a Willow Run B-24 produced by Ford. These were airplanes Charles Lindbergh deemed "the worst piece of metal aircraft construction I have ever seen."

Additionally, from their first day at Hammer Field on October 29, 1943, the 461st Bomb Group suffered a paucity of serviceable aircraft. Many of the airplanes assigned to the Group after its arrival were found to be in poor condition and required long periods of maintenance and a number of engine changes. "A grossly inadequate supply of B-24 parts, which included prop governors, added to the difficulty of maintaining airplanes that had been received in poor condition."

By November 1943, with seventy combat crews to train, the 461st had only twenty-one Liberators. When Brig. Gen. Samuel M. Connell, commanding general of the 4th Bomber Command, visited Hammer Field on November 3, he was annoyed by the "lack of progress in training accomplished by the Group due to slow airplane maintenance." With flight training behind schedule, ground school was curtailed so more time could be allocated to flying. Maintenance now suffered even more, since all twenty-one of the Group's aircraft were constantly in the air.

Magazine writers in 1976 and 1978 erroneously wrote of *Exterminator* being caught in a blinding snowstorm and experiencing a failure of its hydraulic system. This, they say, led to the emergency requiring the crew to bail out. George Barulic believes hydraulic failure was the cause as well. "I imagine the hydraulic system must have gone out, because the bomb bay doors wouldn't open up with the electronics." He was partially correct.

Mike Tanksley sees no connection between *Exterminator* losing its hydraulic system and the plane crash. Referring to the B-24 Liberator aircraft system schematics, he observes, "The hydraulics on the B-24 are used for systems such as the brakes and the bomb bay doors, but the primary flight controls and engine controls are directly controlled by cables." Hydraulics would therefore have no effect on them. "Also, the hydraulic pump runs off engine #3, which appears to have been operating normally," so problems with engine #2 would have had no effect on the hydraulic system. Why *Exterminator* lost its hydraulic system will never be known, but "Its failure was unlikely to have contributed to any decrement in the ability to control this airplane in the air."

There is a photograph in the *Fresno Bee* archives and another image in the July 1, 1980, *Los Angeles Times* from Gene Forte's failed salvage operation. Both photos show Forte on the Dutra Construction Company barge. Beside him is one of *Exterminator's* engines. A winter 1990 photograph taken by Big Creek School fourth-grade teacher, Robert Crider, shows an unbent propeller blade poking out of icy Huntington Lake waters when the lake level was lowered to effect repairs on the dam.

One of the first lessons accident investigators learn about propeller aircraft involves what happens during a crash landing. If all of the props are bent back during a crash landing, it means the engines were running and the props were engaged. If just one or two props are bent, the engine

The low water level of Huntington Lake reservoir during the winter of 1990–1991 exposed this propeller wreckage of *Exterminator*. PHOTO IN AUTHOR'S COLLECTION, COURTESY OF BIG CREEK SCHOOL 4TH GRADE PROJECT

was shut down and the props were feathered. Since *Exterminator* was making a water landing, what makes the newspaper photos especially interesting is that one prop (likely the top one) is not bent at all. It's feathered. The two lower props are slightly bent, and feathered. Lt. Col. Tom Betts, a retired air force pilot and accident investigator, says, "This would lead to the firm conclusion [that] the props were intentionally feathered. Given that the top prop isn't bent at all, the engine was probably not running."

These three long-unexamined photographs go a long way toward explaining Captain Darden's actions in the fatal ditching of his airplane. The examining board probably decided on their 50/50 ruling of pilot error / undetermined because Darden should have been able to fly *Exterminator* on three engines. A lack of physical evidence and the weak statements as to cause by Lieutenant Settle and Sergeant Barulic account for the other half of the equation.

Lieutenant Settle did tell the accident examining board there was some sort of problem with their #2 engine, but he was not believed. This is expressed by a certain frostiness the board displayed toward Settle during their interview, when halfway through the proceedings they turned from what was happening on board *Exterminator* to discussing the weather. They might have been wondering why the copilot bailed out when he should have been in the cockpit, helping the pilot.

Reasoning for this interpretation is found in both Lieutenant Settle's statement and in the photos of the feathered engines. Settle makes no mention of Captain Darden feathering an engine because Settle was unaware of it. This means the pilot was flying the airplane and troubleshooting the engine problem without assistance. It takes a well-trained team of pilots approximately twenty seconds to feather a Liberator engine: spot the problem and decide what to do (five to ten seconds), shut off fuel to the engine (two to three seconds), set off the fire bottle to extinguish any engine fire (two seconds), feather the engine (two to five seconds), and visually confirm that the engine is feathered (five seconds).

Without a copilot to help him, William Darden broke a cardinal rule of flying: Focusing on the engine issue, he forgot to fly the airplane. Distracted with trying to fix the problem with #2 engine, Darden lost altitude and airspeed. At that point he had no other option but to ditch into the lake. The warning horn Lieutenant Settle heard, and then didn't hear, could have been associated with feathering *Exterminator*'s #2 engine. If an engine is idled with modern aircraft, and the airplane isn't in the landing configuration with gear down and landing flaps in position, a warning horn goes off to help avoid gear-up landings. If Darden had shut down #2 engine in preparation for feathering the props, he would have first pulled the throttles back to idle, perhaps triggering the gear warning horn. This horn will sound when the throttle is closed unless the gear is latched properly in the "Down" position. Therefore, *Exterminator*'s wheels were up since the horn was sounding. In fact, this is what John Marion observed in 1980 during Gene Forte's salvage operation.

These must be the reasons the examining board found Captain Darden culpable. The B-24 had specific procedures for dealing with engine failure, and the flight manual states in no uncertain terms, "There is sufficient power available in three engines to climb the B-24, and all of this power should be used." Pilots were expected to know these procedures in case of emergency so they could be executed "smoothly and efficiently, thus eliminating the need for hurried, unpremeditated moves which constitute the greatest hazard of any emergency operation." The accident examiners must have had this section of the B-24 flight manual firmly in mind when deciding how to assess the degree of pilot error.

In Darden's defense, the examiners didn't have the photographs from 1980 and 1990 of *Exterminator*'s feathered engine. They had no choice but to conclude: "There is no definite evidence to show mechanical difficulties resulting in a lack of power." Here, after more than seventy years, is evidence of engine failure. And, in Settle's defense, it must be said that he told the examiners quite plainly that the pilot had ordered him out of the plane. "All right, hell, get out of here," Darden had said. Culos Settle was reacting to this training and doing as he was told.

George Barulic scoffs at the story told around campfires that Captain Darden was attempting an emergency landing in a snow-covered meadow. "There was no snow. It wasn't a meadow. It was water there! He [Darden] wasn't thinking about landing. He was telling us to jump out." If Captain Darden had been serious about landing, he wouldn't have come around and pointed *Exterminator* downwind. Darden would have come around upwind. "That plane went crosswise instead of lengthwise when it hit the lake. If he wanted to ditch the plane, he would have turned it around to go lengthwise, right?"

Considering the known factors, it's plausible that the loss of engine power combined with rising terrain, low absolute altitude, and windy conditions conspired to put *Exterminator* in a position where William Darden didn't think he could climb above the mountains ahead of him. He chose instead to attempt a controlled emergency landing on the flattest thing he could find—the reservoir. He instructed the crew to bail out, knowing his effort was highly risky, but stayed with the plane himself. Perhaps Darden was trying to turn around to ditch *Exterminator* properly, upwind and along the length of Huntington Lake. Downwind landings, even on a runway, are dangerous. Throwing in low airspeed guaranteed disaster. Unfortunately, Darden ran out of time and lift, and only two of the boys made it out. Hitting the surface of the reservoir would have been roughly the same thing as colliding with a brick wall.

—◦—

Had the Hammer Field boys not died in California, would they have survived combat? While many of them did, the numbers were against them. Drawing from the *Army Air Forces Statistical Digest*, in *USAAF Handbook, 1939–1945*, Martin W. Bowman counts 63,410 casualties in the European Theater of Operation (ETO). Fifty-two percent of all aircrews were casualties, with 19,876 killed in action, 8,413 wounded, and 35,121 missing in action. In comparison, 31,155 of the boys in the Mediterranean Theater of Operation (MTO), or 26 percent, were casualties, with 10,223 killed, 4,947 wounded, and 15,985 missing. During 1944, when Settle, Barulic, and other Hammer Field boys were overseas, 4,470 bombers were lost in the ETO and 2,455 in the MTO.

—◦—

Less than a week before their last flight together, Charles Turvey, Robert Hester, Ellis Fish, William Cronin, Robert Bursey, and Howard Wandtke gathered with two others for a couple of group photographs in front of a Liberator known as *Lucky Lee*, #42-6987. Why there are eight of them in the photos when there should be ten is unknown. As their commanding officer, Colonel Glantzberg told them, "You groups of ten who count so on each other just learned each other's names five weeks ago. Each single man has in his hands the lives of all the other nine, and the fate of the mission as well." That was one goal of their training—to be a tight-knit group of professionals who would do their job and act as one.

In standard form, kneeling in front of *Lucky Lee* are the lieutenants: Cronin, Turvey, Fish, and Hester. Standing in back are the sergeants: Bursey, Wandtke (reversed in the other crew photo), and two unknowns. The boys are casual; tired, maybe. It could be that they'd just that moment returned from a long mission and the photographer had rushed over to catch them before they walked away. All their gear—leather insulated flight suits, parachutes, and their Mae West life vests—are thrown in a

The crew of 463. Front row (L to R): William Cronin, Charles Turvey, Ellis Fish, Robert Hester. Back row (L to R): Howard Wandtke, Robert Bursey, unknown, unknown. COURTESY RON WELCH JR. AND WILLIAM CRONIN FAMILY

jumble off to one side. Four still wear parachute harnesses. Three of the officers sport ties and garrison hats.

For many years, families of the boys would look at those two crew portraits and think that *Lucky Lee* was their own. But the shamrock-sided Liberator was only a backdrop, and many Hammer Field boys had their photos taken with it (see page 78).

What we know about 463 and her accident is comprised of shards of evidence and shreds of truth. Everyone who has visited Hester Lake and studied the site agrees with the initial 1960 hypothesis by James Moore, Frank Dodge, and Leroy Brock: that 463 hit Peak 12,483 south of the lake and then crashed into the water.

Hester Lake (middle ground) and Peak 12,483 behind it, looking south. Conjectured route of 463 is directly at the photograph's viewer. PHOTO BY PETER STEKEL

Stephen DeSalvo's 1989 expedition has the only underwater video available to researchers; it shows 463 upside down in a deep layer of silt. Very little wreckage is recognizable as an airplane except for some propeller blades poking straight out of the muck.

In 1993, when Christopher Thomas visited the lake, at least two of the engines were in fairly shallow water and easily viewed when swimming on the surface. Thomas was therefore able to add something to the accident scenario by spotting one engine with feathered propellers and another engine where the props weren't turning under power when the aircraft hit the water. Just like *Exterminator*, had the propellers been bent back like the dead fronds of a palm tree, they would have been turning with the force of the engine. What Thomas saw were slightly bent props. This means they were only turning with the wind of flight and the engines were not producing power.

Depth of silt in bottom of Hester Lake is evident from this propeller blade. The distance from the ground to the bottom blade was 37 inches. The propeller spun on a diameter of 11 feet, 7 inches. IMAGE CAPTURE FROM VIDEO SHOT BY STEPHEN DESALVO. COURTESY STEPHEN DESALVO

When Bursey nephew David Hill and his companions made their 2003 expedition to Hester Lake, one of the engines in the lake was still visible from shore. By 2015, when the ROV crew arrived at Hester Lake, all the engines had slid into deeper water. Craig Fuller plotted the debris field on land and also examined the ROV data and condition of the airplane debris in the lake bottom. He concluded that the force of 463's crash actually punched the Liberator through the lake ice, if there really was ice at the time. As with *Exterminator*, the impact of 463 hitting the lake surface, covered with ice or not, would have been like hitting a brick wall. The ROV crew found most of the wreckage in water 50 to 70 feet deep.

———

In his statement before the board investigating the disappearance of 463, Lt. John Specht reveals two contributing factors that might explain what happened to the Turvey and Hester Liberator. First is the strong quartering wind Specht encountered while flying north from San Diego to Hammer Field. Second was the lieutenant's comment, based on what another pilot had told him, that the radio compass on 463 was "not in very good operating condition."

Specht says his Liberator encountered 40- to 50-mile-per-hour winds from the northwest (270 to 290 degrees) at 12,000 feet, and was blown 40 miles off course to the southeast. He also encountered "quite a bit of turbulence" above Muroc at 0145, and "outside of a few scattered clouds, it was clear as far north as Hanford," 30 miles south of Hammer Field. He also said it was "dark to the northeast," and he couldn't see what the weather conditions were. Of course it was dark. There were no lights to the east, a storm was moving in, and the last quarter moon wouldn't rise until 4:04 a.m.

Weather conditions along 463's route home from Davis-Monthan called for the wind Lieutenant Specht experienced. Capt. Richard L. Moore, the station weather officer, also suggested that "an error in navigation could have been made in undercompensating for these high winds." If the missing plane was blown off course and ended up as far north as Mono Lake on the Sierra Nevada's east side, they would have encountered "broken cumulus clouds, bases on the mountains, tops twenty to twenty-five thousand," with no visibility, but moderate icing in the clouds.

The accident investigation board decided the cause of 463's disappearance and presumed crash was "undetermined." However, based on Lieutenant Specht's observations and Captain Moore's weather synopsis, they raised a suspicion that "weather was an underlying factor." Even though the board had no evidence for how 463 reacted to "adverse weather conditions," they concluded, "It is also evident that action could have been taken to avoid unfavorable areas."

The aircrews of World War II flew the most sophisticated and advanced aircraft of their time, with the most sophisticated and advanced

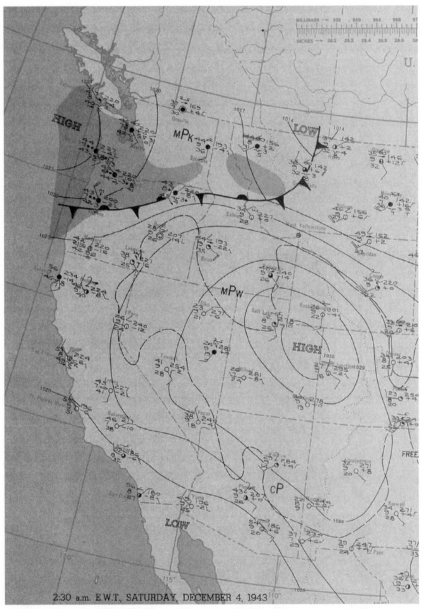

Weather map from December 4, 1943, shows a front moving south that will later impact flights at Hammer Field. UNITED STATES DEPARTMENT OF COMMERCE, WEATHER BUREAU

radios and navigational aids then available. The ubiquitous use of GPS in aviation today allows pilots to accurately locate themselves within a dozen or so feet on a map. In the 1940s it wasn't so easy. Celestial, dead reckoning, and pilotage were the mainstays of aviation navigation, and they took time, practice, and skill to perfect.

On top (and sometimes on the bottom) of any World War II–era airplane is an object that resembles a pointy-ended football. Inside that football is a rotatable loop antenna for the aircraft's automatic direction finder (ADF). The combination of a radio receiver, the ADF, and a needle gauge constituted the aircraft's radio compass. By rotating the loop antenna it's possible for the radio compass to determine the direction, or bearing, toward a radio transmitter relative to the direction the aircraft is headed.

By the time World War II began there were a series of ADF radio beacons established across the continental United States. One series ran from Tucson, Arizona, west to Los Angeles, and then north to Hammer Field and Fresno, continuing north to Seattle. Lieutenant Specht told the accident examining board that "every pilot knows about it." Essentially a pilot could fly from beacon to beacon along this radio "highway." Leaving or losing the beacon would be akin to today's motorists exiting the interstate and striking off on their own without knowing their direction home.

There was no ADF beacon in Owens Valley on the east side of the Sierra Nevada. Leaving Davis-Monthan Army Air Forces Base in Tucson, Turvey and Hester could have easily followed a radio compass highway all the way back to Hammer Field. Lacking a functioning radio compass to check their bearings, they would have been less aware of being pushed east, off course, by the wind.

Lieutenant Specht felt that "For a celestial mission, that could have been a very good reason for them to get quite a ways off course without realizing it."

Had Turvey and Hester flown 463 before December 4, 1943, they would have known about the faulty compass. But training had been delayed by not enough flyable Liberators, so they likely discovered the issue on the way south to Tucson. With confidence in their ability to handle anything that might come up, and confidence in Cronin's ability

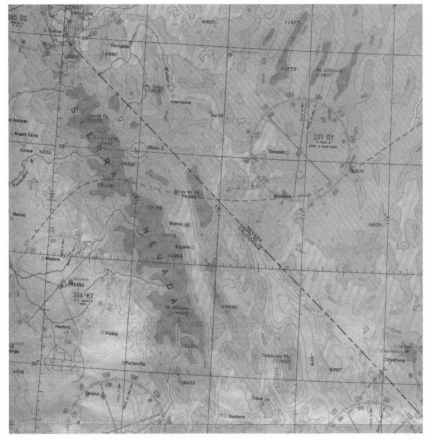

Section of a July 13, 1944, radio direction–finding aeronautical chart showing the lack of radio range stations in Owens Valley. IN AUTHOR'S POSSESSION

to use dead reckoning and pilotage to get them to Tucson and return, they flew on.

Part of every pilot's basic education is to stay away from high mountains—especially when clouds are in the mix, because those clouds are regularly "stuffed with granite." To be on the safe side, pilots keep a 2,000-foot vertical buffer between themselves and the tallest object around. Why, then, were Turvey and Hester flying lower than the Sierra

Nevada? There is one bit of evidence in Sgt. Robert Bursey's IDPF to suggest that the boys in 463 understood their predicament.

As flight engineer, Bursey's position in the air was with the pilots, standing behind them during the flight and helping to monitor gauges, among other duties. When his remains were recovered from Hester Lake in 1960, the mortuary examiners found the impression of a seat belt imbedded in Bursey's flesh. To be wearing his seat belt meant only one thing: The pilots knew they were in danger, and they were preparing for the worst.

If they thought the situation so dire, why didn't the pilots radio for help? Pilots have an old saying: "Flying the airplane is more important than calling a person on the ground for help who is incapable of understanding your plight or doing anything about it." Lt. Col. Tom Betts also points out, "New pilots never want to call for help if they think they can get themselves out of trouble without getting found out." Added to that, for all their sophistication, World War II radios were "crude and unreliable compared to today's equipment." They were restricted to line of sight and therefore exhibited limited range, especially when mountains were involved. Not that it would matter. Christopher Thomas had met R.W. Koch, a freelance aviation writer and earlier visitor to Hester Lake. Koch had found the undeployed long-range radio antenna for 463. Even if they had wanted to send a message, no one would have heard them.

Then, why not bail out? For one thing, it was dark. Forget the lack of training or experience for the moment, and consider what happened to the crew of *Hat in the Ring* over Santa Barbara. While on a night training mission they experienced engine failure over the Pacific Ocean. Two crewmen bailed out prematurely over open water and were never seen again. That's why a crew wouldn't want to jump out of their airplane without the light of day. Not only was it dark, but they were flying in clouds, maybe even in turbulence. And then, it's entirely reasonable to assume that the crew of 463 didn't exactly know where they were. Were they over land? Or water? Mountain, or plain?

The boys had been at Hammer Field long enough, had taken at least one flight there, had examined and studied their charts more than once, and knew there was a big, tall, snowy mountain range running the spine of California from north to south, nearly from Mexico to the Oregon border, and further on north as the Cascade Mountains, all the way to Canada. A hell of a long way to be on the wrong side of anything. For all intents and purposes, lost as they were, and lost as they no doubt realized, 463 and her crew of six were flying blind.

They should have been at Hammer Field, but they weren't. Where they were would have been the big topic of discussion in the cockpit, not how they got there. It was too late for that. Bewildered as they might have been, the pilots were savvy enough to avoid speculating on where they *might* be, though they absolutely knew where they *should* be. "Convincing yourself it is such a place simply because it is due to appear means the beginning of your end if it happens to be some other hamlet," wrote Ernest K. Gann.

This is where crews come together, working toward a common goal, to solve the problem at hand. The crew of 463 had reached their moment of truth. They knew they'd pull through; they had been in plenty of jams before. "Hope always persists beyond reason." And west into the night they flew.

There are several reasons for explaining why 463 was flying so low in the mountains that have nothing to do with the possibility of one or more malfunctioning engines. Engine failure could have been what finally cooked their goose. Using pilotage and dead reckoning, they may have thought they knew where they were. If they were flying in bad weather, as some researchers have thought, or plowing through clouds, they had no way of knowing they were on the wrong side of the mountains. They may have decided to drop some altitude for a look-see. Or, since they were supposed to be at Hammer Field at 0300, the pilots may have decided it was time to begin their descent, hoping to punch out of the clouds at a lower altitude.

Another possibility for being so low has to do with how physically uncomfortable it was for heavy bomber crews operating in unpressurized aircraft. Maintaining altitudes above 10,000 feet meant wearing an oxygen mask and breathing supplemental oxygen. Either that or suffer anoxia—death through "oxygen starvation."

The last radioed position for 463 was above Muroc in the Mojave Desert, flying at 18,500 feet, a place where the phrase "bitter cold" loses all meaning. The temperature inside of the airplane was the same as outside—something approaching 40 degrees below zero. "At that temperature, warm skin making contact with bare metal forms an instant, inseparable bond. Breath literally crystallizes; perspiration forms beaded icicles." Even with their electrically heated suits and gloves to protect them, a wind equal to their forward speed—say, 200 miles per hour—whipped through the open gun ports of the Liberator's fuselage. The noise was deafening, too. Dropping to a lower altitude meant warmth and freeing themselves from wearing oxygen masks. Or, maybe, 463 was building up a load of wing ice, so the boys decided to lose some altitude and get to warmer air.

Assuming the pilots realized their navigational error, and knowing they were on the east side of the Sierra Nevada, Turvey and Hester would have made sure to stay pretty high to avoid any pesky granite mixing in the clouds. But at 12,000 or so feet, the boys may have decided to fudge matters a bit and drop their oxygen masks. Nobody was going to die of anoxia at that altitude. The worst they could expect was a little lightheadedness. Crossing the Sierra, they would have done what pilots always do when crossing high mountains: They would have had their navigator tell them the highest point around and then added a cushion of 2,000 feet—just in case. At that time they would have put their oxygen masks on for what the pilots would have considered a brief hop over the mountains, from Owens Valley to Hammer Field.

If the weather had been clear enough in the Owens Valley for the boys to know where they were, they could have landed at the AAF auxiliary field in Bishop, or farther south, in Manzanar. They chose not to. This could either mean they didn't know where they were, or they knew where they were, and had no qualms about crossing the Sierra Nevada. Maybe they were anxious to sleep in their own beds that night. Clouds were dancing along the tops of the mountains at the time, so Turvey and Hester would not have crossed the Sierra without a cushion of altitude below them. What sounds most reasonable is that they were confident of what they were doing.

But something happened.

⊸ ⚬ ⚬ ⚭

The final question has to do with how 463 ended up on the wrong side of the Sierra Nevada. William Lansford spent time chewing that over for an article he wrote, and he also shared his thoughts privately with Bob Hester's sister, Janet. From their last recorded position near Muroc, the boys turned to 210 degrees for their approach to Bakersfield before their final shot home. But they were bucking a 40- to 50-mile-per hour northwesterly wind (blowing from 270 to 290 degrees) they knew nothing about. Even though the nose of their Liberator was pointed at 210 degrees, this wind caused the heavy bomber to "crab" to their right. Working without the benefit of a radio compass, they really had no immediate way of knowing they were drifting off course.

⊸ ⚬ ⚬ ⚭

Any fear for the future is gone now; there isn't time. Charlie Turvey knows they're in trouble. There's too much to do to allow for any second-guessing about using the auxiliary field in Bishop when they could see it. Charlie and Bob are doing what they were trained to do, what they are supposed to do. They are flying the airplane. And they have to get over these mountains with one engine feathered. That should be no problem.

If there was time when they arrived at Hammer Field they would complain about the sorry state of this kite. The radio compass! Turvey and Hester understood the problems inherent with keeping enough planes in the air; everyone at the Field knew about the shortage of engines, engine parts, and tools. The mechanics worked around the clock. But there could be no excuse for the radio compass not working. Adding insult to injury was the fact that no one had told them about it. On the hop from Hammer Field to Davis-Monthan, it hadn't mattered. It sure mattered now. Bill Cronin did his best to figure out where they were, and his best was pretty good. At least they knew Bishop was down there, and that meant they knew which side of the Sierra Nevada they were on.

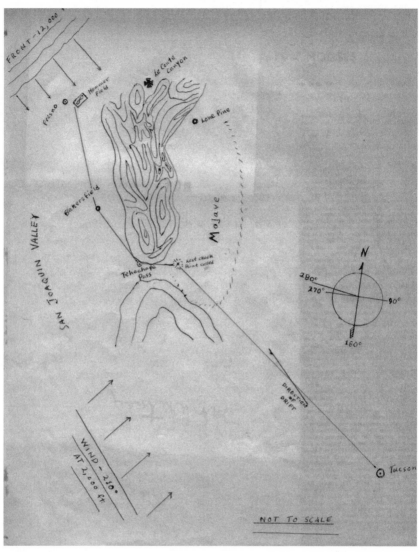

Sketch map drawn by William Lansford to explain to Janet Hovden his theory about how her brother's B-24 drifted off course. COURTESY OF JANET HOVDEN AND ROBERT HESTER FAMILY

Charlie has his radio operator, Howard Wandtke, transmit a message to Hammer Field with their position. Also, to ask about the weather conditions in the San Joaquin Valley. It has been a bumpy, but clear, ride all the way from Muroc, and now, the weather is changing. Cronin can't see stars anymore for celestial navigation. Charlie and Bob talk about that briefly and agree that if the stars are blotted out, there are going to be clouds hugging the Sierra Nevada peaks. What was that saying they heard during training? "It's impossible to have too much altitude *beneath* you." They agree on an extra cushion for comfort, and Charlie lifts the nose of 463. On the interphone Charlie calls to his crew to make sure oxygen masks are on and secure.

You do what you can do. That's what the two pilots on 463 have learned. They're pretty much cocky about it, too. Confident they can guide this big bird home. Charlie knows that Bob has superior piloting skills, and he wasn't afraid to admit that in a letter to his mother. He knows Bob still rankles at being assigned as copilot when he obviously has the talent needed to be first pilot. The army moves in strange ways. Charlie can't help but think how lucky he was to get a copilot like Bob, and he knows Bob feels that way about him. Lucky he's flying with somebody he can trust to do the right thing. Bob had a chance to leave the crew, but chose to stay. They're a team now, he and Bob. It's a great team.

And Bill Cronin, their navigator. His big brother tried to talk him into a safe job with transport, but Bill declined. He wanted to be with the guys he flew with. What a gang! They liked Bill almost as much as all the pretty girls who were always hanging around him. That was fine with Charlie. He has his sweetheart back home, and Bob has Miriam, his wife, and their baby daughter. Ellis has a son, but he doesn't talk much about his family life. He's a great guy, though. Happy, with some kind of inner glow or awareness he's going places. So what if not that long ago they were all strangers. They're a crew now.

The army doesn't expect officers to fraternize with enlisted men, but any pilot worth anything wants to get to know his flight engineer. He could be the most important boy on a Liberator. Sure, sure; the pilot flies the aircraft, and he needs his copilot to do everything he can't do. But without a flight engineer checking your fuel levels, monitoring the gauges, and keeping an eye on the engines aloft and on the ground, you're no better than a bird with clipped wings. That's what is so great about Bob Bursey. He has a certain nervousness about him because he wants everything to work just right. Importantly, Bursey has that innate sensitivity of someone who understands engines, machines, and tools a whole lot better than he understands people.

So, there they are. On their way back in the darkness of early morning on a celestial training mission from here to there and from there to here. Six boys flying west with the night. Confident in their abilities, as determined by the US Army Air Forces, and sure of those abilities. Their instructors would be proud.

And then the second engine quits.

—◆—

World War II slips further away from us with each passing day. The number of United States soldiers serving during the war was 16,112,566. Depending on the source of information, how the data are calculated, and the year in which the results were published, as many as 1,100 World War II veterans die every day today. With their deaths passes not only an era in our nation's history, but also their personal stories and family histories.

Of the 16.1 million Americans who served during the war between December 1, 1941, and December 31, 1946, there were a total of 405,399 deaths across the four branches of service. The army suffered 318,274 (78 percent) of those deaths, with 234,874 killed in action (KIA). Non-battle deaths were 83,400. Of army deaths, 89,119 (28 percent) were from the USAAF. There were 52,173 soldiers in the Army Air Forces KIA, and 35,946 who were non-battle deaths.

Rolled into official numbers for those KIA in all branches of service are 9,256 non-battle deaths, representing "persons who died of disease or other non-battle causes while in a captured, interned, or missing in action status." The 83,400 figure for non-battle deaths comprise those who died due to disease, accident, health issues, or other causes not related to combat. It's a staggering 26 percent of all US armed forces deaths during the war. More staggering is the 41 percent of USAAF personnel deaths that were not KIA. As dangerous as aerial combat was, four out of every ten flight-line personnel and ground crew did not die in combat.

Sifting through the numbers even more, the *Army Air Forces Statistical Digest* shows what a dangerous business war can be, even for those people not engaged in battle. Between 1941 and 1945 there were 54,249 airplane accidents in the continental United States (see Table 2), resulting in 14,899 fatalities in 6,127 fatal accidents, with 13,992 aircraft wrecked. Nearly 60 percent of the wrecked aircraft were combat types. The remainder were used for training or transport. Flying airplanes was dangerous!

There were more accidents in pursuit aircraft than in any other airplane type. However, the greatest number of accidental deaths were in the ten-man-crew, four-engine B-24 Liberator and B-17 Flying Fortress heavy bombers, followed by the six-man-crew, two-engine B-25 Mitchell and seven-man-crew B-26 Marauder medium bombers (see Table 1).

In his compendium of fatal USAAF aviation accidents, compiled from all extant accident reports, Anthony Mireles comes up with slightly higher numbers for crew losses. He shows that between 1941 and 1945, there were 15,530 pilots, crew members, and ground personnel killed in accidents while training in the United States. "During World War II, the air over the continental United States was a virtual third front."

Navy losses were equally as bad. Their total aviation deaths from all causes were 12,133, with 3,618 from enemy action, and 8,515 deaths from training accidents, losses while ferrying aircraft, and other, non-aviation-related causes. More than 4,500 American aircraft were lost in battle against Japanese army and naval forces, but this is still less, by a ratio of 3:1, than the number of aircraft lost by the USAAF during training within the United States (see Table 2).

The loss of the boys from 463 and *Exterminator* echoes and reverberates through the years, although sometimes it seems they are largely forgotten to all but their families. Images of the boys still prominently grace fireplace mantels or adorn walls covered with family photographs. Over time, following their deaths, others were named in their honor. That tradition continues into later generations. Whereas the dead of World War II and the cause and reason for their ultimate sacrifice may

Table 2. Airplane Accidents in the Continental United States, Number and Rate: 1939–1945

Army Air Forces Statistical Digest World War II
Second Printing, December 1945, Page 308
Prepared by Office of Statistical Control
Table 212 -Airplane Accidents in Continental United States, Number and Rate: 1939-1945
(Rates are per 100,000 flying hours.)

Year	All Accidents	Rate	Fatal Accidents	Rate	Fatalities	Rate	Aircraft Wrecked	Rate
1939	389	53	32	4	52	7	86	12
1940	478	51	46	5	90	10	100	11
1941	1304	58	116	5	199	9	228	10
1942	5612	74	582	8	1096	14	1259	17
1943	15652	70	1779	8	4209	19	3854	17
1944	20883	54	2272	6	5616	14	5387	14
1945	10798	42	1378	5	3779	15	3264	13
TOTALS 1939-45	55116		6205		15041		14178	
TOTALS 1941-45	54249		6127		14899		13992	

1939 and 1940 data includes continental US and overseas accidents

(Army Air Forces Statistical Digest for World War II)

go unrecognized today by those who did not suffer the loss, their families have not forgotten. The dead are still remembered with respect, because that is what our dead deserve. These boys, these young men, too soon gone, have powerful claims upon us today. Lest we forget, those claims are very strong indeed.

That some lived and others died haunted the survivors. George Barulic knew it had everything to do with good fortune. "Luck is just like that when you're flying," he said. There in *Exterminator*, with the Liberator falling from the sky, he realized he'd gone aboard without a parachute. Only luck can explain how he found a parachute close by. But did that mean one of the other boys on board lost his chance to bail out?

No one aboard 463 or *Exterminator* was any more or less heroic or dedicated to the task than any other man who fought during the war. British bomber pilot Guy Gibson struggled for a reason to explain why some made it back alive from battle while others did not. What he finally decided upon is neither profound nor poetic but this is how he saw it and he was there. "Some were unlucky."

Epilogue

For those of us who need to touch history to truly appreciate, understand, and experience it, it's easy to reach Huntington Lake from Fresno on State Route 168. To find the crew memorial installed for *Exterminator* by the Big Creek School fourth graders, continue along the main road, following the north shore of the reservoir. Pass through the resort community of Lakeshore and drive to the extreme eastern end of the reservoir, turning northeast onto Kaiser Pass Road. From there,

Monument plaque to *Exterminator*'s crew at Huntington Lake presented by Mr. Bob Crider and his Big Creek School fourth grade students. PHOTO BY PETER STEKEL

immediately turn right into a large asphalt parking lot at the Eastwood Ranger Station.

A few steps from the ranger station at the west end of the parking lot is a white granite stone with a 15-by-20-inch brass plaque memorializing the crew of *Exterminator*. The rock squats in a clearing, surrounded by small lodgepole and yellow pines.

———

Multiple dams impound the waters of Huntington Lake. Beginning at the western end of the reservoir, it's an easy 1-mile walk to the concrete spill-way of the Big Creek Hydroelectric Project Dam #1 along the Southern California Edison access road. Below you, in the deep azure lake waters, lies *Exterminator*. Above the concrete spillway is a large outcrop of gran-

Someone has added a personal memorial to this benchmark placed by the Southern California Edison Company. The benchmark is located on a rock above *Exterminator*'s crash site, but is not associated with the aircraft in any way. PHOTO BY PETER STEKEL

ite where Tom Spangle observed the army in 1955 as they brought the remains of his big brother and other of Richard Spangles's fellow crew members to shore.

Near Dam #1 is a site haunted by a geocachers located at N37 14.098 W119 12.507. A faint path leads through the forest and underbrush to a Southern California Edison benchmark, and a less-imposing monument than the granite-and-brass testament to the crew of *Exterminator*. Somebody has etched a cross into the marker.

Close to Clint Hester's house in Lone Pine is the memorial and mass grave to the 1872 Owens Valley earthquake victims. On the plateau behind the memorial are a few dozen houses of various vintages. Clint's house is a modified barn-like structure, built in 1947, according to the Inyo County records department, of faux adobe brick and wood. A

Clint Hester's home in Lone Pine, California. "Lone Pine's a beautiful spot for a retired man. I won't have to go so far to look for Bob." PHOTO BY PETER STEKEL

cottonwood rail fence surrounds the house, and aged cottonwood trees provide shade. The flagpole erected by Clint, so that Bob would know he was there, looking, is still there, north of the house. Despite the proximity of neighbors, it's as isolated and lonely a spot as Mrs. Turvey described in her letter to Janet Hester in 1961. The property is in private ownership, and the current residents would probably appreciate not being haunted by the curious.

With a long, low, brown hill of broken rock between Clint's Lone Pine house and the eastern Sierra crest, Clint Hester could not claim to live in the shadow of Mount Whitney. But his views—south to the Horseshoe Meadow road, north up the Owens Valley, and east to the White and Inyo Mountains—were breathtaking nevertheless. The open country no doubt reinforced in his mind the enormity of his search. Although he was convinced that Bob's B-24 lay somewhere in the Mount Whitney country, in actuality, it could have come down anywhere. It took a tremendous amount of what—faith, certainty, obsession—to focus all of his energy in one place.

The Phantom Rider. His only son.

Hester Lake will always be a difficult and inaccessible place to reach. Getting there is everything they say it is, from the trip over Bishop Pass, through Dusy Basin, and down to LeConte Canyon Ranger Station, to traveling up the steeply forested and waist-high manzanita slopes, to below the Notch. That crack in the granite wall is nothing special by Sierra Nevada standards—a solid Class 3 climb for 328 vertical feet. The hardest part is actually the 300 or so feet of unconsolidated talus below the Notch, which requires excellent route-finding and unquestionable balance.

Beyond and above the Notch, a steep incline leads across granite slabs, implausible meadows, and a watery slope, to Hester Lake. The lake is in a pothole, surrounded by cliffs rising as high as 100 feet, and there is very little shoreline that doesn't plunge directly to the bottom of the

Ruins of the parachute pulled to shore by James G. Moore in 1960.
PHOTO BY PETER STEKEL

lake. The water has a liquid cobalt blue cast to it; sunlight hitting bits and pieces of twisted and deformed aluminum below the water's surface shines and twinkles. Sparkles. The pressure of winter snow and ice push more and more of that debris into deeper water every year. Soon there will be nothing left to see. The parachute pulled to shore in 1960 by James Moore is still there. All that's left are shreds of shrouds and harness.

The place used by the army divers in 1960 to stage their equipment is easy to find, because it's the only reasonably flat place around the lakeshore, albeit far from level. It's no bigger than someone's backyard deck. Most of the area is covered by vegetation, but closer to the water there are slabs of cracked and broken granite poking out from the mountain heather, sedges, and grasses.

The soldiers at Hester Lake in 1960 certainly had lots of time on their hands while the divers probed beneath the water. The soldiers mon-

Along the shore of Hester Lake this natural cleft in the rock has been modified by an unknown person into a cross (probably a member of the 1960 army diving team). PHOTO BY PETER STEKEL

itored what they had to monitor. Watched the air pump, making sure nobody starved for air. Listened to what needed to be heard. Wondered if they'd be able to cook dinner that night or not.

Those army guys had lots of time to think about what they were doing. And they had lots of time to think about how what they were doing would mean something to the families of the aviators in the lake. Because one of them, or maybe more, found a flat-faced rock on the lakeshore, just a couple of inches above the water's surface. It was right where the divers entered and left the lake, so all of them had to have seen this rock over and over again.

This particular rock had a deep cleft in it that extended nearly perfectly horizontally for many inches. A perfect, natural piece of art. Somebody thought of a way to perfect nature. They chipped another cleft on the vertical axis of that crack, turning nature's work of art into a cross.

What a memorial. If you wanted a monument to your death, wouldn't you want to be recognized by those who had served with you? Or searched for you? Those boys on the not-so-lucky *Lucky Lee*, #987. What we know as the crew of 463. And the crew of *Exterminator*. Those boys, too. All of them. They would have liked that.

And the rest of us? We're haunted by those waters as surely as we haunt them ourselves.

ACKNOWLEDGMENTS

I AM DEEPLY INDEBTED TO THE FAMILIES OF THE BOYS FROM 463 AND *Exterminator* for opening their hearts and sharing their family stories and treasures. As William Shakespeare wrote in *Richard II*, "Where words are scarce, they are seldom spent in vain / For they breathe truth that breathe their words in pain."

From the crew of 463, my gratitude and profuse thanks goes to Janet Hovden, Bob Hovden (who also reviewed portions of the manuscript), and Marilyn Tierney, for sharing the Hester family archives and stories about Clint Hester and Bob Hester. Many thanks to Diane Coombes for sharing the family photographs and history of her parents, Bob and Miriam Hester. Many thanks to Ronald Welch Jr. (who also reviewed the manuscript) and Eileen Cronin Welch, for sharing photographs of William Cronin. Thank you to David Hill for sharing photographs of Robert Bursey and other precious memorabilia. Eileen and Ron Welch and David Hill guided me through the hometowns of Bill Cronin and Bob Bursey, giving me unparalleled insight into the lives of these two boys. Thank you to Debbie Coulter for sharing photographs of her grandfather, Ellis Fish. And thank you to Joan Walker as well, for her contributions.

From the crew of *Exterminator* my gratitude goes to David Mayo (who also reviewed portions of the manuscript), Richard Mayo, and Walker Mayo for sharing their uncle Dick Mayo's photographs, diary, and other family papers, including letters written by their grandmother. Thank you to Thomas Spangle for sharing photographs and other papers relating to his big brother, Richard, and to Mary Condo as well, for her memories of Richard Spangle. Thank you to Oscar Traczewitz for sharing photographs of Donald Vande Plasch and the marriage between Donald and Leona Traczewitz. Thank you to William Root for photographs of

Culos Settle. Being able to interview George Barulic at the beginning of my research in 2011, the only living survivor from the two lost B-24 Liberators, was an especially meaningful experience.

Aviation archaeologist Pat Macha was ever-giving of his time, expertise, and support. Thank you to aviation archaeologists Nick Veronico, Brian Linder, and Craig Fuller. Thanks also to Kent Schneider and so many others who keep these stories alive.

Thank you to Michael Sledge for his seminal book, *Soldier Dead*. For all those times we got together to exchange ideas and compare notes about this profession of ours, my writers' group deserves appreciative words: David B. Williams, Beth Geiger, Michele Solis, Julie Monahan, and Cassia Herman. A big shout-out to Diane Sepanski, writer and editor, who helped turn my book proposal into a winning proposition. Thank you to Roslyn Bullas for believing in me so many years ago.

Mike Robbins, Dick Shipley, John Boothe, Karl Hufbauer, Dawn Meekhof, David Graber, and William Tweed read, reviewed, and commented on early and late versions of either major portions or the complete manuscript. Thank you for your eagle eyes, feedback, and contributions toward making this a better book.

Thank you to Hughes Glantzberg for his work in organizing the 461st Bombardment Group (H) website and publishing the 461st Group records. I leaned heavily on Lt. Col. Tom Betts (US Air Force, Ret.) and CW2 Fred Smyth (US Army, Ret.). They were my go-to guys for all questions military and aeronautical, and they always managed to make this neophyte understand the difficulties, dangers, and joys of flying airplanes. It was the same with CW4 Thomas Sandbakken, Mike Tanksley, John Matthews, Bill McKensie, and Sgt. Maj. Joseph R. Menard Jr. Any mistakes that squeaked past their fine eyes are, of course, mine.

Ann and Paul McCoy provided essential information about the Hester Lake divers. Robert Specht supplied me with photos and background information about his uncle, John Specht. I also want to acknowledge the fine detective work and dedication to the crew of 463 by Christopher Thomas.

Thank you to Douglas H. Clark, PhD, at Western Washington University for his glaciology expertise; James G. Moore, PhD; librarians

Debra Cox at the Seattle Public Library and Molly Bernard; Museum of Flight archivist Jessica Jones and assistant curator, John Little; Susan Robinson at Big Creek School; and Mary Laura Cloudy and Lisla Danasat with the Virginia Military Institute and VMI Alumni Association. Thank you to Ward Eldredge, museum technician, with Sequoia & Kings Canyon National Parks, for assistance with the National Park Service archives relating to Hester Lake.

Thank you to three wonderful friends: Richard Stowell, for introducing me to the Sierra Nevada, and Gregg Fauth, for our years of exploring in the Range of Light. Also Michele Hinatsu, who was with me on Mendel Glacier in 2007 when this whole airplane journey began, and who accompanied me on my first trip to Hester Lake. Jim Meadowcroft, Greg Juhl, and Rick Sanger were also either on my first Hester Lake trip, or the second. All have helped me with my everlasting desire to see beyond the first ridge to the last.

Thanks to everyone at Camp Wolverton BSA, alas no more, in Sequoia National Park. Though the physical place no longer exists, there are memories which cannot be so easily wiped away.

Susan M. Kilianski, government release specialist with the Freedom of Information Act / Privacy Act Office Human Resources Command HQ Department of the Army, was extremely helpful in processing my FOIA requests and providing the IDPFs for the crews of 463 and *Exterminator*. Thank you to Steve Ivey, who took me for airplane rides so I could see Hester Lake the way the crew of 463 may have seen it.

Portions of this book were written or edited on Lopez Island at the home of David Flotree and Ellen Hauptmann. What great friends! I am thankful for the three original maps which grace these pages, designed and created by Jim Reed, PhD. Thanks also to Kevin Callahan for the music.

Aviation museums such as Seattle's Museum of Flight, California's Planes of Fame, Hiller Aviation Museum, Castle Air Museum, the Yankee Air Museum in Willow Run, the Historic Flight Foundation and Flying Heritage Museum in Washington, and hundreds more not only preserve our history, they keep it alive. If there is an aviation museum near where you live, adopt it as your own and support it with your volunteer time and your money.

This book is a direct outgrowth of my previous work, *Final Flight*. I want to thank all my readers who wrote with their ideas and appreciative words. Writers work alone; it is wonderful to know when we have touched another person's life with our own. In the course of writing *Beneath Haunted Waters* I interviewed over three score people, sometimes multiple times. You will find their names in the references section, but I want to collectively thank them here for answering my questions and sharing their memories, stories, and expertise.

I'm grateful to my editor at Lyons Press, Eugene Brissie, for recognizing the value of this project, and to John Burbidge, at FalconPress, for being the catalyst that brought us together. Lyons Press production editor Lynn Zelem and copy editor Melissa Hayes did fabulous work.

Lasting thanks to those who served and those who continue to serve. And to the many who never came back, both overseas and right here. Let us remember *Taking Chance*.

As before, my thanks to the Sierra Nevada, the best friend a boy ever had.

To Jennie Goldberg, of course. What is love if not for you?

Endnotes

Note: Arranged by page number.

Prologue

x. Three letters received by Mrs. Roger Hovden (Janet Hester) document the naming of Hester Lake as a memorial to her father, Clint Hester, and her brother, Robert Hester:

> George W. Abbott, US Department of the Interior, Assistant Secretary of the Interior. Letter to Mrs. Roger A. Hovden, January 20, 1961.
>
> J. O. Kilmartin, US Department of the Interior, Board on Geographic Names. Letter to Mrs. Roger Hovden, May 3, 1961.
>
> Maurice Webster, Vice President and General Manager KCBS, San Francisco, California. Letter to Mrs. Roger Hovden, February 17, 1961.

Chapter 1: Discovery in a High Sierra Lake

1. After finding a yellow oxygen bottle. Leroy Brock interview, November 1, 2011.
1. Dodge and Moore. James Moore, "Mystery at Hester Lake" (unpublished manuscript).
3. "map part of the east side." Ibid.
3. It was July 27, 1960. Monthly Superintendent's Report, Sequoia & Kings Canyon National Parks, July 1960.
3. six-month-old daughter. Brock interview, November 1, 2011. "We spent the summer out there with her, and the packer would come in with a string of mules and I would be carrying her. She could reach and grab a mule by the lip and tug on it. When we got out in the fall and she got in a car, she got scared and got to crying. She could handle the mules but not a car."
3. In its second year. Extract from LeConte Canyon Ranger Station log, 1991.
4. on horseback. Brock interview, November 1, 2011. Brock rode a horse he called Mex and packed all his food and supplies on a mule named Mose.
4. Brock had met. Ibid. Brock would be out of the backcountry occasionally for a few days, conducting business in Bishop, and Moore and Dodge would leave their boots at LeConte Ranger Station for him to take to town for resoling. "Believe it or not, they were going through a set of boots every week or so. My God, they went through a lot of soles! There was an old bootmaker in Bishop at the time,

and I'd drop them off, pick them up the next time [he was in town]. I don't know how many pair they had, but they were really covering the Sierra!"

4. "I wanted to go." Ibid.
4. "We'd go by there." Frank Dodge interview, July 25, 2011.
4. "He kept bugging us." Ibid.
4. "The next day." Ibid.
4. Opportunities for injury. Crawford Coates, "Tragedy Near Hester Lake" (unpublished manuscript); Karl Hufbauer, "[Charles] Bays Locker (1931, Newton, Iowa—1952, Peak 12,360, Fresno Co., Calif.)" (unpublished manuscript).
6. barely lit. www.calendar-12.com/moon_calendar/1952/july.
6. In the meantime. Karl Hufbauer e-mail, February 27, 2014.
6. the recovery effort. Coates, "Tragedy Near Hester Lake."
6. Dudley Boothe. Boothe ran the Rainbow Pack Station with his wife, Alice, between 1950 and 1975, when it was sold to the current owners. Besides being sheriff, Joplin did some ranching on the side and left the area a decade or so later. Denton, known and revered locally as Dr. Bob, had moved to Bishop in 1950 to practice medicine, and continued to do so for fifty-seven years. Douglas Carl Engelbart later invented the computer mouse and played a leading role in the invention of the Internet. His wife, Ballard, never went on a hiking or wilderness trip again. Hufbauer, "[Charles] Bays Locker."
6. telephones. Donald F. Griffin, "Trail Building in the High Sierras" (unpublished manuscript).
9. stainless-steel bicycle chain. Brock interview, November 1, 2011.
9. "Jim Moore or Frank Dodge." Ibid.
9. Farther up. Ibid.
9. Moore decided. Moore, "Mystery at Hester Lake."
10. "It was a flight boot." Ibid.
10. "Our first reaction." Ibid.
10. "Around the lake." Brock interview, November 1, 2011.
10. It was difficult. Ibid.
10. "Papers within." Moore, "Mystery at Hester Lake."
11. Putting it all together. Moore, "Mystery at Hester Lake"; James Moore interview, April 9, 2011; Brock interview, November 1, 2011; Leroy Brock interview, November 30, 2011; and Dodge interview, July 25, 2011.
12. "We returned the boot to the lake." Moore, "Mystery at Hester Lake."
12. Leroy Brock filled them in. Ibid.
12. December 4, 1943. Monthly Superintendent's Report, Sequoia & Kings Canyon National Parks, August 1960.
12. "Clinton Hester, the father." Moore, "Mystery at Hester Lake."

CHAPTER 2: THE REPORTERS
14. At 5:00 a.m. John Boothe interview, August 31, 2011.
14. "grim corner of the High Sierra." James Benét, "*Chronicle* Team Reaches B-24 in Sierra Lake," *San Francisco Chronicle*, August 1, 1960, page 1.

14. "After a quick breakfast." John Boothe, "John Boothe's Accounting of Trips to Plane Crash Site Discovered in July of 1960" (unpublished manuscript).

15. Leroy Brock and the Boothes. Brock interview, November 30, 2011.

15. "sheer side of the canyon." Boothe, "John Boothe's Accounting."

15. "bits of sheet metal." Benét, "*Chronicle* Team Reaches B-24."

15. spry and enthusiastic. James Benét interview, August 8, 2011. A graduate of Stanford University, Benét was a veteran of the Abraham Lincoln Brigade during the Spanish Civil War. He initially drove ambulances before volunteering for combat, staying in Spain for fifteen months. He said, "Spain made a man of me." Following the war, Benét took part in John Dollard's study, *Fear in Battle*, which was used to create a template for morale education in the US Army before World War II.

A committed antifascist and admitted political "radical," Benét believed his job as a journalist was "seeing through the rhetoric of politicians and trying to get the real story out." He worked as a correspondent for the New York bureau of TASS (the Soviet news agency) during World War II, which led to his investigation by the House on Un-American Activities Committee when it visited San Francisco in May 1960, shortly before the Liberator was found in Kings Canyon National Park. Benét refused to cooperate and testify, but was not punished or jailed for his silence.

During the 1960s, he covered the Free Speech movement, and later became a journalism professor at UC Berkeley and San Francisco State University, along with writing a guidebook to San Francisco and two mystery novels. All of this in addition to his twenty years at the *San Francisco Chronicle* and later work with the independent television and radio station, KQED.

Benét was the son of poet, William Rose Benét, and the nephew of the Pulitzer Prize–winning writer, Stephen Vincent Benét. His grandfather and great-grandfather were both high-ranking officers in the US Army. After his mother's death in the 1919 Spanish influenza outbreak, he was raised by his aunt, novelist Kathleen Thompson Norris. James Benét died on December 16, 2012, at the age of ninety-eight, from a blood infection.

15. "It was one of those things." Benét interview, August 8, 2011.

15. "We know the B-24." Benét, "*Chronicle* Team Reaches B-24."

17. Benét reports. Ibid.

17. "Some moving parts." Boothe, "John Boothe's Accounting."

17. "The flesh and even the hair." Ibid.

17. "It is quite common." Ibid. Drought and climate change have made it less common in recent years.

18. "Well, you know the way." Ibid.

18. two mules. Fred Goerner, "The Angry Mountains: A Radio Newsman Fights the High Sierra," *San Mateo Times*, August 6, 1960.

18. "You made it this far." Boothe interview, August 31, 2011.

18. "The photographer." Brock interview, November 30, 2011.

18. ferried in. The park service headquarters at Three Rivers is located on the west side of the Sierra Nevada Mountains, at an elevation of 1,723 feet. The helicopter

flight to the lake crash site, at 11,255 feet, can be made in less than thirty minutes. Even the hardiest and most well-conditioned mountaineer has difficulty in making that sort of elevation transition without exhibiting symptoms of altitude sickness (headache, nausea, fatigue). Symptoms of altitude sickness are known to experienced hikers. Personal conversations with park rangers provides the approximate flight time from park HQ to crash site.

18. "I don't know." Boothe interview, August 31, 2011.

18. "wound up doing." Boothe, "John Boothe's Accounting."

18. a front-page. Anonymous, "Find Clues to Bomber Crash," *San Mateo Times,* August 2, 1960.

18. John Boothe says. John Boothe e-mail, July 11, 2014. Brock's wife agrees that the photo of the man in the water is her husband.

19. heading northeasterly. Anonymous, "Find Clues to Bomber Crash." Also, "Sierra Lake Preserves Bodies of Bomber Crew," *Oxnard Press-Courier,* August 4, 1960.

19. "We found the lake." Goerner, "The Angry Mountains."

20. "The day we went up there." John Boothe e-mail, March 13, 2014.

20. "Under the water." James Benét, "Lake Yields Its Secret," *San Francisco Chronicle,* August 1, 1960.

20. Goerner returned. Anonymous, "Find Clues to Bomber Crash."

21. Other items. Ibid.

21. "by this paper's Amelia Earhart expedition." Ibid.

21. "assault on that 3,000 feet." Goerner, "The Angry Mountains."

21. "We scrambled." Ibid.

21. "Bob Fischer." Ibid.

22. "I managed." Ibid. John Boothe says, "As for Goerner's falling on the way down and injuring his ankle, that just plain never happened." Boothe e-mail, March 13, 2014.

22. "They traveled all night." Brock interview, November 1, 2011.

22. "God must love them very much." Goerner, "The Angry Mountains."

CHAPTER 3: THE DIVERS

23. Stephen Lukacik. "Copter to Fly Team to B-24 Thursday," *Inyo Register,* August 4, 1960. Stephen Lukacik, who assisted in the recovery of Charles Bays Locker's body in 1952, in the lake basin immediately south of the airplane in the lake, was a major in the Bishop Squadron of the Civil Air Patrol.

23. "large cargo parachute." Ibid.

24. Later that summer. Leroy Brock e-mail, June 3, 2014; Leroy Brock interview, June 4, 2014.

24. Major John E. Thayer. "Sierra Lake Preserves Bodies of Bomber Crew," *Oxnard Press-Courier,* August 4.

24. Lt. Robert C. Hartmann. William Lansford, "If My Son Is Alive—I'll Track Him Down," *Stag,* 12:7 (July 1961).

24. 561st Engineering Company. "Divers to Study Lost Bomber," *San Francisco Chronicle,* ND.

25. a crew of twelve men. "Heavy Duty Diving Gear Now Being Used To Recover B-24 Bodies," *Inyo Register*, August 11, 1960.
25. risking their life. Robert Mester and Mark Allen interview, December 10, 2015.
26. "Oxygen and nitrogen." Robert Mester e-mail, December 26, 2015.
26. environmental factor. Peter Hunt interview, November 18, 2015.
26. delivers air to the diver. Mester and Allen interview, December 10, 2015.
28. lead-weighted shoes. Bill Bekemeier, telephone interview, March 29, 2014.
28. the angle of attack. Lt. Col. Tom Betts e-mail, March 10, 2014.
29. Piasecki H-21. Photographs, Numbers 00001–00017, in Sequoia & Kings Canyon National Parks archives, ND; and letter from US Army to Hester family, August 31, 1960. If you were allowed to fly to the crash site today, the preferred machine would be the jet-powered single-engine French Aérospatiale Alouette III. Betts, March 10, 2014.
29. "The service ceiling." Betts e-mail, March 10, 2014. Having to fly over the 11,972-foot Bishop Pass to LeConte Canyon meant the pilot was pushing his luck.
29. "This also allows." Ibid.
29. "The HH-43 would not." Ibid.
29. "This made the little helo." Ibid.
30. which was quite cumbersome. Ibid.
30. The HH-43 from the late 1940s. Ibid.
31. "The HH-43 is not comfortable." Ibid.
31. vibration of the rotor system. Ibid.
31. "The flight to the site." Ibid.
31. Reaching the lake. Letter from US Army to Janet Hovden, August 31, 1960.
32. "inadequate for a complete job." Ibid.
32. "They were told." Paul McCoy interview, March 29, 2012.
32. The air compressor and hoses. Photographs, Numbers 00001–00017, Parks archives.
32. all cooking. McCoy interview, March 29, 2012.
32. The soldiers at Little Pete. Brock interview, November 30, 2011.
32. "My wife said, 'Why don't you.'" Ibid. Rainbow Pack Outfit owner, Dudley Boothe, showed up around this time with a string of horses, which were admired by the Little Pete Meadow Army men. Boothe offered to take them for a ride.

The army men were keen to show off their horse skills. "And so the whole string ran with a military guy on them and Dudley in the lead. I saddled up and took my horse and followed them up in the rear down to Grouse Meadow," about 3 miles below the ranger station.

They met some backpackers on the trail who were both interested and amazed by what they saw. Army troops on horses! The military guys were "characters," as Brock remembers it. They told the backpackers, "This is the last horse unit in the United States Army. We're a special unit." The backpackers replied, "We never knew the army still had horses!" Brock kept himself in check. "I just acknowledged it and kept moving."

32. the lake bottom was searched. Letter from US Army to Janet Hovden, August 31, 1960.
33. "crystal clear." McCoy interview, March 29, 2012.
33. Douglas McCoy told his son. Ibid.
34. found in 35 feet of water. Letter from US Army to Janet Hovden, August 31, 1960.
34. "Other remains." Ibid.
34. "The various commanders." Mark Allen e-mail, December 28, 2015.
34. "The team decided." "Search for B-24 Bodies Called Off," *Inyo Register*, August 18, 1960.
34. "Reference your brother. Office of the Quartermaster General, Department of Army. Telegram to Janet Hovden, August 21, 1960.
35. "Now come the newspapermen." Benét, "Lake Yields Its Secret."
35. "I feel that I'm doing a service." Brock interview, November 30, 2011.
35. A few years after. Ibid.
35. "One was the brother." Brock interview, November 1, 2011.
36. The man in the orange flight suit. Ron Welch interview, October 26, 2011.

CHAPTER 4: ONE OF OUR AIRPLANES IS MISSING

37. B-24 #41-28463. "Report of Aircraft Accident" for B-24 #41-28463, December 17, 1943.
37. Built at a cost. Steve Birdsall, *Log of the Liberators*, page 312.
37. In her short life. Record of B-24 #41-28463.
37. proper duty station. Extract: Special Order #315, Wendover Field, Utah. November 11, 1943, in archives of 461st Bombardment Squadron (Heavy) (www.461st .org).
38. On takeoff. Graeme Douglas, *Consolidated B-24 Liberator 1939 Onwards (All Marks) Owners' Workshop Manual*, page 134.
38. "[a] critical and a very risky game." Truman Smith, *The Wrong Stuff*, page 259.
38. "I firmly believed." Ernest K. Gann, *Ernest K. Gann's Flying Circus*, page 191.
39. "The workload is demanding." Douglas, *Consolidated B-24 Liberator Manual*, pages 135–36.
39. C-1 autopilot. Anonymous, *Pilot Training Manual for the B-24 Liberator*, page 163.
39. Cylinder head gauges. Philip Ardery, *Bomber Pilot*, page 47.
39. At 0210. "Report of Aircraft Accident" for B-24 #41-28463.
40. 463's nose. The optimal rate of descent to land in a B-24 is at 200 feet/minute and at less than 200 mph. "Letting down 10,000 feet at 200 feet a minute requires fifty minutes." Therefore, "Start the letdown about an hour out." From 20,000 feet, "start one hour and forty minutes out." William Carigan, *Ad Lib: Flying the B-24 Liberator in World War II*, page 47.
40. High scattered clouds. "Report of Aircraft Accident" for B-24 #41-28463.
40. Weather creeps. William Langewiesche interview, May 24, 2007.
40. "Flight is a forward progression." Ibid.

41. "It comes at you." Ibid.
41. "There are many times." Smith, *The Wrong Stuff*, page 250.
42. "A B-24 does not fly backward." Louis Falstein, *Face of a Hero*, page 127.
42. altitude is an ally. Smith, *The Wrong Stuff*, page 32.
42. at 0300 on December 5. "Report of Aircraft Accident" for B-24 #41-28463.
43. One reason for the delay. "Search Sierra for Missing Bomber," *Inyo Register*, December 10, 1943, page 1.
43. Lieutenant Zumsteg's mishap. Ibid., page 6.
43. "I believe, though." Charles A. Watry, *Washout! The Aviation Cadet Story*, page 96.
43. "pervasive sense of danger." John Boeman, *Morotai: A Memoir of War*, page 56.
44. fifty major airfields in California. en.wikipedia.org/wiki/California_World_War_II_Army_Airfields.

CHAPTER 5: ANOTHER OF OUR AIRPLANES IS MISSING
45. On the morning. "Report of Aircraft Accident" for B-24 #42-7674, December 16, 1943.
45. It was piloted. Ibid.
45. The pattern was also determined. "Report of Aircraft Accident" for B-24 #41-28463.
48. "The compass radio." Statement by 2nd Lt. John K. Specht, "Report of Aircraft Accident" for B-24 #41-28463.
48. Starting from Hammer Field. "Report of Aircraft Accident" for B-24 #42-7674.
48. From Mariposa. Ibid.
49. Approaching 0950. Lt. Culos Settle statement, "Report of Aircraft Accident" for B-24 #42-7674.
49. Settle's usual copilot. Roster List of the 461st Bomb Group, 765th Squadron (www.461st.org). Lieutenant Behrens, Lieutenant Ostrander, and Staff Sergeant Barulic later flew with Lieutenant Settle once the 461st Bombardment Group reached their European base at Torretta, Italy.
50. "it sounded all right." Culos Settle statement, "Report of Aircraft Accident" for B-24 #42-7674.
50. "All right, hell, get out of here." Ibid.
50. and then changed his mind. Ibid.
50. Magneto failure. Roger Freeman, *B-24 Liberator at War*, page 90. A magneto provides electrical current to the engine's spark plugs.
50. Sergeant Nyswonger must have struggled. Ibid. Pages 106–107.
50. There are several. Anonymous, *Pilot Training Manual for the B-24 Liberator*, page 212.
50. Another exit point. Barry Ralph, *The Crash of* Little Eva, page 53.
50. To manually open. Ibid., page 54.
51. Lieutenant Settle couldn't get. Culos Settle statement, "Report of Aircraft Accident" for B-24 #42-7674.
51. "I could hear him yelling." Sgt. George Barulic testimony. 1943, 16 December. "Report of Aircraft Accident" for B-24 #42-7674.

51. Barulic succeeded. George Barulic interview, August 5, 2011

51. He crawled toward. Ibid.

51. "You know, luck is just." Ibid.

53. "Where the low-wing B-17." Frederick A. Johnsen, *B-24 Liberator: Rugged But Right*, page 29.

53. "as the bomb bay doors." Douglas, *Consolidated B-24 Liberator Manual*, page 100.

53. mentioned in war memoirs. Falstein, *Face of A Hero*, page 130. According to Falstein everybody aboard a B-24 knew it was not designed nor built for crash landings.

53. Ditching was also covered. Anonymous, *Pilot Training Manual for the B-24 Liberator*, page 210.

53. George Barulic chose to follow. Barulic interview, August 5, 2011.

54. Between 300 and 500 feet. Culos Settle statement, "Report of Aircraft Accident" for B-24 #42-7674.

54. "When I jumped." Barulic interview, August 5, 2011.

54. "We were going down." Culos Settle statement, "Report of Aircraft Accident" for B-24 #42-7674.

54. "We had changed direction." Ibid.

54. Considered an experienced officer. "Report of Aircraft Accident" for B-24 #42-7674.

54. Leaving Virginia Military Institute. Letter from W. B. Darden to Lt. Gen. Charles E. Kilbourne, February 2, 1944. Darden's father wrote, "If the nearness of war had not prevented it, it was his purpose and that of both his mother and myself, to send him back to liquidate the deficiency."

54. Darden enlisted. US World War II Army Enlistment Records, 1938–1946.

54. received his wings. Letter from W. B. Darden to Lt. Gen. Charles E. Kilbourne, February 10, 1944.

54. He had 1,453.05 hours. "Report of Aircraft Accident" for B-24 #42-7674.

56. Questioned about whether. Settle statement, December 16, 1943.

56. "only a cloud." Ibid.

56. "Was there very much." Ibid.

56. The forecast for the search route. "Report of Aircraft Accident" for B-24 #42-7674.

56. "Was any mention made." Culos Settle statement, "Report of Aircraft Accident" for B-24 #42-7674.

57. "I figured since everybody." Barulic interview, August 5, 2011.

57. They couldn't figure out. G. Pat Macha and Don Jordan, *Aircraft Wrecks in the Mountains and Deserts of California, 1909–2002*, page 398.

57. "Somebody checking." Barulic interview, August 5, 2011.

57. Lieutenant Settle called Hammer Field. Macha and Jordan, *Aircraft Wrecks in the Mountains and Deserts*, page 398.

57. badly damaged oxygen bottles. December 8, 1943, T.W.X. from Col. Guy Kirksey, Commanding Officer at Hammer Field, to Director of Flying Safety, Winston-Salem, North Carolina, in "Report of Aircraft Accident" for B-24 #42-7674.

57. Settle ventured out. Culos Settle statement, "Report of Aircraft Accident" for B-24 #42-7674.
58. blowing east to west. Ibid.
58. "still missing." December 8, 1943, T.W.X. from Col. Guy Kirksey.
58. "Pilot 50%." "Report of Aircraft Accident" for B-24 #42-7674.
58. for sensing "some difficulty." Ibid.
58. "A strong wind." Ibid.
59. Salinas Army Air Base. Robert A. Burtness, *The Santa Barbara B-24 Disasters*, page 31.
59. only forty-four hours. Ibid., page 47.
59. Point Arguello. The California coast is mostly north-south, but between Santa Barbara and Point Arguello, it trends west-east.
59. San Miguel Island. Burtness, *The Santa Barbara B-24 Disasters*, page 71. Bad luck plagued efforts to recover the crew from #42-7160. Though most of the crew's remains were brought home after their March 16, 1944, discovery, more remains were found by campers on San Miguel Island in September of 1954. On October 2, 1954, a Coast Guard cutter with a forensic team was dispatched to the island from Los Angeles harbor. Near Point Mugu, the 125-foot cutter collided with a 60-foot ketch, sinking it and killing two of the five passengers. A few scattered bones were eventually recovered from the crash site of the B-24 on San Miguel Island.

CHAPTER 6: THE PHANTOM RIDER

61. it was losing his mother. Janet Hovden interview, November 8, 2014. Frances Hester died from uremia. Today, she would be treated with kidney dialysis. There was no such thing in 1938.
61. She lived just long enough. Ibid.
61. he was heartbroken. Janet Hovden interview, September 5, 2011.
61. Clint had always wanted. Ibid.
61. Miriam Puranen. Diane Coombes interview, August 3, 2014. As a teenager, Miriam Puranen worked as an usher in a movie house in Juneau. This is where she met Bob Hester. Their daughter, Diane Hester Coombes, remembers her mother saying, "A friend of my dad had a date with a girl, and he asked his girlfriend if he could find a date for my dad. It turned out to be my mom."
62. "I'm going to find them." Lansford, "If My Son Is Alive," page 65. Lansford's original title for the article, according to a letter he sent to Janet Hovden on November 4, 1960, was the more-appropriate "The Long Search," which became the title of an anonymously penned article for an August 15, 1960, issue of *Time*.
62. Clint Hester received a letter. Mrs. Charles W. (Margaret) Turvey, Letter to Clinton W. Hester, January 4, 1944.
62. "It seems as though." Ibid.
62. "I can think of nothing worse." Ibid.
62. "In early 1943." Marlyn Pierce, "Earning Their Wings: Accidents and Fatalities in the United States Army Air Forces During Flight Training in World War Two," page 200.

62. American public. Ibid.
63. Reginald H. Thayer Jr. Stuart Leuthner and Oliver Jensen, *High Honor: Recollections by Men and Women of World War II Aviation*, page 173.
63. "The accident problem." Pierce, "Earning Their Wings," page 200.
63. A public relations campaign. Ibid., page 201.
63. Henry Neil Henson. Michele Aucoin e-mail, November 1, 2007. Henson's mother facilitated his death by corroborating his lie. For years she refused to believe he was dead.
63. Flying is inherently risky. Pierce, "Earning Their Wings," page xiii.
63. Deaths were inevitable. Ibid., page xv.
64. Arthur Artig. Leuthner and Jensen, *High Honor*, page 157.
64. "Death in combat." Pierce, "Earning Their Wings," page xv.
64. "I wouldn't take anything." Mrs. Charles W. (Margaret) Turvey, Letter to Clint Hester, June 11, 1944. Clint probably sent a map of his search area in the Sierra Nevada in addition to the probable route of 463 from Davis-Monthan Field to Hammer Field.
64. "Bob is a fine fellow." Turvey letter to Hester, June 11, 1944.
64. "We are still so broken up." Ibid.
65. Clint Hester wasn't a wealthy man. Lansford, "If My Son Is Alive," page 66.
65. "You'll never know just what." Mrs. Charles W. (Margaret) Turvey, Letter to Clint Hester, June 28, 1944.
66. "The program was one." Dominick A. Pisano, *To Fill the Skies With Pilots*, back jacket cover.
66. 11237 Graham Place. The house no longer exists. It was torn down to provide a connection between the eastbound Santa Monica Freeway (I-10) to the southbound San Diego Freeway (I-405).
66. Retz R-10. Photograph in Hester Family Archives. Built for speed, the Retz R-10 was a single-seat biplane with a radial engine. An advanced, or at least experimental, design for the era, there were no wing struts between the tandem wings. This reduced drag, or wind resistance, that would slow down the airplane.
66. Al Hanes wanted to buy it. Lansford, "If My Son Is Alive," page 66. Hanes eventually purchased Bob Hester's Retz R-10, converting it to the experimental H-1 Midget Racer, tail number NX-68379. The H-1 was a one-person mid-wing monoplane with an enclosed cockpit and an 85-horsepower Continental C-85 in-line engine.
66. Hanes lived. Ibid.
67. "Why not hunt." Ibid.
67. Starting at Clover Field. Ibid.
67. "But I can't give up." Ibid.
67. Clint Hester remarried in 1948. The date is calculated in two ways. First, the death certificate of Gladys Estelle Hester states she was a resident of Los Angeles for two years before her death. Next, Clint's daughter, Janet Hovden, told me during an interview on September 5, 2011, that Gladys died a year after she and Clint were married.

67. During the summer of 1947. Janet Hovden interview, September 5, 2011. Janet Hovden says that Clint "had a motorcycle *all* his life except for when he'd have his accidents, and then he'd have to give up the motorcycle and buy a new one later on." She's positive the accidents weren't from driving too fast. She remembers a time when Clint was hit by a truck that turned in front of him. "And then he had a couple of accidents coming home from Lone Pine, searching for Bob."

67. only thirty-five years old. Certificate of Death, Gladys Estelle Hester, July 20, 1949. Cause of death was a "cerebral hemorrhage" twelve days after suffering a "ruptured aneurysm." She was buried on July 23, 1949, in Forest Lawn Memorial Park (Glendale), Plot: Graceland, Lot 5647, Space 1. A large tree arches over her gravesite, giving shade during the hot southern California summers.

67. Though he never smoked. Hovden interview, September 5, 2011.

68. In 1950, Clint Hester. Inyo County. General Index, Grantors, A–K. July 1958–June 1971 (microfiche) and Inyo County. General Index, Grantors, A–K. July 1948–June 1958 (microfiche), Inyo County Assessor's Office. Assessor's Map Bk. 26 Pg.04, 1950. Clint built his home under the shade of some large, old cottonwood trees. The selling price of the house in 1954 was $19,500.

68. "Lone Pine's a beautiful spot." Lansford, "If My Son Is Alive."

68. "I won't have to go." Anonymous, "California: The Long Search," *Time*, August 15, 1960.

68. Every morning. Lansford, "If My Son Is Alive." The current owner was amazed to learn the history of his house when I met him in August of 2014.

68. "He was never a strict father." Hovden interview, September 5, 2011.

69. in the early 1920s. Janet Hovden, Letter to Peter Stekel, December 2014.

69. Laurel Canyon. Ibid.

69. Eight homes later. Ibid.

69. "Our dead are never dead." George Eliot, *Adam Bede*. The passage incorporating the quote is from Book 1, Chapter 10.

69. heart attack. Lansford, "If My Son Is Alive," page 67.

69. In September of 1954. Ibid.

69. US Air Force contacted. In 1947, the US Army Air Forces was spun off from the army and into the US Air Force.

69. A search of records. "Report of Aircraft Accident" for B-24 #41-28463.

70. TWENTY-FIVE DEGREES. December 8, 1943, T.W.X. from Col. Guy Kirksey.

70. A further note. Morse code for "2" is dot-dot-dash-dash-dash and for "3" is dot-dot-dot-dash-dash. It's easy to see how an inexperienced radio operator could have mis-keyed a dot or a dash either in transmission or reception.

70. OBVIOUSLY THIS POSITION REPORT. "Report of Aircraft Accident" for B-24 #41-28463.

70. On February 16, 1959. California Death Index, 1940–1997. Clinton William Hester. He's buried in Woodlawn Cemetery, Santa Monica, California, in Mausoleum—J, Old Section, Unit 2 / Fourth Addition, Niche #169.

70. Clint's military history. Clinton W. Hester military history in the files of the US National Homes for Disabled Volunteer Soldiers, 1866–1938.
71. Mrs. Turvey never forgot. Mrs. Charles (Margaret) Turvey, Letter to Mrs. Roger (Janet) Hovden, April 25, 1961.
71. "that he [Clint] was recognized." Ibid.
71. "It looked so lonesome." Ibid.
71. One of the most complete. Lansford, "If My Son Is Alive."
71. In a letter. William D. Lansford, Letter to Mrs. (Janet) Hovden, January 2, 1961. William Lansford was an interesting fellow. His mother was from Juarez, Mexico. His father was an Irish-Anglo ex-Texas cowboy and, later, a rough-and-tough police captain in Los Angeles. While still in his teens, Lansford enlisted in the marines and fought with the Second Marine Raider Battalion (Carlson's Raiders) in the South Pacific. At war's end he was discharged as a sergeant with the Navy Commendation Medal, a Purple Heart, and two Presidential Citations.

     After World War II, he enlisted again, this time in the army, and served during the Korean Conflict. He served nine years with the army, where he earned his officer commission. He also served as an 8th Army military correspondent. He ended his army career as a first lieutenant, with a Bronze Star and sixteen other awards and decorations.

     Lansford found little glory in battle. In his January 2, 1961, letter to Janet Hovden, Lansford wrote, "It is difficult for me to relate the foul extermination of human life with words like 'heroic' and 'gallant.'" He found better descriptive words, such as "sad" and "useless," writing that he resigned from the army after his stint in Korea, "after two wars, and at the tender age of thirty, because I had already begun to sense—more instinctively than intellectually, perhaps—that something was wrong; that it was nothing short of immoral to send young men out to meet well-ordered deaths, the way one orders willing children out to run an errand to the grocery store."
71. "But each time." Ibid.
72. The inescapable fact. Ibid.
72. "Everywhere you look." Turvey letter to Hester, June 28, 1944.
73. "for we've come to join them." Lansford letter to Hovden, January 2, 1961.

CHAPTER 7: TRAINING FOR WAR
74. Not everyone was surprised. Since October 1940, men between the ages of twenty-one and thirty-five were subject to the military draft. Col. Bettie Morden USA (Ret.) in, Maj. Gen. Jeanne M. Holm, *In Defense of a Nation: Servicewomen in World War II*, page 39.
74. self-interest and parochialism. Holm, *In Defense of a Nation*, page 143.
75. "American weakness." Eric M. Bergerud, *Fire in the Sky: The Air War in the South Pacific*, page 49.
75. "Americans cut corners." Ibid.
75. the army expected. Martin W. Bowman, *USAAF Handbook 1939–1945*, page 79.
76. "Between July 1939 and August 1945." Watry, *Washout!*, page 144.

76. "Planning factors." Ibid., page 6.
76. "Cadet recruiting." Ibid.
77. The pass rate. Ibid. Washout rates rose toward the end of the war because fewer pilots were needed.
77. "In 1938, the Air Corps." Ibid., page 47.
77. The fact that all of these boys. Girls, too; the Women's Army Corps (WAC) and Women's Army Auxiliary Corps (WAAC) trained around 150,000 young women during the war, many of whom were injured or died during training accidents and while on transport or other flying duty.
78. "in whose hands." Leonard Cheshire, *Bomber Pilot*, page 32.
78. "Bombing is technical." Ibid., pages 32–41.
79. "If you become annoyed." John J. Hibbits, *Take 'Er Up Alone, Mister!*, page 210.
80. "the pilot remained." Bernard C. Nalty, John F. Shiner, and George M. Watson, *With Courage: The U.S. Army Air Forces in World War II*, pages 170–72.
80. cadets were introduced. Ibid.
80. "the only ones." Ralph, *The Crash of* Little Eva, page 6.
81. and a gentleman: more pay. Hibbits, *Take 'Er Up Alone, Mister!*, page 208. "My base pay as second lieutenant was $150. My flying pay was one-half my base pay, or $75. Since my quarters were provided, the $40 single-quarters allowance was withheld. There was also a $21 ration allowance. After I'd paid my bills, I still have slightly over $200 left, and, compared to my cadet pay, felt independently wealthy." Newly commissioned officers also received a $250 clothing allowance.
81. specialized schools. Rebecca Hancock Cameron, *Training to Fly: Military Flight Training, 1907–1945*, pages 409–10.
81. "Now I discovered." Hibbits, *Take 'Er Up Alone, Mister!*, page 203.
81. "It sounded as if half a dozen." Ibid.
81. "They were still." Ibid., page 208.
81. the number of boys. Bowman, *USAAF Handbook 1939–1945*, page 79.
82. Even in combat. Bergerud, *Fire in the Sky*, page 418.
82. an additional 125 hours. Cameron, *Training to Fly*, page 411.
82. "Because bombing operations." Ibid., pages 458–59.
82. 613 total hours ... 235 hours. "Report of Aircraft Accident" for B-24 #41-28463; "Report of Aircraft Accident" for B-24 #42-7674.
83. That means that as unit training. Carigan, *Ad Lib*, page 74.
83. Ninety-seven hours ... forty hours. "Report of Aircraft Accident" for B-24 #41-28463; "Report of Aircraft Accident" for B-24 #42-7674.
83. "Flying was strictly." Frederick P. Graham and Harold W. Kulick, *He's in the Air Corps Now*, page 81.
83. "the science of getting." Ibid., page 124.
84. "But on-board instruments." Bergerud, *Fire in the Sky*, page 137.
84. a twenty-week course. Bowman, *USAAF Handbook 1939–1945*, page 83. Navigator training was a constantly moving target as the need for better-prepared navigators made itself known. First it was ten weeks, then twelve, then fifteen, eighteen, and finally, twenty. In the European Theater of Operation, the 8th Air Force mostly

gave up on individual navigators and had fleets of bombers play follow-the-leader, with one well-versed and reliable navigator in front of the bomber stream.

85. 202 hours. Cameron, *Training to Fly*, page 339.
85. "the road that leads." Beryl Markham, *West with the Night*, page 186.
85. Between 1938 and 1939. Bowman, *USAAF Handbook 1939–1945*, page 85.
85. 1.4 million persons. Nalty, et al., *With Courage*, page 175.
85. "Things, parts malfunctioned." Barulic interview, August 5, 2011.
86. thirty-four separate. Bowman, *USAAF Handbook 1939–1945*, page 86.
87. a tight fit everywhere. Freeman, *B-24 Liberator at War*, pages 95–110.
87. "The pilot gives." Carigan, *Ad Lib*, pages 68–70.
88. "Never leave it up." Ibid., page 60.
88. Darden was described. 461st Bomb Squadron history, Chapter IV, and crew roster (www.461st.org).
89. "I never had." Barulic interview, August 5, 2011.
89. paratrooper selection. Graham and Kulick, *He's in the Air Corps Now*, page 140.
89. during his sixteen weeks of training. Ibid., pages 142 and 165.
89. Leonard Cheshire's initial thoughts. Cheshire, *Bomber Pilot*, page 92.
89. A six-month survey. Johnsen, *B-24 Liberator: Rugged But Right*, page 29. The sample size of the survey was small: just fifty planes.
90. only 16.8 percent of B-17 crews. Ibid.
90. "I have felt." Gordon Forbes, *Goodbye to Some*, page 219.
90. Forbes then recounts. Ibid.
91. "Sometimes a plane." Bergerud, *Fire in the Sky*, page 107.
91. September 20, 1944 Johnsen, *B-24 Liberator: Rugged But Right*, page 29. Also, Raymond Long, "B-24 'Ditched' to Experiment on Structures," *Daily Press of New Port News*, September 21, 1944. There is a video of the test at www.youtube.com/watch?v=WjadMxpXprk.
91. "The peak was in." Bowman, *USAAF Handbook 1939–1945*, page 84.
93. "air power had new meaning." Graham and Kulick, *He's in the Air Corps Now*, page 21.
93. "The Nazis unleashed." Ibid.
93. Gone were the requirements. Ibid., page 22.
94. "reduce the number of accidents." Cameron, *Training to Fly*, page 320.
94. "War has little respect." Graham and Kulick, *He's in the Air Corps Now*, page 22.
94. "The training task." H. H. Arnold, *Global Mission*, page 359.
94. "at a rate." Ibid.
95. "Another disturbing element." Ralph, *The Crash of Little Eva*, page 19.
95. but for every navy. Navy Department Library, Aviation Personnel Fatalities in World War II.

CHAPTER 8: NOT *EXACTLY* A DEATH TRAP

96. Within five and a half years. Douglas, *Consolidated B-24 Liberator Manual*, page 15.
96. "characterized by a high-aspect ratio." Ibid., page 59.

96. Royal Air Force figures. Ibid., page 28.
97. "surpassed the production." Martin Bowman, *The B-24 Liberator 1939–1945*, page 6. According to Bowman, 19,256 were produced.
97. Consolidated Aircraft Company licensed production. Birdsall, *Log of the Liberators*, pages 312–13.
97. Captain Darden's *Exterminator*. Ibid.
98. just like pilots. Pierce, "Earning Their Wings," page 56. As General H. H. "Hap" Arnold explained, "The Air Corps was going into 'mass-production' of flyers." In its recruiting manual the Air Corps took it a step further and compared the training regimen of pilots and crew to an "assembly line."
98. "Willow Run finally created." Douglas, *Consolidated B-24 Liberator Manual*, page 59.
98. the use of dies. Ibid., page 56.
98. "the worst piece." A. J. Baime, *The Arsenal of Democracy*, page 176.
98. a B-24 training conference. Pierce, "Earning Their Wings," pages 173–74.
99. "We have more." Baime, *The Arsenal of Democracy*, page 177.
99. "Heavy on the controls." Carigan, *Ad Lib*, page 9.
99. "We started with war-weary B-24Ds." Ibid., page 74.
99. The lower-octane fuel. 461st Bomb Group History, Chapter 4, "Training, Inspection, and Preparation for Overseas Movement" (www.461st.org), page 11.
99. Through all of its variants. Birdsall, *Log of the Liberators*, page 315.
100. In 1941 the cost to produce. Douglas, *Consolidated B-24 Liberator Manual*, page 67. After the war, surplus Liberators could be purchased by schools and civic groups for memorial display from the Reconstruction Finance Corporation for $350.00, plus shipping costs. Nicholas A. Veronico, *Hidden Warbirds II*, page 180.
100. "My first impressions." John Musgrave, quoted in Freeman, *B-24 Liberator at War*, page 37.
100. "crew or even aircraft survival." Freeman, *B-24 Liberator at War*, page 11.
100. "The design of military aircraft." Pierce, "Earning Their Wings," pages 20 and 170.
100. For basic bodily crew comfort. Baime, *The Arsenal of Democracy*, page 176.
100. "Relief tubes were a devilish device." Smith, *The Wrong Stuff*, page 63.
100. "He had to take off." Ibid., page 182. Smith's crew was later attacked over their target by German fighter aircraft. Adding insult to humiliation, the flight engineer retrieved his helmet to protect his head. "However, when his head temperature went up from the excitement of battle, his frozen waste thawed out and dribbled down out of his helmet and soiled him badly."
101. "The Stirling was limited." Ronald Bailey, *The Air War in Europe*, page 62.
102. "The wing area was smaller." Douglas, *Consolidated B-24 Liberator Manual*, page 28.
102. "an immediate loss." Bill Holder, *B-24 Liberator*, page 6.
102. "With all power off." Carigan, *Ad Lib*, page 50.
102. "So much so that formation." Douglas, *Consolidated B-24 Liberator Manual*, page 28.
102. "Trimmed properly." Ibid., page 44.

102. "When airspeed was too low." Holder, *B-24 Liberator*, page 6.

102. There were other problems." Freeman, *B-24 Liberator at War*, page 9.

102. With the tremendous weight. Ardery, *Bomber Pilot*, page 154.

103. taxiing B-24s. Birdsall, *Log of the Liberators*, page 10.

103. "carried a spare nosewheel." Ibid., pages 6 and 13.

103. 4,400 landing-gear failures. Pierce, "Earning Their Wings," page 169.

103. "probably the best radials of the war." Freeman, *B-24 Liberator at War*, page 90.

103. 5,500 Liberator accidents. Pierce, "Earning Their Wings," page 169.

103. "and then changed his mind." "Report of Aircraft Accident" for B-24 #42-7674.

103. related to turbochargers." Freeman, *B-24 Liberator at War*, page 90.

103. grossly inadequate. 461st History, Chapter 3, page 14 (www.461st.org).

103. all of its troubles. "Report of Aircraft Accident" for B-24 #42-7674.

104. continually overhaul. 461st History, Chapter 4, page 11 (www.461st.org). Marlyn Pierce comments in his PhD dissertation from December 2013: "This shortage was most critical in 1943 and that for the month of October alone the shortage of high-octane fuel caused the loss of 5,558 flying hours and the reduction in output of 60 pilots and 29 bomber crews." Less experienced pilots meant a greater risk for more accidents.

104. seventy crews at Hammer Field. 461st History, Chapter 3, page 7 (www.461st .org).

104. to provide six hours. Ibid., page 10.

104. "long periods of maintenance." Ibid., page 13.

104. Group airplanes were grounded. Ibid.

104. maintenance errors. Ibid., page 166.

104. it had a faulty compass. John Specht statement, "Report of Aircraft Accident" for B-24 #41-28463.

105. twenty-six gallons of oil. Douglas, *Consolidated B-24 Liberator Manual*, page 133.

105. about six hours. John Specht statement, "Report of Aircraft Accident." for B-24 #41-28463.

105. neither wingtip is visible. Douglas, *Consolidated B-24 Liberator Manual*, page 133.

105. faced with engine lives. Freeman, *B-24 Liberator at War*, page 86.

105. ground crews worked long. Ibid., page 91.

105. the average age. Ibid., page 84.

105. "The group that trained." Ardery, *Bomber Pilot*, page 51.

105. Biggs Field. Located in El Paso, Texas.

106. "The effect of the combination." Ardery, *Bomber Pilot*, page 51.

106. "planning how to meet." Ibid., page 23.

106. "You can fly okay." Ibid., page 49.

106. B-24 pilots like James Davis. James M. Davis, *In Hostile Skies*, page 140.

107. "Fuel seeping from tanks." Freeman, *B-24 Liberator at War*, page 11.

107. "No one smoked." Ibid., page 86.

107. Some B-24s had engine fire extinguishers. Edgar J. Allen, *Pilot from the Prairie*, page 42.

107. "if the brakes were applied." Freeman, *B-24 Liberator at War*, page 40.

107. The abortion rates. Ibid., page 40

107. Each of the big bombers. Graham and Kulick, *He's in the Air Corps Now*, page 107.

107. Long before the cabin crew. Ibid.

108. Before the bomber could leave. Ibid.

108. "Normally the Liberator's." James Dugan and Carroll Stewart, *Ploesti*, pages 66–67.

108. Every sixty hours. Ibid.

108. General Hap Arnold. H. H. Arnold, *Global Mission*, pages 66–67.

108. "There's usually more on the way." Smith, *The Wrong Stuff*, page 32.

109. what prompted Bob Hester. Diane Coombes interview, August 3, 2014.

109. "Survival rates." Douglas, *Consolidated B-24 Liberator Manual*, page 29.

109. describes the experience. Laura Hillenbrand, *Unbroken*, pages 187–91. Like Bill Cronin, Louis Zamperini was born in Olean, New York.

110. fatality rates. Freeman, *B-24 Liberator at War*, pages 11–12.

110. Enemy fighters. Bailey, *The Air War in Europe*, page 114.

110. Pilots and crews also died. Ibid., page 120.

110. "For the majority." Freeman, *B-24 Liberator at War*, page 12.

111. While serving as a B-17 instructor. Starr Smith, *Jimmy Stewart Bomber Pilot*, page 46.

111. Sometimes the famous. "War Writer Killed," *Harrisburg Telegraph*, September 11, 1944.

111. William P. Upshur. Anonymous, "General Upshur, Charlie Paddock Die in Air Crash," *Pittsburgh Press*, July 23, 1943.

111. "Soon afterward." Bailey, *The Air War in Europe*, page 187.

112. "I had nothing else to compare." Freeman, *B-24 Liberator at War*, page 92.

CHAPTER 9: FINDING THE HAMMER FIELD BOYS— *EXTERMINATOR'S* CREW

114. born on March 6, 1918. California Death Index, 1940–1970, Ancestry.com.

114. April 3, 1942. US World War II Army Enlistment Records, 1938–1946, Ancestry .com.

114. National Jewish Welfare Board. AJHS World War II Jewish Serviceman Cards, 1942–1947, Ancestry.com.

114. September 26, 1955. Anonymous, "Lake Yields 4 in '43 Air Crash," *Stars and Stripes*, September 26, 1955.

115. IDPF for Schlosser. Individual Deceased Personnel File (IDPF) for 2nd Lt. Samuel J. Schlosser, 1955.

116. February 23, 1922. New World Descendants, Nyswonger Family, Rootsweb .ancestry.com.

116. locomotive fireman. Ibid.

117. Clark's IDPF. Individual Deceased Personnel File (IDPF) for S/Sgt. Franklin Nyswonger, 1955.

117. telegram dated November 15, 1955. Ibid.

118. Fort Snelling National Cemetery. Ibid.
118. December 9, 1941, issue. Anonymous, Vande Plasch wedding announcement, *Milwaukee Journal*, December 9, 1941.
118. Oscar's reply. Oscar George Traczewitz, Letter to Leona Traczewitz Vande Plasch, January 16, 1944.
119. "She would have made." Oscar Traczewitz II interview, March 19, 2014.
120. born on July 3, 1917. Draft registration card for Culos Marion Settle, #3512, October 16, 1940.
120. Appalachian State University. Anonymous, *Rhododendron—Yearbook for Appalachian State University*, 1940, pages 70, 160, 166, and 168.
120. He also got married. They were married on October 26, 1940. Annie Mae Settle was remarried on November 16, 1962, to Gene Pratt. William Root e-mail, May 6, 2016.
120. draft registration card. Draft registration card for Settle.
120. George Barulic's description. Barulic interview, August 5, 2011.
120. Distinguished Flying Cross. 461st Bomb Squadron history, www.461st.org.
122. At VMI Darden studied. *Bomb*, Yearbook for Virginia Military Institute, 1940.
122. July 26, 1940. William H. U. Darden enlistment record.
122. less than one credit remaining. W. B. Darden, Letter to Lt. Gen. Charles E. Kilbourne, Superintendent, Virginia Military Institute, February 10, 1944. "Captain Darden, who was my son, failed to secure his degree with the Class of '40, if I am not mistaken, by a fraction of a point. If the nearness of war had not prevented, it was his purpose and that of both his mother and myself, to send him back to liquidate the deficiency."
122. Darden married. Wedding announcement for Lt. and Mrs. William H. Darden, Sunday, March 16, 1941.
122. had just separated from his wife. Anonymous, "Marital Troubles Aired at Trial of War Risk Suit." Unknown newspaper article in Virginia Military Institute files of William H. U. Darden, 1944.
122. his radio operator. Barulic interview, August 5, 2011. "He had a reputation. I guess he was rated number one."
122. official paperwork. 461st Bomb Group History, Chapter IV, Training, Inspection, and Preparation for Overseas Movement, page 10, December 1943 (www.461st .org).
123. for $200 in the tiny settlement. Tom Spangle interview, March 30, 2011.
123. Tom Spangle remembers. Ibid.
123. physical examination for flying. Physical Examination for Flying, IDPF for Sergeant Richard L. Spangle, 1955.
124. 5 feet, 10 inches, and 130 pounds. Enlistment record for Richard Lee Spangle, IDPF for Sergeant Richard L. Spangle, 1955.
124. Tom recalls. Spangle interview, March 30, 2011.
124. blue star. Begun in 1945 after World War II, a blue star was used on service flags (an official banner that family members of service members can display) to denote a service member fighting in the war. Since that time blue stars also include

Memorial Markers, Memorial By-ways, and National Cemeteries, parks, veterans' facilities, and gardens.

124. Tom Spangle's daughter, Lori. Lori Spangle interview, March 30, 2011.

124. Tom's wife. Audria Spangle interview, March 30, 2011.

124. Losing her husband. Mary Condo interview, August 22, 2011.

125. "The Best." Address book for Richard Lee Spangle.

125. "It was a good place." Condo interview, August 22, 2011.

125. In 1946 Mary married. Ibid.

126. "Richard never really." Ibid.

126. "I think Richard's death." Ibid.

126. October 8, 1942. Enlistment record for Dick E. Mayo.

127. Washington and Lee University. David Mayo interview, July 29, 2014. The campus is a thirty-minute walk away from Virginia Military Institute, where Capt. William Darden attended college.

127. without finishing his bachelor's degree. This was not unusual at the time. Walker Mayo e-mail, March 14, 2016.

127. "Sgt. Mayo volunteered." Anonymous, "Five Floyd Countians Missing or Dead, Reports Received Here State," *Floyd County Times*, December 9, 1943.

127. Older brother Louis Harkey Mayo. David Mayo e-mail, July 28, 2014.

127. Younger brother Walker Porter Mayo. Ibid.

127. According to his nephew. Ibid.

128. He didn't have to choose. Of all the boys on the two B-24s, Dick Mayo is the only one who had no initial intention of joining the air service when he enlisted. This is confirmed by an entry in his diary from February 14, 1943.

128. Dick Mayo's diary. This and other quotes by Dick Mayo are from the diary of Dick Erwin Mayo.

129. Southern boy, John Waites. John B. Waites (January 1, 1921–September 6, 2005) finished the war as a corporal. One big reason he could have been so homesick at Christmas was that he missed his wife back home in Russell County, Alabama.

131. "As far as the eye can carry." Chapter 2, "The Salt Flats at Wendover," History of 461st Bomb Group (www.461st.org).

132. "I've had a lot of tragedy." This and other quotes are from Barulic interview, August 5, 2011.

133. fifty-two missions. Mary Anne Viator e-mail, June 20, 2016.

CHAPTER 10: FINDING THE HAMMER FIELD BOYS—463'S CREW

134. born on November 30, 1923. US Veterans Gravesites, ca. 1775–2006, Ancestry.com.

134. summary of his enlistment record. US World War II Army Enlistment Records, 1938–1946, Ancestry.com.

134. David Valentine, of Toledo, Ohio. "Wrecked B24 Flew From D-M," *Tucson Daily Citizen*, August 4, 1960.

134. August 4, 1960. Ibid.

136. Turvey was a big man. Charles W. Turvey Jr. enlistment record. Patterson Field was renamed Wright-Patterson Air Force Base in 1948.

136. He was a stocky. Ellis H. Fish enlistment record, Individual Deceased Personnel File (IDPF) for 2nd Lt. Ellis H. Fish.

136. August 21, 1943. Official report of death, January 10, 1944, Fish IDPF.

137. Mileage expenses. Schedule of Expenses and Amounts Claimed, Fish IDPF.

137. Rena Mary. At birth the girls were christened Mary Rena and Mary Reta. To avoid confusion they both later decided to invert the names and became Rena Mary and Reta Mary. They were known in their hometown as "the Bursey Twins."

137. February 17, 1942. Vermont marriage record for Mary Rena Bursey and Carroll James Hill.

137. "Uncle Bob emulated." David Hill interview, January 27, 2016.

138. enlistment physical. Robert O. Bursey enlistment record, September 12, 1942, in Individual Deceased Personnel File (IDPF) for Robert O. Bursey, October 6, 1960.

138. August 23, 1943. Vermont marriage record for Reta Mary Bursey and Richard J. Allen.

138. Laredo Army Field. Located in Laredo, Texas. Diploma, US Army Air Forces. August 7, 1943.

139. Bob's parachute. Doesn't it seem odd that the army would have allowed Bob to travel with his parachute?

139. a phone call to CJ. David Hill interview, January 27, 2014.

139. "We have been scheduled." Dick Mayo diary, November 15, 1943.

140. Only one letter. Robert O. Bursey, Letter to his mother, ND, Bursey Family Archives.

140. Robert Bursey graduated. There are three newspaper clippings of unknown attribution in the Bursey Family Archives that cover Bob's life between high school and his disappearance in 463. The first records his return to Houlton Air Base in Houlton, Maine, after a holiday furlough. That must be from Christmas, 1942. The other two report on Bob's recent disappearance and must be from December, 1943. The first clip is untitled. The remaining two are "S/Sgt. Robert Bursey 'Missing in Action,'" and "Sergt. Bursey in Crew of Plane Week Overdue."

140. Bob's nephew. Hill interview, January 27, 2014.

140. conveyed Robert Oakley Bursey's. Bursey IDPF.

141. A solemn requiem Mass. Obituary, Bursey IDPF.

141. October 6, 1960. Ibid.

142. You were more likely. Donald L. Miller, *Master of the Air*, page 471. Loss statistics for Germany and Great Britain began in 1939, which means the United States lost a similar number of aviators in roughly two and a half years' less time.

142. "Only 3 percent." Smith, *The Wrong Stuff*, page 262.

142. Until the spring of 1944. Maj. James J. Carroll, "Physiological Problems of Bomber Crews in the 8th Air Force during WWII," March 1997, page 30.

142. his first combat mission. Barulic interview, August 5, 2011.

143. Consider the famous bad luck boys. Mario Martinez, *Lady's Men*.

143. Patrick J. Cronin. Ron Welch Jr. e-mail, April 7, 2016.
144. St. Bonaventure's College. Since 1950, St. Bonaventure University.
144. "He used to walk." Ronald Welch interview, October 26, 2011.
144. Eileen Cronin Welch, remembers. Eileen Cronin Welch interview, May 1, 2014.
144. "I can see him." Eileen Cronin Welch interview, June 20, 2012.
145. "He could do so much." Ibid.
145. "We were good friends." Charlotte Y. Murphy interview, October 8, 2014.
145. "We didn't have any place." Welch interview, May 1, 2014.

CHAPTER 11: THE PLANE IN THE LAKE

146. Telegrams were dispatched. F. E. Glantzberg, Telegram to Mrs. Merle Spangle, December 6, 1943.
146. Debris collected. December 8, 1943, T.W.X. from Col. Guy Kirksey.
146. "in case personnel." Ibid.
147. "[the] base furnish men." Ibid.
147. Colonel Glantzberg. Col. Frederic E. Glantzberg, Letter to Mrs. Reba E. Mayo, December 14, 1943.
149. In one of his first duties. James C. Dooley, Commanding Officer, 766th Bombardment Squadron, Hammer Field, Letter to Mr. and Mrs. Mayo, December 17, 1943.
149. However, the scope of the search. "Search for Plane Pressed," *Oakland Tribune*, December 8, 1943
149. Also with the search team. Glantzberg letter to Mayo, December 14, 1943.
149. According to data. National Oceanic and Atmospheric Administration, Record of Climatological Observations for Huntington Lake, California, December 1 1943– January 31, 1944.
149. The sky was CAVU. "Informal Report of Aircraft Accident" written December 12, 1943, by Alexander E. Sprout, Capt. M.C. AME, Squadron Surgeon, 461st Bombardment Group (H), Office of the Group Surgeon, Hammer Field, Fresno, California, in "Report of Aircraft Accident" for B-24 #42-7674.
151. A partial financial accounting. IDPF for 2nd Lt. Samuel J. Schlosser.
151. found nothing. Sherman Spangle, Letter to Mr. and Mrs. Mayo, December 22, 1943. Huntington Lake Road follows the reservoir's north shore fairly closely, but there is no shoreline road on the south side except where it crosses two of the reservoir's four dams. As it happens, the wreckage would be found on the south shoreline of the lake near Dam #1.
151. Porter and Reba Mayo. Ibid. Dick's father, Walker Porter Mayo, was always referred to as "Porter" by his family.
152. as they carried bombs. Ibid.
152. On December 31, 1943. 461st Bombardment Group History (www.461st.org).
152. "Approximately 43 inches." January 5, 1944, T.W.X. "Report of Aircraft Accident" for B-24 #42-7674.
152. search was suspended. Ibid., January 7, 1944.

152. "As you know." H. M. Beemer, Special Agent, Letter to Mrs. W. P. Mayo, January 10, 1944.

153. Col. Guy Kirksey. Col. Guy Kirksey, Letter to Mrs. Reba E. Mayo, January 13, 1944. Kirksey was a veteran of World War I and flew with Billy Mitchell.

153. a new message. Sherman Spangle, Letter to Mr. and Mrs. Mayo, January 14, 1944.

153. Not even a week later. Sherman Spangle, Letter to Mr. and Mrs. Mayo, January 20, 1944.

154. Citing the large snowpack. Col. Guy Kirksey, Letter to Mr. W. P. Mayo, February 29, 1944.

154. This was reiterated. Major Leland F. Johnson, Letter to Mrs. Reba E. Mayo, April 20, 1944.

154. Meanwhile, word came. Sherman Spangle, Letter to Friends (Mr. and Mrs. Mayo), March 15, 1944.

154. chaplain John W. Knoble. Chaplain John W. Knoble, Letter to W. B. Marriott, pastor, June 27, 1944.

154. Mrs. Mayo was advised. 1st Lt. Robert H. Finical, Letter to Mrs. Reba E. Mayo, July 11, 1944.

154. "After you left." H. M. Beemer, Letter to Mr. Mayo, July 15, 1944.

155. "If you can come." Ibid.

155. He wrote to Hammer Field. Lt. Col. Frank G. Millard, Letter to Mr. W. Porter Mayo, December 20, 1945.

156. company town. As of the 2010 census, the population of Big Creek was 175. There is an elementary school, some restaurants, and over 100 housing units. Other than working for Southern California Edison, the main employment for the town centers around working at the school or servicing the tourists.

157. "His heart." Mrs. W. P. Mayo, Letter to Mr. and Mrs. Spangle, January 16, 1947.

157. "While in the full participation." Ibid.

157. "In view of the fact." Reba (Mrs. W. P. Mayo) Mayo, Letter to Commanding General, Hammer Field, Fresno, California, October 20, 1947.

157. Secretary of War. Mrs. W. P. Mayo, Letter to Secretary of War, April 26, 1948.

158. frost-proof the dams. "Utility Company to Lower Level of Lake," *Bakersfield Californian*, June 13, 1955.

158. Don and Bill. Don Ekhoff e-mail, May 8, 2015.

158. "I handed it." Ibid.

158. Ronald White. "Huntington Yields '43 Plane Wreckage," *Fresno Bee*, September 15, 1955.

158. Alameda County Sheriff's Underwater Rescue Unit. "Skindivers in Action," *Oakland Tribune*, September 5, 1955. Alameda County is located in the eastern San Francisco Bay area.

158. September 17-18. "Skin Divers to Hunt Plane in Sierra Lake," *The Independent* (Long Beach, California), September 8, 1955.

158. local fisherman. "1943 Bomber Wreckage Spotted in Sierra Lake," *Oakland Tribune*, September 15, 1955.

158. north of Dam #1. "Huntington Yields '43 Plane Wreckage."

158. September 2, 1955. Merle Spangle, Letter to Mrs. Mayo, September 2, 1955.

159. in ill health. Reba Mayo, Letter to Mrs. Spangle, September 21, 1955.

159. "Three days of diving." Herbert Schlosser, Letter to Director of Military Personnel, September 29, 1955, in IDPF for 2nd Lt. Samuel J. Schlosser.

159. The congressman's office. William M. Gage, assistant, Letter to Col. Robert L. Kelly, October 14, 1955, in IDPF for S/Sgt. Franklin Nyswonger.

159. Melvin Vande Plasch writes. Melvin Vande Plasch, Letter to National Air Force Headquarters, October 3, 1955, in Individual Deceased Personnel Files (IDPF) for Sgt. Donald C. Vande Plasch.

160. An October 28 memo. Helen T. McDonald, memo to Mr. Czarnecki, Office of Congressman Clement J. Zablocki, October 28, 1955, in IDPF for Sgt. Vande Plasch.

160. By November 2. Telegram to Melvin Vande Plasch from Decedent Branch, Memorial Division.

160. "Due to the nature." Telegram from the Deputy Post Commander, Presidio of San Francisco, to Mr. Ernest Vande Plasch, November 5, 1955.

160. Zablocki gets a similar. Memo from Helen T. McDonald, Planning Office, Memorial Division, November 14, 1955.

160. Melvin Vande Plasch. Letter from Colonel J. E. Geiser to Mr. Melvin Vande Plasch, November 17, 1955.

160. they consisted of very little. IDPF for Sgt. Vande Plasch.

160. Mrs. Mayo writes. Reba Mayo, Letter to Mrs. Spangle, November 2, 1955.

161. The IDPF paper trail. Individual Deceased Personnel Files (IDPFs) for Captain William H. Darden, 2nd Lt. Samuel J. Schlosser, S/Sgt. Franklin Nyswonger, Sgt. Richard L. Spangle, and Sgt. Donald C. Vande Plasch.

161. "should remains be recovered." Col. Walter P. Scoggins, Memorial Division, Memorandum for Record, August 18, 1955, in IDPF for Capt. Darden.

161. Other papers. IDPF for Darden.

161. One of them. "Divers Find 2 More Bodies in Old Wreck," *Bakersfield Californian*, September 24, 1955.

161. A letter from Sherman Spangle. Sherman Spangle, Letter to Mrs. Mayo, December 19, 1955.

162. IDPFs for the boys. IDPFs for Darden, Schlosser, Nyswonger, Spangle, and Vande Plasch. The IDPF for Dick Mayo supports Mr. Spangle's observation.

162. The divers. Memo, "Recovery and Disposition of Remains, Huntington Lake, California," from L. P. Day, September 15, 1955, in IDPF for Vande Plasch.

162. There were a couple. Paul McCoy interview, March 29, 2012; McCoy e-mail, March 4, 2012.

162. Captain Darden's remains. IDPF for Darden.

162. the mud. Tom Spangle interview, March 30, 2011.

162. "and they would." Ibid.

163. Sherman Spangle explained. Spangle, Letter to Mrs. Mayo, December 19, 1955.

163. You can tell. Ibid.

163. John Marion was spending his honeymoon. John Marion interview, November 21, 2011.

163. A local historian. Ibid.

164. "some of the bodies recovered." "Fatal Plunge . . . 37-year-old Crash into Lake Is Recalled by Flier," *Fresno Bee*, July 9, 1980.

164. "the bodies of three crewmen. "Divers Seek to Recover Plane," *Los Angeles Times*, July 1, 1980, and Gene Rose, "Raising a Liberator," *Fresno Bee*, June 27, 1980.

164. "Fresno County." "Divers Seek to Recover Plane."

164. "I know a lot of pieces." "Raising a Liberator."

164. Led by Dan Webb. Ibid.

164. "I think the recovery." Ibid.

165. Salvage II. Investment Summary, Salvage II, A California Limited Partnership.

165. Spangle and his wife. Subscription Agreement between Salvage II and Thomas Spangle and Audria Spangle, June 2, 1980.

165. 30-ton crane. "Effort to Raise Old Bomber Goes Under," *Los Angeles Times*, July 13, 1980.

165. "They had pulled." John Marion interview, November 21, 2011.

165. "a backer had lied." "Effort to Raise Old Bomber Goes Under."

165. Dutra Construction stopped work. Ibid.

165. Forte sued Dutra. David Paul Steiner, Esq., Letter to Mr. and Mrs. Tom Spangle, June 23, 1981. At this point in the salvage saga, the Spangles may have looked at their Subscription Agreement and Section 10, where it reminded them they could get their money back if Salvage II was not successful in selling all twenty units of the limited partnership. In an October 26, 1981, letter to the Spangles, a contrite Gene Forte wrote, "I state the fact that I never intended to cause you to loose [*sic*] money, or gain by any such loss. If I had the money personally, I would allow you to withdraw your investment."

165. GTY Investment Planning. "Effort to Raise Old Bomber Goes Under."

166. US Navy Reserve. Robert Palomares, "Search Comes Up Empty," *Fresno Bee*, 1990. Month unknown.

166. In the early 1990s. Cyndee Fontana and Mark Grossi, "Huntington Lake Still Holds Crash Mystery," *Fresno Bee*, September 14, 2008.

166. In 2008 Matt Finnegan. Ibid.

166. A short video. 2013. Rachel Zurcher, "In Search of the Huntington Liberator," www.youtube.com/watch?v=xusZGpOdMKU.

166. Zurcher grew up. Dan Zurcher interview, August 9, 2016.

166. a fourth-grade student. George F. Gruner, *Into the Night: Hammer Field . . . Camp Pinedale . . . Fresno Fairgrounds—Central California in World War II*, page 169.

167. "the likes of which." Gene Rose, "Warplane's Icy Death Brings New Life to Fourth Graders' Lessons," *Fresno Bee*, April 29, 1991.

167. "They are acquiring." Ibid.

167. they dedicated a monument. Gene Rose, "Pupils Honor WWII Fliers Lost at Lake," *Fresno Bee*, December 7, 1991.

168. later donated around 2012. Mary Jean Crider interview, June 14, 2016.
168. the artist is unsure. Michael J. Rasmussen interview, November 17, 2011.
169. They published. Bob Crider, ed. Untitled booklet by the 1991 and 1992 Fourth-Grade Classes of Big Creek School, ND.
169. In a letter of appreciation. "Winnie" Mason, Letter to Jean Brynn and other children at Big Creek School District, May 12, 1991.

CHAPTER 12: THE SEARCHERS

171. "granite friction face." Brother William McCall, Letter to Gordon Boyd, High Sierra Ranger, Sequoia & Kings Canyon National Parks, November 1, 1972.
171. "of a service aircraft." Ibid.
172. "I found an old." Ibid.
172. "hopelessly lost." S. Samuel Boghosian, "Another One of Our B-24s is Missing!" *Air Classics* Vol. 12, No. 9 (September 1976), page 22.
172. "the lake doesn't freeze." Marion, interview, November 21, 2011.
172. his Hester Lake article. S. Samuel Boghosian, "The Tragic Tale of the Lake Hester Liberator," *Air Classics* Vol. 15, No. 6 (June 1979), pages 56–59.
173. another magazine story. R. W. Koch, "The Deadly Storm," *Air Classics* Vol. 14, No. 2 (February 1978), pages 88–91.
173. "Found about enough aluminum." Extract from LeConte Ranger Station log, September 22, 1986, in Sequoia & Kings Canyon National Parks archives.
174. "Gathered up pieces." Extract from LeConte Canyon Ranger Station log, August 31, 1987, LeConte Canyon Ranger Station, LeConte Canyon, Kings Canyon National Park.
174. "How did that plane." Ibid.
174. "Carried last load. Ibid., September 20, 1987.
174. "the deep past." Ibid., July 26, 1988.
174. They could see. Stephen DeSalvo interview, July 9, 2011.
175. DeSalvo wrote to. Stephen C. DeSalvo, DDS, Letter to Superintendent J. Thomas Ritter, Sequoia & Kings Canyon National Parks, August 7, 1989.
175. "Much of the wreckage was removed." William L. Bancroft, Acting Superintendent, Sequoia & Kings Canyon National Parks, Letter to Felix J. Stalls III, Major, USAF, August 9, 1989.
175. "authorizes you to use." William L. Bancroft, Acting Superintendent, Sequoia & Kings Canyon National Parks, Letter to Dr. Stephen C. DeSalvo, DDS, August 17, 1989. Alden Nash, Sierra Sub-District Ranger, had direct supervision over the Kings Canyon National Park wilderness at this time, and was kept completely in the dark about plans for private citizens to be helicoptered in to Hester Lake. Alden Nash e-mail, March 29, 2016.
176. "high-grading." Then, as today, collectors as well as aviation museums will pay well for instrumentation from a Liberator cockpit.
176. Speaking about the private flight. John Kraushaar interview, April 3, 2016.
176. Kraushaar also remembers. Ibid.

176. "There is no interest." Maj. William G. Anderson Jr., Letter to William L. Bancroft, Acting Superintendent, Sequoia & Kings Canyon National Parks, August 24, 1989.

177. "fabulous shape." DeSalvo interview, July 9, 2011.

177. video DeSalvo shot. Stephen DeSalvo, video recording of his Hester Lake dive, September, 1989.

177. the handwritten memo. Notes to the File, October 24, 1990, in Sequoia & Kings Canyon National Parks archives.

178. "After all." Steve (Stephen) DeSalvo, Letter to Sierra District Ranger Paul Fodor, Sequoia & Kings Canyon National Parks, September 13, 1990.

179. Fodor's reply. Paul Fodor, Letter to Stephen DeSalvo, March 8, 1991.

179. "They wanted to have." Christopher Thomas interview, July 14, 2011.

179. main wing spar. "The spar is the main structural component of a wing, running from wingtip to wingtip. Sometimes they terminate at the fuselage where each is bolted to a structural box. Sometimes there is a 'carry-through' that serves to attach spar to spar. There are two spars in the B-24 wing, one near the leading edge and the other near the trailing edge. They are attached to each other, fore to aft, with ribs, the upper and lower shapes of which dictate the shape of the wing when the skin is attached. The larger of the wing spars is called the main wing spar." Fred Smyth e-mail, March 30, 2016.

179. Christopher Thomas wrote. Christopher R. Thomas, Letter to Superintendent, Sequoia & Kings Canyon National Parks, October 22, 1993.

179. Nearly four months later. J. Thomas Ritter, Letter to Christopher R. Thomas, February 1, 1994.

180. We completely underestimated. Christopher Thomas interview, October 23, 2011.

180. "interesting" pieces. Ibid.

180. "You'd kick." Ibid.

180. the bumper. Anonymous, *Flight Manual for B-24 Liberator.*

180. "severely mangled." Christopher Thomas interview, July 14, 2011.

180. "One engine." Ibid. Spinning propellers show impact damage; especially the edges, from where they've hit something. Stationary propellers don't show impact damage.

182. blackout conditions. "The blackout rules generally only applied to coastal areas in the United States, since there was no danger of air raids or the need to avoid backlighting ships far from the coast. All cities, including Tucson, did conduct blackout drills from time to time, but even the coastal cities did not have total blackouts all the time." James Stemm e-mail, November 13, 2012.

182. "One of the gentlemen." Thomas interview, July 14, 2011. The gentleman he spoke with was R.W. Koch, author of magazine articles about the Hester Lake and Huntington Lake B-24s.

183. "They made a bad decision." Ibid.

183. "he ran out." Ibid.

183. "But once you put." Ardery, *Bomber Pilot*, page 50.

184. "The Jackass Expedition." Paul Sweinhagen, "The Jackass Expedition, Part One," *Mad Diver*, ND.

184. "and all the little stuff." Paul Sweinhagen interview, March 16, 2012.

184. "At the trailhead." Ibid.

184. "It looked like." Ibid.

184. "They were the right guys." Ibid.

184. Marine Expeditions International. Kevin Neal, "Lake Hester Expedition 2003," Marine Expeditions International. Unpublished manuscript, 2003.

185. "We had injury. We had death." Kevin Neal interview, April 13, 2012.

185. "tasted funny." Ibid.

185. "It was hard." Ibid.

185. "It's a touch of human tragedy." Ibid.

186. 70 pounds. Ben Draeger interview, July 9, 2011.

186. "I saw it." Mike Groves interview, July 9, 2011.

186. "It was like." Draeger interview, July 9, 2011.

186. "As we came." David Hill e-mail, July 17, 2011.

187. "She was just so pleased." David Hill interview, July 11, 2011.

187. "They were really." Martin McClellan interview, February 23, 2016.

187. "Horses are limited." Ibid.

187. $10,000 per dive. Ibid.

188. producing a film. Peter Fulks interview, January 28, 2012.

188. remotely operated vehicle (ROV). Walt Holm interview, August 19, 2014.

188. They were joined. Walt Holm interview, September 9, 2015.

189. The deepest part. Ibid.

189. "The main body of wreckage." Ibid.

189. Diane Coombes. Barbara Ferrey, "Downed B-24 Pilot's Daughter to See Crash Site, Namesake Lake," *Inyo Register*, September 7, 1990.

189. unperturbed by climbing. Diane Coombes interview, August 3, 2014.

190. "one of the things." Ibid.

CHAPTER 13: WHAT THEY FACED

191. Over 52,000 airmen. William T. Y'Blood, et al., eds. 2000. *Reflections and Remembrances*, page ix.

191. Losses greater. Ibid., page 10.

191. Only two of the boys. Enlistment records in IDPFs for Darden and Nyswonger.

192. enlisted on April 3, 1942. According to Schlosser's enlistment record, he was "single without dependents." Enlistment record for Samuel J. Schlosser (aad.archives .gov).

192. Robert Hester enlisted. Enlistment record in IDPF for Hester.

192. The requirement. Donald L. Miller, *Masters of the Air*, page 164.

192. May 26, 1942. Enlistment record for Culos M. Settle.

192. Charles Turvey enlisted. Enlistment record for Charles W. Turvey.

192. July 6, 1942. Enlistment record for Richard Lee Spangle.

192. He'd been married. Mary Condo interview, August 22, 2011.

193. Robert Bursey waited. Enlistment record for Robert O. Bursey.
193. Three members of *Exterminator*. Enlistment records for Dick E. Mayo, George Barulic, and Donald Vande Plasch.
193. Donald Vande Plasch, was married. Oscar Traczewitz II interview, March 19, 2014.
193. Howard Wandtke. Enlistment record for Howard Wandtke.
193. the last of the boys. Enlistment record for William Cronin.
193. "It crept into." Ardery, *Bomber Pilot*, page 6.
193. "From that day." Boeman, *Morotai*, page 1.
193. "In the thirties." Samuel Hynes, *Flights of Passage: Reflections of a World War II Aviator*, pages 13–14.
194. "a tearful parting all." Allen, *Pilot from the Prairie*, page 7.
194. "I had to relinquish." Ibid., page 8.
194. "merely a state of mind." Winston Groom, *The Generals*, page 227.
195. General George C. Marshall. Ibid., page 261.
195. Salary of $1,800 per year. Miller, *Masters of the Air*, page 164.
196. "Bombing was certainly." James L. Stokesbury, *A Short History of Air Power*, page 83.
196. Some bombing occurred. Ibid., pages 77–78.
196. the revulsion people felt. Ralph Barker, *The Thousand Plane Raid*, pages 24–25.
196. "the realization that Britain." Ibid.
196. "bomber dream." Robin Neillands, *The Bomber War*, page 12.
196. Douhet believed. Miller, *Masters of the Air*, page 34.
197. "civilians lack the fortitude." Ibid., page 35.
197. "a few gas bombs." Quoted in Miller, *Masters of the Air*, page 35.
197. "Don't talk to me." Adolf Galland, *The First and the Last*, page 55.
197. psychological effects. Miller, *Masters of the Air*, page 473.
197. Over 35 percent. Adam Hochschild, *To End All Wars*, page xiv.
198. twenty-one million. Ibid., page xv.
198. By 1918. Ibid., page 310.
198. By its end. Ibid., page 257.
198. "The Royal Air Force." W. G. Sebald, *On the Natural History of Destruction*, page 1.
198. "A sustained and unremitting." Stokesbury, *A Short History of Air Power*, page 198.
198. "Its only tests." Bailey, *The Air War in Europe*, page 81.
198. "There must not have been." Groom, *The Generals*, page 363.
198. During clear weather. Berry, *The Crash of Little Eva*, page 45.
199. "could not claim." Ibid.
199. antiaircraft flak. The term "flak" comes from the German word for "aircraft defense cannon," *Flugabwehrkanone*.
199. "Bomber" Harris. Some within the RAF preferred the sobriquet "Butcher" Harris.
199. "persisted despite intense pressure." Bailey, *The Air War in Europe*, page 187.
199. Joseph Goebbels wrote. Yuki Tanaka, *Bombing Civilians: A Twentieth-Century History*, pages 1–7.
199. "Thereafter, Japanese bombers." Ibid., page 5.

200. "Three and a half million." Miller, *Masters of the Air*, page 472.

200. another 800,000 Germans. Ibid.

200. The 8th Air Force's staggering losses. Ibid., page 471. According to Miller, "There are no reliable figures for casualties in the Fifteenth Air Force (working out of North Africa and Italy), and even the more carefully documented Eighth Air Force casualties are subject to challenge." He also states, "There are no separate official casualty figures for the Eighth and Fifteenth Air Forces." Miller goes on to say that Army Air Forces losses in both the European Theater of Operation and the Mediterranean were about 35,800 men dead, 13,700 wounded, and 33,400 captured or interned and, "5,900 missing, i.e., killed." He also says these numbers are for two- and four-engine bombers and fighters (Miller, page 598).

200. Only submariners. In *The Price of Admiralty: The Evolution of Naval Warfare*, John Keegan gives a maximum of 40,900 American submariners lost throughout the war, with 28,000 definitely killed ("gone down with their boats"), for a death rate of 68 percent. Keegan rounds up to 70 percent. Casualty numbers (soldiers killed, wounded, or missing) can be misleading and confusing, because they are often equated with soldier deaths. Ron Welch Jr. email, July 27, 2016.

200. "two-thirds of them." Stokesbury, *A Short History of Air Power*, page 243.

200. "The redemptive quality." Ibid., page 46. Governments and militaries during the Great War were convinced a parachute would lead pilots to "abandon government property and let it be destroyed prematurely. Many a young pilot or observer carried a pistol not so he could shoot the enemy, but so he could shoot himself when his plane caught fire" (Stokesbury, page 45).

201. "For some reason." Guy Gibson, *Enemy Coast Ahead*, page 158. By his death in combat at age twenty-six, in 1944, Wing Commander Guy Penrose Gibson had flown over 170 operations.

201. "Later that day." John L. Stewart, *The Forbidden Diary*, pages 59–61.

201. nearly an impossible accomplishment. Bowman, *USAAF Handbook 1939–1945*, page 225. Morale for combat crews throughout 1942 was abysmal because the boys recognized the odds were against them. At an average loss of 5 percent per mission (then considered a conservative estimate), they were unlikely to complete twenty missions.

201. "individual missions." Ibid.

201. at least fifty missions. Ibid., page 226.

202. "I was aware of the fairness." Ardery, *Bomber Pilot*, page 220.

CHAPTER 14: ACCIDENTS: WHY THERE WERE SO MANY

203. Lt. Thomas Selfridge. Clayton Knight and K. S. Knight, *Plane Crash*, page 37. Selfridge was an experienced pilot for his day, having flown dirigibles and his own personally designed powered aircraft.

203. a statistical digest. Office of Statistical Control, *Army Air Forces Statistical Digest for World War II*, Table 214.

203. Recent research. Anthony J. Mireles, *Fatal Army Air Forces Aviation Accidents in the United States, 1941–1945*.

203. ten deaths. Pierce, "Earning Their Wings," page x.
204. "the Air Service." Ibid., pages 25–26.
204. 10 percent of army strength. Ibid., page 229.
204. almost fraternal. Ibid., page 1.
204. fifty-one fatalities. Ibid., page xvi.
204. "number of cadets." Ibid., page 51.
205. "Often, in the early part." Ibid., page 9.
205. "The resulting crash." Ibid., page 107. Flying with all four engines feathered meant all four engines were shut down. As quoted earlier, "With all power off, the B-24 glides almost straight down." Carigan, *Ad Lib*, page 50.
205. "Man is out of his element." Boeman, *Morotai*, page 19.
205. "It is the mistakes." Smith, *The Wrong Stuff*, page 9.
205. "right to make mistakes." Markham, *West with the Night*, page 189.
205. "weak sisters." Chuck Yeager and Leo Janos, *Yeager: An Autobiography*, page 20.
206. "gruesome weeding-out process." Ibid., pages 20–21.
206. Accidents directly attributable. Pierce, "Earning Their Wings," page 153.
206. In his memoir. Stewart, *The Forbidden Diary*, page 69.
207. "Thoughts of getting killed." Ibid.
207. planes were required. Pierce, "Earning Their Wings," page 123.
207. Joseph William Loftus. War Department, Missing Air Crew Reports #4086 and #4087.
207. Wilson ordered his crew. War Department, Missing Air Crew Report #4087.
208. "Sometimes the sky." Stewart, *The Forbidden Diary*, pages 100–01.
208. "the accident rate." Pierce, "Earning Their Wings," page 116.
208. "Between 1943 and 1945." Hillenbrand, *Unbroken*, page 79; [Data is from Tables 100 and 161 in the *Army Air Forces Statistical Digest for World War II* and represents all types of aircraft].
208. "There was a near unanimous." Pierce, "Earning Their Wings," page 92.
209. "In these maneuvers." Ibid., page 140.
209. the scale of the accidents. Ibid., page 47.
209. More than half of their reports. Ibid., page 11.
209. During the first half. Ibid.
209. Solutions to accidents. Ibid., pages 195–96.
210. "Throughout the war." Ibid., page 169.
210. The anticipated washout rate." Watry, *Washout!*, page 203.
210. psychomotor and psychological. Pierce, "Earning Their Wings," page 204.
211. too much confidence. Ibid., page 124.
211. significant coordination issues. Watry, *Washout!*, page 114.
211. "The planes are powerful." Pierce, "Earning Their Wings," page 125.
211. accident report for *Exterminator*. "Report of Aircraft Accident" for B-24 #42-7674.
211. Turvey began Primary. "Report of Aircraft Accident" for B-24 #41-28463.
214. The first part involved. Pierce, "Earning Their Wings," page 129.

214. But Hester also. Eugene Fletcher, *Mister: The Training of an Aviation Cadet in World War II*, page 126.
214. every five months! Pierce, "Earning Their Wings," page 50.
214. "I didn't know then." Boeman, *Morotai*, page 6.
214. "In FY 1941." Pierce, "Earning Their Wings," page 56.
214. the pool of candidates. Ibid., page 56.
215. As the war progressed. Ibid., pages 78–79.
215. "Weather conditions." Allen, *Pilot from the Prairie*, page 41.
215. "Over 2,700 accidents." Pierce, "Earning Their Wings," page 155.
215. "Even [General] Arnold." Ibid., page 82.
215. after three years. "Report of Aircraft Accident" for B-24 #42-7674.
215. The accident report for 463. "Report of Aircraft Accident" for B-24 #41-28463.
216. "The transition to single-seat." Pierce, "Earning Their Wings," page 128.
216. Army Air Forces Statistical Digest. Office of Statistical Control, *Army Air Forces Statistical Digest for World War II*, Table 214.
216. 2,068 in 1942. Pierce, "Earning Their Wings," page 146. The War Department reported that in the first nine months of the year, the fatality rate was 0.017 percent (seventeen per 100,000 flying hours). That sounds pretty good until the *number* of fatalities is counted. That was 1,279.
216. Naval aviators suffered equally. Navy Department Library, "Aviation Personnel Fatalities in World War II" (www.history.navy.mil/library/online/aviation_fatal.htm).
217. "In 1943 in the Pacific." Hillenbrand, *Unbroken*, page 80.
217. how low the rate. Pierce, "Earning Their Wings," page 141.
217. fifty per year. Ibid., page 142.
217. "their own safety." Ibid., page 141.
217. But combat losses. Ibid., pages 142 and 208.
217. "By the time." Ardery, *Bomber Pilot*, page 3.
217. "When we got there." Jim Wright, *The Flying Circus: Pacific War 1943 as Seen Through a Bombsight*, pages 16–21.
218. "More than 75,000 Americans." Audra Jennings. "The Human Machinery of War" (ehistory.osu.edu/exhibitions/machinery/index).
218. "confounding situations." Boeman, *Morotai*, page 185.
218. that some pilots felt. Ibid.
218. "had been concentrated." Ibid.
218. "The heavy accident toll." Pierce, "Earning Their Wings," page 208.

Chapter 15: Some Were Unlucky

219. were four weeks away from. 461st Bomb Group History, Chapter 5, "Overseas Movement, January and February, 1944" (www.461st.org), page 1.
220. "100 percent undetermined." "Report of Aircraft Accident" for B-24 #42-7674.
220. "50 percent pilot error, 50 percent unknown." Ibid.
220. "sounded all right." Statement made by copilot, "Report of Aircraft Accident" for B-24 #42-7674.

220. "get out of here." Ibid.
220. Opened manually by Sergeant Barulic. Ibid. Settle said the bomb bay doors were opened by the engineer, but George Barulic said it was he who did it. George Barulic interview, August 5, 2011.
220. "The engines were putting." Ibid.
220. The weather forecast. Weather forecast, "Report of Aircraft Accident" for B-24 #42-7674.
221. "over the lake." Statement made by copilot, "Report of Aircraft Accident" for B-24 #42-7674.
222. The weather map. US Department of Commerce Daily Weather Map, December 5, 1943.
223. "While it is less common." Michael Tanksley e-mail, November 25, 2011.
223. "the worst piece." Baime, *The Arsenal of Democracy*, page 176.
223. Many of the airplanes. 461st Bomb Group History, Chapter 3, "The Morning Fogs of Hammer Field" (www.461st.org), page 13.
223. "A grossly inadequate." Ibid., page 14.
224. "lack of progress." Ibid., page 16.
224. Magazine writers. Boghosian, "Another One of Our B-24s is Missing!"; and Koch, "The Deadly Storm."
224. George Barulic believes. Barulic interview, August 5, 2011.
224. Referring to the B-24. Tanksley e-mails, November 25 and November 30, 2011.
225. "This would lead." Lt. Col. Tom Betts e-mail, August 24, 2016.
226. twenty seconds to feather. Ibid.
226. If an engine is idled with modern aircraft. Mike Tanksley e-mail, August 26, 2016.
226. in the "Down" position. Anonymous. *Flight Manual for B-24 Liberator*, page 145.
226. "There is sufficient power." Ibid., page 92.
227. "All right, hell, get out of here." Statement made by copilot, "Report of Aircraft Accident" for B-24 #42-7674.
227. "There was no snow." Barulic interview, August 5, 2011.
227. "That plane went crosswise." Ibid.
228. colliding with a brick wall. Groom, *The Aviators*, page 352.
228. 63,410 casualties. Bowman, *USAAF Handbook, 1939–1945*, pages 230–32.
228. "You groups of ten." 461st Bomb Group History, Chapter 4, "Training, Inspection, and Preparation for Overseas Movement" (www.461st.org), page 5.
230. had the propellers been bent back. Lt. Col. Tom Betts e-mail, January 9, 2008.
232. In his statement. John Specht statement, "Report of Aircraft Accident" for B-24 #41-28463.
232. the last quarter moon. "Sun, Moon, and Tide," *Oakland Tribune*, December 3, 1943.
232. Weather conditions. "Base Weather Station," December 17, 1943, "Report of Aircraft Accident" for B-24 #41-28463.
234. The combination of a radio receiver. Army Air Forces, *Instrument Flying: Advanced Theory and Practice.*

234. By rotating the loop antenna. Mike Abbot and Liz Kailey, *Jeppesen Guided Flight Discovery: Private Pilot*, pages 9–35.

234. "every pilot knows about it." John Specht statement, "Report of Aircraft Accident" for B-24 #41-28463.

234. There was no ADF beacon. US Coast and Geodetic Survey, Aeronautical Chart for Radio Direction Finding, #24 DF, July 13, 1944.

236. "New pilots never want." Betts e-mail, January 9, 2008.

237. "Convincing yourself." Gann, *Ernest K. Gann's Flying Circus*, page 46.

237. "Hope always persists." Markham, *West with the Night*, page 46.

238. "At that temperature." Arthur Weingarten, *The Sky Is Falling*, page 110.

239. an article he wrote. Lansford, "If My Son is Alive."

239. shared his thoughts. William D. Lansford, Letter to Mrs. (Janet) Hovden, November 4, 1960.

241. Bob still rankles at being assigned as copilot. Bob Hester, Letter to Clint Hester, October 16, 1943.

242. during the war was 16,112,566. Nese F. DeBruyne and Anne Leland, *American War and Military Operations Casualties: Lists and Statistics*, Congressional Research Service, page 2.

242. Depending on the source. A May 30, 2001, article in *Slate* says 1,100. On May 24, 2008, Fox News reported the number was 1,000. On the website for the National World War II Museum in New Orleans, the number is 430 as of 2016.

242. a total of 405,399 deaths. DeBruyne and Leland, *American War and Military Operations Casualties*, page 2.

242. Non-battle deaths. US Adjutant General, *Army Battle Casualties and Non-battle Deaths in World War II*, Department of the Army, pages 5–8.

242. Of Army deaths. DeBruyne and Leland, *American War and Military Operations Casualties*, page 2.

242. "persons who died of disease." US Adjutant General, *Army Battle Casualties*, pages 5–8.

243. Between 1941 and 1945. Office of Statistical Control, *Army Air Forces Statistical Digest for World War II*, Table 212, page 308.

243. there were 15,530 pilots. Mireles, *Fatal Army Air Forces Aviation Accidents*.

243. "During World War II." Ibid.

243. Navy losses were equally as bad. Navy Department Library, Aviation Personnel Fatalities in World War II.

243. More than 4,500. Mireles, *Fatal Army Air Forces Aviation Accidents*.

245. "Luck is just like that." Barulic interview, August 5, 2011.

245. "Some were unlucky." Gibson, *Enemy Coast Ahead*, page 337.

References

Interviews

Alexander, Gil. Telephone interview. January 24, 2013.
Allen, Mark. Email. December 28, 2015.
Barulic, George. Telephone interview. August 5, 2011.
Bekemeier, Bill. Telephone interview. March 29, 2014.
Bekemeier, Bill. E-mail. January 9, 2014.
Benét, James R. Telephone interview. August 8, 2011.
Betts USAF (Ret.), Lt. Col. Tom. E-mail. August 24, 2016.
Betts USAF (Ret.), Lt. Col. Tom. E-mail. October 23, 2014.
Betts USAF (Ret.), Lt. Col. Tom. E-mail. October 20, 2014.
Betts USAF (Ret.), Lt. Col. Tom. E-mail. March 10, 2014.
Betts USAF (Ret.), Lt. Col. Tom. E-mail. January 9, 2008.
Boothe, John. E-mail. July 11, 2014.
Boothe, John. E-mail. March 13, 2014.
Boothe, John. E-mail. March 12, 2014.
Boothe, John. Interview. Bishop, California. August 31, 2011.
Brock, Leroy. Interview. Bishop, California. August 11, 2014.
Brock, Leroy. Telephone interview. June 4, 2014.
Brock, Leroy. E-mail. June 3, 2014.
Brock, Leroy. Telephone interview. November 30, 2011.
Brock, Leroy. Telephone interview. November 1, 2011.
Calderon, Vikkie. Telephone interview. March 9, 2011.
Condo, Mary. Interview. Granite Bay, California. August 22, 2011.
Condo, Mary. Telephone interview. July 25, 2011.
Coombes, Diane. Interview. Klamath Falls, Oregon. August 3, 2014.
Coombes, Diane. Telephone interview. May 28, 2014.
Crider, Mary Jean. Telephone interview. June 14, 2016.
Densmore, Eugene. Interview. Billy Creek Museum, Huntington Lake, California.
    August 23, 2011.
DeSalvo, Stephen. Telephone interview. July 9, 2011.
Disterdick, John (Billy). Telephone interview. November 29, 2016.
Dodge, Frank. Telephone interview. July 25, 2011.
Draeger, Ben. Telephone interview. July 9, 2011.
Durkee, George. E-mail. March 28, 2016.

Fish, David. Telephone interview. February 7, 2013.

Fletcher, Sherry. Telephone interview. August 23, 2016.

Fulks, Peter. Telephone interview. January 4, 2015.

Fulks, Peter. E-mail. December 20, 2014.

Fulks, Peter. E-mail. August 27, 2014.

Fulks, Peter. Telephone interview. January 28, 2012.

Fulks, Peter. E-mail. January 26, 2012.

Fuller, Craig. Telephone interview. August 20, 2014.

Groves, Mike. Telephone interview. July 9, 2011.

Gruner, George. Telephone interview. July 31, 2014.

Hill, David. Interview. Rutland, Vermont. May 2, 2014.

Hill, David. Interview. January 27, 2014.

Hill, David. E-mail. November 4, 2011.

Hill, David. E-mail. July 17, 2011.

Hill, David. Telephone interview. July 11, 2011.

Holm, Walt. E-mail. November 2, 2015.

Holm, Walt. E-mail. October 15, 2015.

Holm, Walt. Telephone interview. September 9, 2015.

Holm, Walt. Telephone interview. August 19, 2014.

Hovden, Janet. Telephone interview. November 6, 2014.

Hovden, Janet. Telephone interview. June 19, 2014.

Hovden, Janet. Interview. Roseville, California. September 5, 2011.

Hovden, Robert. E-mail December 23, 2012.

Hovden, Robert. E-mail. August 26, 2012.

Hovden, Robert. E-mail. August 23, 2012.

Hovden, Robert. E-mail. January 11, 2012

Hovden, Robert. E-mail. January 7, 2012.

Hovden, Robert. Telephone interview. December 15, 2011.

Hufbauer, Karl. E-mail. February 28, 2014.

Hufbauer, Karl. E-mail. February 27, 2014.

Hufbauer, Karl. Interview. Seattle, Washington. February 19, 2014.

Hunt, Peter. Interview. Oak Harbor, Washington. November 18, 2015.

Hyatt, Gary W. E-mail. November 12, 2014.

Jones, John Edward. E-mail. April 15, 2016.

Jordan, Don. Telephone interview. August 28, 2016.

Kraushaar, John. Telephone interview. April 3, 2016.

Kraushaar, John. E-mail. March 30, 2016.

Langewiesche, William. Seattle, Washington. May 24, 2007.

Lindner, Brian. E-mail. September 18, 2014.

Lindner, Brian. E-mail. September 15, 2014.

Lindner, Brian. E-mail. July 3, 2014.

Lindner, Brian. E-mail. September 28, 2010.

Lucak, Brad. E-mail. November 24, 2014.

Macha, Pat. E-mail. April 5, 2016.

Marion, John. Telephone interview. November 21, 2011.

Mayo, David. E-mail. March 6, 2016.

Mayo, David. Telephone interview. July 29, 2014.

Mayo, David. E-mail. July 28, 2014.

Mayo, Richard. E-mail. March 12, 2016.

Mayo, Walker. E-mail. March 14, 2016.

McClellan, Martin. E-mail. April 8, 2016.

McClellan, Martin. Telephone interview. February 23, 2016.

McCoy, Paul. Telephone interview. March 29, 2012.

McCoy, Paul. E-mail. March 4, 2012.

McKenzie, Bill. Telephone interview. December 5, 2014.

Menard, Joe. Telephone interview. November 1, 2014.

Menard, Joe. E-mail. November 1, 2014.

Mester, Robert and Mark Allen. Interview, Olympia, WA. December 10, 2015.

Mester, Robert. Email. December 26, 2015.

Moore, James G. Telephone interview. October 24, 2014.

Moore, James G. Telephone interview. April 9, 2011.

Moore, James G. E-mail. February 4, 2011.

Nash, Alden. E-mail. March 29, 2016.

Neal, Kevin. Telephone interview. April 13, 2012.

Newman, Jeanette. Telephone interview. May 25, 2016.

Piwowar, Glenn R. E-mail. April 13, 2016.

Poole, Steve. E-mail. April 14, 2016.

Rasmussen, Michael J. Telephone interview. November 17, 2011.

Root, William. E-mail. May 15, 2016.

Root, William. E-mail. May 11, 2016.

Root, William. E-mail. May 6, 2016.

Root, William. E-mail. April 27, 2016.

Root, William. Interview. Bothell, Washington. April 26, 2016.

Smyth, Fred. E-mail. March 31, 2016.

Smyth, Fred. E-mail. March 30, 2016.

Spangle, Tom. Interview. Weed, California. March 30, 2011.

Specht, Robert. Telephone interview. October 2, 2011.

Spivey, Leonard. Telephone interview. April 8, 2014.

Stemm, James. E-mail. November 13, 2012.

Stone, Randy. Telephone interview. August 4, 2014.

Storey, Mark. Interview. Seattle, Washington. July 20, 2011.

Sweinhagen, Paul. Telephone interview. March 16, 2012.

Tanksley, Mike. E-mail. August 26, 2016.

Tanksley, Mike. E-mail. November 30, 2011.

Tanksley, Mike. E-mail. November 25, 2011.

Thomas, Christopher. Telephone interview. October 23, 2011.

Thomas, Christopher. Telephone interview. July 14, 2011.

Thurlow, Fred. Interview. Wallingford, Vermont. May 2, 2014.

Traczewitz II, Oscar. Telephone interview. March 19, 2014.

Walker, Joanne. E-mail. March 14, 2016.

Viator, Mary Anne. E-mail. June 20, 2016.
Welch, Eileen Cronin. Interview. Eldred, Pennsylvania. May 1, 2014.
Welch, Eileen Cronin. Telephone interview. June 20, 2012.
Welch Jr., Ron. E-mail. July 27, 2016.
Welch Jr., Ron. E-mail. April 15, 2016.
Welch Jr., Ron. E-mail. April 14, 2016.
Welch Jr., Ron. E-mail. April 7, 2016.
Welch Jr., Ron. E-mail. September 3, 2012.
Welch Jr., Ron. E-mail. September 1, 2012.
Welch Jr., Ron. E-mail. December 15, 2011.
Welch Jr., Ron. E-mail. December 10, 2011.
Welch Jr., Ron. E-mail. December 10, 2011.
Welch Jr., Ron. E-mail. October 26, 2011.
Welch Jr., Ron. Telephone interview. October 26, 2011.
Woods, Lillian Cronin. Telephone interview. December 20, 2011.
Zellerbach, Merla. Telephone interview. March 6, 2011.
Zurcher, Dan. Telephone interview. August 9, 2016.

LETTERS AND TELEGRAMS

Abbott, George W. US Department of the Interior, Assistant Secretary of the Interior. Letter to Mrs. Roger A. Hovden. January 20, 1961.
Anderson, Jr., William G., Major USAF. Letter to William L. Bancroft, Acting Superintendent Sequoia & Kings Canyon National Parks. August 24, 1989, in Sequoia & Kings Canyon National Parks archives.
Bancroft, William L., Acting Superintendent Sequoia & Kings Canyon National Parks. Letter to Dr. Stephen C. DeSalvo, DDS. August 17, 1989, in Sequoia & Kings Canyon National Parks archives.
———. Acting Superintendent Sequoia & Kings Canyon National Parks. Letter to Felix J. Stalls III, Major, USAF. August 9, 1989, in Sequoia & Kings Canyon National Parks archives.
Beemer, H. M. Letter to Mr. Mayo. July 15, 1944.
———. Letter to Mrs. W. P. Mayo. January 10, 1944.
Cronin, Mrs. P. J. Letter to Mrs. Florence Housen, Acting Home Service Chm., American Red Cross. March 29, 1945.
Darden, W. B., Letter to Lt. Gen. Charles E. Kilbourne, Superintendent, Virginia Military Institute, February 10, 1944.
———. Letter to Lt. Gen. Charles E. Kilbourne, Superintendent, Virginia Military Institute, February 2, 1944.
DeSalvo, Steve. Letter to Sierra District Ranger Paul Fodor, Sequoia & Kings Canyon National Parks. September 13, 1990, in Sequoia & Kings Canyon National Parks archives.
———. Letter to Sierra District Ranger Paul Fodor, Sequoia & Kings Canyon National Parks. July 17, 1990, in Sequoia & Kings Canyon National Parks archives.

———. Letter to Superintendent J. Thomas Ritter, Sequoia & Kings Canyon National Parks. August 7, 1989, in Sequoia & Kings Canyon National Parks archives.

Dooley, James C. Letter to Mrs. & Mrs. Mayo. December 17, 1943.

Finical, 1st Lt. Robert H. Letter to Mrs. Reba E. Mayo. July 11, 1944.

Fodor, Paul. Letter to Stephen DeSalvo. March 8, 1991.

Glantzberg, Col. Frederic E. Letter to Miss Lillian Cronin. December 21, 1943

———. Letter to Mrs. Mayo. December 14, 1943.

———. Telegram to Clinton W. Hester. December 9, 1943.

Headquarters, Department of the Army, Office of the Quartermaster General. Letter to Mrs. Janet A. Hovden. August 31, 1960.

Hester, Bob. Letter to Clint Hester. October 16, 1943.

Hovden, Janet. Letter to Peter Stekel. December, 2014.

Johnson, Major Leland F. Letter to Mrs. Reba E. Mayo. April 20, 1944.

Kilmartin, J. O., US Department of the Interior, Board on Geographic Names. Letter to Mrs. Roger Hovden. May 3, 1961.

Kirksey, Col. Guy. Telegram to Clinton W. Hester. ND.

———. Letter to Mr. W. P. Mayo. February 29, 1944.

———. Letter to Reba Mayo. January 13, 1944.

———. Telegram to Clinton W. Hester. December 6, 1943.

Knoble, Chaplain John W. Letter to Pastor W. B. Marriott. June 27, 1944.

Koch, R. W. Letter to Superintendent J. Thomas Ritter, Sequoia & Kings Canyon National Parks. October 17, 1989, in Sequoia & Kings Canyon National Parks archives.

Lansford, William D. Letter to Mrs. (Janet) Hovden. January 2, 1961.

———. Letter to Mrs. (Janet) Hovden. November 4, 1960.

———. Letter to Mrs. (Janet) Hovden. October 12, 1960.

Mayo, Reba. Letter to Mrs. Spangle. September 21, 1955.

Mayo, Mrs. W. P. Letter to the Secretary of War. April 26, 1948.

———. Letter to Mr. and Mrs. Spangle. January 16, 1947.

———. Letter to Commanding General, Hammer Field. October 20, 1947.

McCall, Brother William. Letter to Gordon Boyd, High Sierra Ranger, Sequoia & Kings Canyon National Parks. November 1, 1972, in Sequoia & Kings Canyon National Parks archives.

Millard, Lt. Col. Frank G. Letter to Mr. W. Porter Mayo. December 20, 1945.

Office of the Quartermaster General, Department of Army. Telegram to Janet Hovden. August 21, 1960.

Ritter, J. Thomas. Letter to Christopher R. Thomas. February 1, 1994.

Spangle, Merle. Letter to Mrs. Mayo. September 2, 1955.

Spangle, Mrs. Sherman. Letter to Mrs. Mayo. December 19, 1955.

Spangle, Sherman. Letter to Mr. and Mrs. Mayo. March 15, 1944.

———. Letter to Mr. and Mrs. Mayo. January 20, 1944.

———. Letter to Mr. and Mrs. Mayo. January 14, 1944.

———. Letter to Mr. and Mrs. Mayo. December 22, 1943.

Thomas, Christopher R. Letter to Superintendent Sequoia & Kings Canyon National Parks. October 22, 1993.

Turvey, Mrs. Charles (Margaret). Letter to Mrs. Robert (Janet) Hovden. April 25, 1961.

———. Letter to Clinton W. Hester. January 4, 1944.

———. Letter to Mr. (Clint) Hester. June 28, 1944.

———. Letter to Mr. Hester. June 11, 1944.

Webster, Maurice, Vice President and General Manager KCBS, San Francisco, California. Letter to Mrs. Roger Hovden. February 17, 1961.

BOOKS

Abbot, Mike, and Liz Kailey. *Jeppesen Guided Flight Discovery: Private Pilot.* Englewood, CO: Jeppesen, 2007.

Allen, Edgar J. *Pilot from the Prairie.* Bothell, WA: Book Publishers Network, 2002.

Ambrose, Stephen. *The Wild Blue: The Men and Boys Who Flew the B-24s Over Germany.* New York: Simon & Schuster, 2001.

Anonymous. *B-24 Liberator Pilot's Flight Operating Instructions.* Reprinted by Periscope Film, LLC, 1942.

———. *Flight Manual for B-24 Airplane.* Appleton, WI: Reprinted by Aviation Publications, 1942.

———. *Military Aircraft Crash Sites.* London, England: English Heritage, 2002.

———. *Pilot Training Manual for the B-24 Liberator.* US Army Air Forces, 1945.

———. *Survival.* Airlines War Training Institute, 1943.

Ardery, Philip. *Bomber Pilot.* Lexington: The University Press of Kentucky, 1978.

Arnold, H. H. *Global Mission.* New York: Harper & Brothers, 1949.

Bailey, Ronald H., and the editors of Time-Life Books, *The Air War in Europe.* Alexandria, VA: Time-Life Books, 1981.

Baime, A. J. *The Arsenal of Democracy.* Boston: Houghton Mifflin Harcourt, 2014.

Barker, Ralph. *The Thousand Plane Raid.* New York: Ballantine Books, 1966.

Bergerud, Eric M. *Fire in the Sky.* New York: Basic Books, 2009.

Birdsall, Steve. *The B-24 Liberator.* New York: Arco Publishing Company, Inc., 1968.

———. *Log of the Liberators.* Garden City, NY: Doubleday & Company, Inc., 1973.

Boeman, John. *Morotai: A Memoir of War.* Garden City, NY: Doubleday & Company, Inc., 1981.

Bowman, Martin W. *B-24 Combat Missions: First-Hand Accounts of Liberator Operations Over Nazi Europe.* London, England. Elephant Book Company, 2009.

———. *The B-24 Liberator 1939–1945.* Chicago: Rand McNally & Company, 1979.

———. *Consolidated B-24 Liberator.* Wiltshire, England: Crowood Press, 1998.

———. *USAAF Handbook 1939–1945.* Sparkford, Great Britain: Sutton Publishing, 1997.

Burtness, Robert A. *The Santa Barbara B-24 Disasters.* Charleston, SC: The History Press, 2012.

Cameron, Rebecca Hancock. *Training to Fly: Military Flight Training, 1907–1945.* Washington, DC: US Government Printing Office, 1999.

Carigan, William. *Ad Lib: Flying the B-24 Liberator in World War II.* Manhattan, KS: Sunflower University Press, 1988.

Carr, Edward C. *On Final Approach: Recollections of a World War II B-17 Air Crew.* Centralia, WA: Gorham Printing, 2002.

Cass, William F. *The Last Flight of Liberator 41-1133*. [no location given]: The Wings Aloft Press, 1996.

Cheshire, Leonard. *Bomber Pilot*. Granada, Hertfordshire: Mayflower, 1975.

Childers, Thomas. *Wings of Morning*. Reading, MA: Addison-Wesley Publishing Company, 1995.

Clark, Ronald W. *The Role of the Bomber*. New York: Thomas Y. Crowell Company, 1977.

Cowart, Clarence P. *A Fallen Eagle*. Indianapolis, IN: Dog Ear Publishing, 2009.

Crider, Bob, ed. Untitled booklet by the 1991 and 1992 Fourth-Grade Classes of Big Creek School. Big Creek, CA. ND.

Davis, James M. *In Hostile Skies*. Denton: University of North Texas Press, 2006.

Deighton, Len. *Bomber*. United Kingdom: 1970. [Reprint edition, New York: Sterling, 2011.]

Douglas, Graeme. *Consolidated B-24 Liberator 1939 Onwards (All Marks) Owners' Workshop Manual*. Sparkford, Yeovil, Somerset, United Kingdom: Haynes Publishing, 2013.

Dugan, James, and Carroll Stewart. *Ploesti*. New York: Bantam, 1963.

Eliot, George. *Adam Bede*. Online version from Classic Literature (about.com).

Falstein, Louis. *Face of a Hero*. South Royalton, VT: Steerforth Press, 1998.

Fletcher, Eugene. *Mister: The Training of an Aviation Cadet in World War II*. Seattle: University of Washington Press, 1992.

Forbes, Gordon. *Goodbye to Some*. New York: Orion Books, 1989.

Freeman, Roger. *B-24 Liberator at War*. London, England: Ian Allan, 1983.

———. *The U.S. Strategic Bomber*. London, England: Macdonald and James, 1975.

Friendly, Capt. Alfred. *The Guys on the Ground*. New York: Eagle Books, 1944.

Galland, Adolf. *The First and the Last*. New York: Ballantine Books, 1957

Gann, Ernest K. *Ernest K. Gann's Flying Circus*. New York: Macmillan Publishing Co., Inc., 1974.

Gardner, Flight Lt. Charles. *The 'Gen' Book*. London, England: Hutchinson & Co., 1943.

Gibson, Guy. *Enemy Coast Ahead*. New York: Bantam, 1979.

Graham, Frederick P., and Harold W. Kulick. *He's in the Air Corps Now*. New York: Robert M. McBride & Company, 1942.

Green, William. *Famous Bombers of the Second World War*. Garden City, NY: Hanover House, 1959.

Groom, Winston. *The Generals*. Washington, DC: National Geographic, 2015.

Gruner, George F. *Into the Night: Hammer Field . . . Camp Pinedale . . . Fresno Fairgrounds—Central California in World War II*. Clovis, CA: Clovis Veterans Memorial District, 2012.

Gunston, Bill. *Bombers*. London, England: Hamlyn Publishing Group, 1978.

Herman, Arthur. *Freedom's Forge: How American Business Produced Victory in World War II*. New York: Random House, 2012.

Hibbits, John J., as told to F. E. Rechnitzer. *Take 'Er Up Alone, Mister!* New York: Whittlesey House / McGraw-Hill, 1943.

Hillenbrand, Laura. *Unbroken*. New York: Random House, 2010.

Hochschild, Adam. *To End All Wars*. Boston: Houghton Mifflin Harcourt, 2011.

Hoffman, Carl. *Hunting Warbirds*. New York: Ballantine Books, 2001.

Holder, Bill. *B-24 Liberator*. Carrollton, TX: Squadron/Signal Publications, 2005.

Hynes, Samuel. *Flights of Passage—Reflections of a World War II Aviator*. Boston: G. K. Hall & Co., 1989.

———. *The Soldiers' Tale: Bearing Witness to a Modern War*. New York: Penguin, 1998.

Johnson, Frederick A. *B-24 Liberator: Rugged But Right*. New York: McGraw-Hill, 1999.

Keay, Danny I. P. *Roscoe Red Three Is Missing*. Indianapolis, IN: Dog Ear Publishing, 2012.

Kinzey, Bert. *B-24 Liberator In Detail*. Carrollton, TX: Squadron/Signal Publications, 2000.

Knight, Clayton, and K. S. Knight. *Plane Crash*. New York: Greenberg, 1958.

Lay, Jr., Berne. *I Wanted Wings*. New York: Harper & Brothers, 1937.

Macha, G. Pat, and Don Jordan. *Aircraft Wrecks in the Mountains and Deserts of California, 1909–2002*, 3rd ed. Lake Forest, CA: Info Net Publishing, 2002.

Markham, Beryl. *West With the Night*. San Francisco, CA: North Point Press, 1983.

Martinez, Mario. *Lady's Men*. South Yorkshire, England: Pen & Sword Aviation, 2011.

Miller, Donald L. *Masters of the Air*. New York: Simon & Schuster, 2006.

Mireles, Anthony J. *Fatal Army Air Forces Aviation Accidents in the United States, 1941–1945*. Jefferson, NC: McFarlane & Company, 2006.

Nalty, Bernard C., John F. Shiner, and George M. Watson. *With Courage: The U.S. Army Air Forces in World War II*. Washington, DC: US Government Printing Office, 1994.

Neillands, Robin. *The Bomber War*. New York: Overlook Press, 2001.

Perkins, Paul, Michelle Crean, and Dan Patterson (photography). *The Soldier: Consolidated B-24 Liberator*. Charlottesville, VA: Howell Press, 1994.

Pisano, Dominick A. *To Fill the Skies with Pilots*. Washington, DC: Smithsonian Institution Press, 2001.

Raleigh, Sir Walter Alexander. *The War in the Air, Vol. 1, The Part Played in the Great War by the Royal Air Force*. Kindle Edition, 2012.

Ralph, Barry. *The Crash of* Little Eva. Louisiana: Pelican Publishing, 2006.

Sebald, W. G. *On the Natural History of Destructions*. New York: Random House, 2003.

Sheehan, Susan. *A Missing Plane*. New York: Berkley Books, 1988.

Sledge, Michael. *Soldier Dead: How We Recover, Identify, Bury, and Honor Our Military Fallen*. New York: Columbia University Press, 2007.

Smith, Starr. *Jimmy Stewart, Bomber Pilot*. St. Paul, MN: Zenith Press, 2005.

Smith, Truman. *The Wrong Stuff*. Norman: University of Oklahoma Press, 2002.

Stekel, Peter. *Final Flight: The Mystery of a WWII Plane Crash and the Frozen Airmen in the High Sierra*. Berkeley, CA: Wilderness Press, 2010.

Stewart, John L. *The Forbidden Diary*. New York: McGraw-Hill, 1998.

Stokesbury, James L. *A Short History of Air Power*. New York: William Morrow and Company, 1986.

———. *A Short History of World War II*. New York: William Morrow and Company, 1980.

Tanaka, Yuki, and Marilyn B. Young, eds. *Bombing Civilians: A Twentieth-Century History*. New York: The New Press, 2009.
Veronico, Nicholas A. *Hidden Warbirds*. Minneapolis, MN: Zenith Press, 2013.
———. *Hidden Warbirds II*. Minneapolis, MN: Zenith Press, 2014.
Veronico, Nicholas A., et al. *Wreckchasing 101: A Guide to Finding Aircraft Crash Sites*. Minneapolis, MN: Stance & Speed, 2011.
Watry, Charles A. *Washout! The Aviation Cadet Story*. Carlsbad, CA: California Aero Press, 1983.
Weingarten, Arthur. *The Sky Is Falling*. New York: Grosset & Dunlap, 1977.
Y'Blood, William T., et al., eds. *Reflections and Remembrances*. Air Force History and Museums Program, 2000.
Yeager, Chuck, and Leo Janos. *Yeager: An Autobiography*. New York: Bantam Books, 1985.

MANUSCRIPTS
Boothe, John. ND. "John Boothe's Accounting of Trips to Plane Crash Site Discovered in July of 1960." Unpublished manuscript.
Coates, Crawford. ND. "Tragedy Near Hester Lake." Unpublished manuscript.
Griffin, Donald F. 1990. "Trail Building in the High Sierras." Unpublished manuscript.
Hufbauer, Karl. 2014. "[Charles] Bays Locker (1931, Newton, Iowa—1952, Peak 12,360, Fresno Co., Calif.)." Unpublished manuscript.
Moore, James. ND. "Mystery at Hester Lake." Unpublished manuscript.
Nance, Kirt. ND. Untitled and unpublished manuscript.
Neal, Kevin. 2003. "Lake Hester Expedition 2003." Marine Expeditions International. Unpublished manuscript.
Thomas, Christopher. ND. "B-24E-14-DT Serial #41-28463." Unpublished manuscript.

PERIODICALS AND RESEARCH PAPERS
Anonymous. "California: The Long Search." *Time*. August 15, 1960.
Boghosian, S. Samuel. "Another One of Our B-24s is Missing!" *Air Classics* Vol. 12, No. 9 (September 1976): 20–26.
———. "The Tragic Tale of the Lake Hester Liberator." *Air Classics* Vol. 15, No. 6 (June 1979): 56–59.
Carroll, Major James J. "Physiological Problems of Bomber Crews in the 8th Air Force during WWII," page 30. Research paper presented to Research Department, Air Command and Staff College, March 1997.
Hammer, Joseph. "Mail Call." *The 461st Liberaider* (1994): 3–4.
Hendrix, Lin. "Requiem for a Heavyweight." *Wings* Vol. 8, No. 1 (February 1978): 20–37.
Koch, R. W. "The Deadly Storm." *Air Classics* Vol. 14, No. 2 (February 1978): 88–91.
———. "The Mystery of the Saline Valley Liberator." *Air Classics* Vol. 15, No. 6 (June 1979): 31–35.

Lansford, William D. "If My Son Is Alive—I'll Track Him Down." *Stag* 12:7 (July 1961): 26–66.

Moore, James G. "Airplanes Down in the Sierra." *Geologic Division Retirees Newsletter* Vol. 50 (Spring 2015).

Pierce, Marlyn. "Earning Their Wings: Accidents and Fatalities in the United States Army Air Forces During Flight Training in World War Two." PhD dissertation, Kansas State University, December 2013.

Sweinhagen, Paul. "The Jackass Expedition, Part One." *Mad Diver*. ND.

"Warplane's Icy Death Brings New Life to Fourth Graders' Lessons." *The 461st Liberaider* 9:1 (1992): 1–2.

NEWSPAPERS

"AF, Rangers Stumped by Plane Ruins," *Star-News*. July 28, 1960.

Anonymous. "War Writer Killed," *Harrisburg Telegraph*, Harrisburg, Pennsylvania. September 11, 1944.

———. Untitled article about Max R. Turvey. *Washington Court House Record-Herald*. August 31, 1944.

———. "Sun, Moon and Tide," *Oakland Tribune*. December 3, 1943.

———. "General Upshur, Charlie Paddock Die in Air Crash," *The Pittsburgh Press*. July 23, 1943.

Benét, James. "*Chronicle* Team Reaches B-24 in Sierra Lake," *San Francisco Chronicle*. August 1, 1960.

———. "Lake Yields Its Secret," *San Francisco Chronicle*. August 1, 1960.

"Bodies of 6 in '43 B-24 Crash Sought," *Oakland Tribune*. July 29, 1960.

Bodine, Mike. "Hester Lake Saga to Be Subject of New Book," *Inyo Register*. September 1, 2011.

"B-24 Lost 12 Years Found in Sierra Lake," *The Independent*. September 15, 1955.

"Copter to Fly Team to B-24 Thursday," *Inyo Register*. August 4, 1960.

"Divers Find 2 More Bodies in Old Wreck," *Bakersfield Californian*. September 24, 1955.

"Divers Recover Four Bodies Out of B-24 Bomber," *Fresno Bee*. September 24, 1955.

"Divers Seek to Recover Plane," *Los Angeles Times*. July 1, 1980.

"Divers to Go After '43 Air Crash Bodies," *Oakland Tribune*. July 30, 1960.

"Effort to Raise Old Bomber Goes Under," *Los Angeles Times*. July 13, 1980.

"Expert Divers to Probe Lake for 6 Bodies," *Bakersfield Californian*. September 17, 1955.

Ferrey, Barbara. "Downed B-24 Pilot's Daughter to See Crash Site, Namesake Lake," *Inyo Register*. September 7, 1990.

"Find Clues to Bomber Crash," *San Mateo Times*. August 2, 1960.

"Fisherman Spots Bomber Wrecked 12 Years Ago," *Uriah Daily Journal*. September 15, 1955.

"5 US Airmen Buried 17 Years After Local Crash," *Inyo Register*. October 6, 1960.

Goerner, Fred. "The Angry Mountains: A Radio Newsman Fights the High Sierra," *San Mateo Times*. August 6, 1960.

"Heavy-Duty Diving Gear Now Being Used to Recover B-24 Bodies," *Inyo Register.* August 11, 1960.

"High Sierra Air Wreckage Puzzle to Remain Unsolved, Says Air Force," *Inyo Register.* October 6, 1960.

Hoekstra, Fred. "Rutland Airman's Body Found After 17-Year Search in Sierras," *Schenectady Gazette*, page 28. August 29, 1960.

"Huge Bomber Makes Emergency Landing at Manzanar Field," *Inyo Register*, page 6. December 10, 1943.

"Huntington Yields '43 Plane Wreckage," *Fresno Bee.* September 15, 1955.

"Lake Yields 4 in '43 Air Crash," *Fresno Bee.* September 25, 1955.

"Lake Yields World War II Air Crash Clues," *Independent.* July 28, 1960.

Long, Raymond. "B-24 'Ditched' to Experiment on Structures," *Daily Press of New Port News.* September 21, 1944.

"Lost Olean Flier of World War II, 5 Others Buried," *Dunkirk Evening Observer.* October 4, 1960.

McCarthy, Charles. "B-24 Buff Seeks a Sunken Treasure," *Fresno Bee.* September 4, 2006.

"Names of Crewmen of Missing Bomber Released by Army," *Inyo Independent.* December 24, 1943.

"1943 Bomber Wreckage Spotted in Sierra Lake," *Oakland Tribune.* September 15, 1955.

"Opening Crowd Fiesta Thrills," *San Mateo Times.* August 6, 1960.

Palomares, Robert. "Search Comes Up Empty," *Fresno Bee*, 1990 [month unknown].

"Plane Mystery Solved," *New York Times.* July 29, 1960.

"Rites Honor Fliers Lost 17 Years," *Pasadena Independent.* October 4, 1960.

"Search for B-24 Bodies Called Off," *Inyo Register.* August 18, 1960.

"Search for Plane Pressed," *Oakland Tribune.* December 8, 1943.

"Search Sierra for Missing Bomber," *Inyo Register*, page 1. December 10, 1943.

"17 Years' Anxiety Over for Mother," *Times-Union.* August 30, 1960.

"Sierra Lake Named for Father, Long-Lost Son." *Bakersfield Californian.* December 12, 1960.

"Sierra Lake Preserves Bodies of Bomber Crew," *Oxnard Press-Courier.* August 4, 1960.

"Skindivers in Action," *Oakland Tribune.* September 5, 1955.

"Skin Divers to Hunt Plane in Sierra Lake," *The Independent.* September 8, 1955.

"A Small Lake in Kings Canyon National Park Will Be Named Hester Lake," *Pasadena Star-News.* December 15.1960

"Tragedy Lake Gets a Name," *San Mateo Times.* January 4, 1961.

"Two Bombers from Fresno Sought," *Oakland Tribune.* December 7 [year unknown]

"2 Bombers Lost in Valley Area," *San Mateo Times.* December 7, 1943.

"Two Safe from Two Lost Planes," *San Mateo Times.* December 8 [year unknown]

"Underwater Rescue Team Awaits B-24 Salvage Order," *Daily Review.* September 16, 1955.

"Utility Company to Lower Level of Lake," *Bakersfield Californian.* June 13, 1955.

"World War II Fresno Bomber Is Found in Sierra Lake," *The Fresno Bee.* July 28, 1960.

"World War II Plane Found in Remote Lake," *Bakersfield-Californian*. July 28, 1960.
"Wreckage of Old B-24 Found in Sierra Lake," *Humboldt Standard*. July 28, 1960.
"Wrecked B-24 Flew From D-M," *Tucson Daily Citizen*. August 4, 1960.

GOVERNMENT SOURCES

Army Air Forces. *Instrument Flying: Advanced Theory and Practice*. 1943.
———. *Instrument Flying: Technique in Weather*. 1943.
Barber, Lt. Com. Stuart B., et al. *Naval Aviation Combat Statistics: World War II*. June 17, 1946.
Brinegar, J. B., et al. *Contact Class of 43-I, Fifth Army Air Force Flying Training Detachment*. Ryan School of Aeronautics. May 1943.
California Death Index, 1940–1997. Clinton William Hester, March 30, 1894– February 16, 1959.
Certificate of Death. Gladys Estelle Hester, July 20, 1949.
DeBruyne, Nese F., and Anne Leland. *American War and Military Operations Casualties: Lists and Statistics*. Congressional Research Service. January 2, 2015.
Extract from LeConte Canyon Ranger Station log, 1991, in Sequoia & Kings Canyon National Parks archives.
Extract from LeConte Canyon Ranger Station log, 1988, in Sequoia & Kings Canyon National Parks archives.
Extract from LeConte Canyon Ranger Station log, 1987, LeConte Canyon Ranger Station, LeConte Canyon, Kings Canyon National Park.
Extract from LeConte Canyon Ranger Station log, 1986, in Sequoia & Kings Canyon National Parks archives.
Farabee, Butch. Memorandum to Paul (Fodor), in Sequoia & Kings Canyon National Parks archives. August 12, 1989.
Flight Manual for B-24D Airplane. 1942. Reprinted 2006 by Periscope Film, LLC.
Individual Deceased Personnel Files (IDPFs) for Capt. William H. Darden, 2nd Lt. Samuel J. Schlosser, S/Sgt. Franklin Nyswonger, S/Sgt. Dick Erwin Mayo, Sgt. Richard L. Spangle, and Sgt. Donald F. Vande Plasch. 1955.
Individual Deceased Personnel Files (IDPFs) for 2nd Lt. Charles W. Turvey, 2nd Lt. Robert M. Hester, 2nd Lt. William T. Cronin, 2nd Lt. Ellis H. Fish, S/Sgt. Robert O. Bursey, and S/Sergeant Howard Wandtke. 1960.
Inyo County. Assessor's Office. Assessor's Map, Book 26, page 4, 1950.
———. General Index, Grantors, A–K. July 1958–June 1971 (microfiche).
———. General Index, Grantors, A–K. July 1948–June 1958 (microfiche).
Kohn, Leo J. *Flight Manual for B-24 Liberator*. 1942. Reprinted 1977 by Aviation Publications.
Monthly Superintendent's Report, Sequoia & Kings Canyon National Parks, August 1960, in Sequoia & Kings Canyon National Parks archives.
Monthly Superintendent's Report, Sequoia & Kings Canyon National Parks, July 1960, in Sequoia & Kings Canyon National Parks archives.
National Oceanic and Atmospheric Administration Weather Maps for December 5, 1943, and December 6, 1943.

Notes to the File, October 24, 1990, in Sequoia & Kings Canyon National Parks archives.

Office of Statistical Control. *Army Air Forces Statistical Digest, World War II.* 1945. Second Printing.

Photographs, Numbers 00001-00017, in Sequoia & Kings Canyon National Parks archives. ND.

Report of Aircraft Accident for B-24 #41-28463. December 17, 1943. In author's possession.

Report of Aircraft Accident for B-24 #42-7674. December 16, 1943. In author's possession.

US Adjutant General, Department of the Army. *Army Battle Casualties and Non-Battle Deaths in World War II.* 1953.

US Army. *Survival.* 1943.

US Department of Commerce, National Oceanic and Atmospheric Administration. US Weather Bureau, "Record of Climatological Observations," December 1943.

US National Homes for Disabled Volunteer Soldiers, 1866–1938. Record #40343, Military History for Clinton W. Hester.

US Weather Bureau. Daily weather maps for December 5, 1943, and December 6, 1943.

War Department. Missing Air Crew Report #4086 for AAF Serial Number 42-52388.

———. Missing Air Crew Report #4087 for AAF Serial Number 41-29336.

The War Eaglet. 14th AAFFTD Polaris Flight Academy, Class of 43-I. July 1943.

MAPS

US Coast and Geodetic Survey. Aeronautical Chart for Radio Direction Finding, #24 DF, July 13, 1944.

———. Aeronautical Chart for Radio Direction Finding, #21 DF, April 6, 1944.

US Geological Survey, 15-foot Mount Goddard Quadrangle, 1948 edition with minor corrections, 1957.

MOVIES, DOCUMENTARIES, AND VIDEOS

B-24 Liberator, "Ditching of a B-24 Airplane into the James River," 1944 NACA World War II. www.youtube.com/watch?v=WjadMxpXprk

DeSalvo, Stephen. Video recording of his Hester Lake dive, September 1989.

ONLINE SOURCES

Carroll, Peter N. "James Walker Benét (1914–2012). www.albavolunteer.org/2013/03/james-walker-benet-1914-2012-2/. March 19, 2013.

Enlistment Record for Samuel J. Schlosser, aad.archives.gov.

Faber, Sebastian. "Obituary: Jim Benét, journalist, internationalist and soldier, veteran of the Abraham Lincoln Brigade." www.organizedrage.com/2013/01/obituary-jim-benet-1914-2012-journalist.html. January 3, 2013.

Fifteenth Air Force, www.15thaf.org (various links).

461st Bombardment Group, www.461st.org (various links).

Jennings, Audra. The Human Machinery of War. ehistory.osu.edu/exhibitions/machinery/index.

Lansford, William Douglas. www.williamdouglaslansford.com.

Macha, Gary P. "B-24E 12/5/43." www.aircraftwrecks.com/pages/b24e%2012-5-43.htm. ND.

National Oceanic and Atmospheric Administration. Weather Maps, December 5 and 6, 1943, www.lib.noaa.gov/collections/imgdocmaps/daily_weather_maps.html.

Rojas, Leslie Bernstein. "WWII Veteran Bill Lansford, 90, Fought for the Recognition of Fellow Latino Vets." www.scpr.org/news/2013/05/31/37515/wwii-veteran-bill-lansford-90-fought-for-the-recog. May 31, 2013.

Shoulder Sleeve Insignia of Army Air Forces. www.angelfire.com/md2/patches/airforce2.html.

US Navy Department Library. Aviation Personnel Fatalities in World War II. www.history.navy.mil.

US World War II Army Enlistment Records, 1938–1946, www.ancestry.com.

"William Douglas Lansford: A True Hollywood Pioneer and American Cultural Treasure." *Latin Heat Entertainment*. www.latinheat.com/tag/william-douglas-lansford-a-true-hollywood-pioneer. May 23, 2013.

Williams, Nadya. California Vets: Del Berg and Jim Benét. www.albavolunteer.org/2012/07/california-vets-del-berg-and-jim-benet/. July 2, 2012.

Index

About the Author

Peter Stekel is the author of *Final Flight: The Mystery of a World War II Plane Crash and the Frozen Airmen in the High Sierra*, *Best Wildflower Hikes Western Washington* (FalconGuides), *Best Hikes Near Seattle* (FalconGuides), and two novels, *Growing Up White in the 60s* and *The Flower Lover*.

He has published over seven hundred feature and news stories in magazines and newspapers, including articles on aviation, science and nature, Olympic sports, outdoor adventure and recreation, history, theater arts and entertainment, and celebrity profiles.

In 1975, Stekel received a BA in botany from the University of California, Davis. He conducted graduate work in ecology at Humboldt State University and in 1982 received a secondary teaching credential in life science. He has worked as an educator, outdoor adventure guide, laboratory technician, botanist, and plant ecologist.

Stekel lives in Seattle, Washington. Visit BeneathHauntedWaters .com.